# THE STAR
# THROWER

ALSO BY LOREN EISELEY

PROSE

*The Immense Journey,* 1957
*Darwin's Century,* 1958
*The Firmament of Time,* 1960
*The Unexpected Universe,* 1969
*The Invisible Pyramid,* 1970
*The Night Country,* 1971
*The Man Who Saw Through Time,* 1973
*All the Strange Hours,* 1975

POETRY

*Notes of an Alchemist,* 1972
*The Innocent Assassins,* 1973
*Another Kind of Autumn,* 1977

# THE STAR THROWER

## Loren Eiseley

### Introduction by W. H. Auden

Times
BOOKS

Designed by Beth Tondreau

**Library of Congress Cataloging in Publication Data**

Eiseley, Loren C., 1907–1977.
  The star thrower.

  I. Title.
PS3555.I78S75 1978   818'.5'408   77–87827
ISBN 0-8129-0746-9

FOR MABEL

# Contents

# CONTENTS

# Editor's Preface

Loren Eiseley died in the summer of 1977. During the last year of his life, he selected and arranged some of his favorite writings for publication. The result is this anthology, which contains a large number of essays and poems that have never appeared in a book before and which add greatly to the total of his work.

The essays the author liked best were the early ones. These were more anecdotal, popular, and shorter than his later writings. As he became better known, he was sought after as a public speaker by universities and other groups, and his lectures, which were necessarily more scholarly, served as the basis of his later books. With the publication of *All the Strange Hours*, his autobiography and last major prose work, he returned to the shorter essay form.

In *The Star Thrower*, there is a generous sampling of the essays from the early books: *The Immense Journey*, which established his reputation as a literary naturalist, *The Firmament of Time*, and *The Unexpected Universe*, which contains the essay that provides the title for the present collection.

It was the publication of *The Unexpected Universe* that prompted W.H. Auden to write the review, "Concerning the Unpredictable," which appeared in *The New Yorker* in 1970. In this review, which is broader in scope than a critical account of a single book, Auden observed that he had read everything of Eiseley's he could find. It seemed appropriate, therefore, to use this essay by Auden, who subsequently became Eiseley's friend, to introduce *The Star Thrower*.

In 1972, Eiseley's first book of poems was published. His editor had encouraged him to collect his early poems for publication. This he did, but then one of those unpredictable things that happen occasionally in publishing occurred: before the manuscript could be sent to the printer, he wrote a whole new book of poems! These were published under the title of *Notes of an Alchemist,* and two other collections followed.

The poems included here are from the unpublished manuscript. Written in the years 1930–1942, most of them were first printed in "little magazines" and are not now available. They serve as a link to his later more modern poetry and were the inspiration for that body of work. As an evolutionist, Loren Eiseley recognized their merit and included them in the anthology.

More than half of this collection consists of essays which have never been published before or which have appeared only in magazines or scientific journals. Although some of them were selected by the author for inclusion, others were discovered by his assistant, Caroline E. Werkley, while assembling his papers for the Loren Eiseley conference room at the University of Pennsylvania. "The Dance of the Frogs" and "The Fifth Planet," which have the *Immense Journey* touch, are among the latter. Since he did not publish them, he may not have thought they were as complete as he would have liked them to be.

At the time of his death, Eiseley had plans for half a dozen new books, which were in various states of preparation. "Man Against the Universe," which is included here, is a lecture he had presented around the country many times and had planned to develop into a book. There were bits and pieces of *The Snow Wolf,* a science-fiction novel he was enthusiastic about and which was to be set in the Ice Age. There were his nature notebooks, a textbook on world archaeology, and other projects.

On July 9, 1977, Loren Eiseley "stepped down to lace his bones with ancient dogs and prairie shadows," in the words of another of his admirers, Ray Bradbury. But he has left behind a body of work which will be read and reread for generations.

The essays and poems in *The Star Thrower* appear essentially as they were first published. Since certain dates, such as those relating to the age of the earth and life on it, are constantly being revised, no attempt has been made to make these consistent or to conform to current thinking.

To round out this book, a list of Eiseley's honors and awards has been appended. His election in 1971 to the National Institute of Arts and Letters is a rare achievement among scientists. He won many of the major literary awards and received thirty-five honorary degrees. Modest by nature, he seldom spoke of this, and few of his friends and colleagues knew he had been so widely honored.

Kenneth Heuer

# INTRODUCTION
## Concerning the Unpredictable

> In creation there is not only a Yes but also a No; not only a
> height but also an abyss; not only clarity but also obscurity; not
> only progress and continuation but also impediment and limita-
> tion . . . not only value but also worthlessness. . . . It is true that
> individual creatures and men experience these things in most
> unequal measure, their lots being assigned by a justice which
> is curious or very much concealed. Yet it is irrefutable that
> creation and creature are good even in the fact that all that is
> exists in this contrast and antithesis.
> —Karl Barth in *Church Dogmatics*

Rather oddly, I first heard of Dr. Loren Eiseley not in this country
but in Oxford, where a student gave me a copy of *The Immense
Journey,* since which time I have eagerly read anything of his I could
lay my hands on. His obvious ancestors, as both writers and thinkers,
are Thoreau and Emerson, but he often reminds me of Ruskin,
Richard Jefferies, W. H. Hudson, whom, I feel sure, he must have
read, and of two writers, Novalis (a German) and Adalbert Stifter
(an Austrian), whom perhaps he hasn't. But I wouldn't be sure.
Some of the quotations in *The Unexpected Universe* surprised me.
I would not have expected someone who is an American and a
scientist to have read such little-known literary works as the *Völuspá,*
James Thomson's *The City of Dreadful Night,* and Charles Wil-
liams's play *Cranmer.* . . .
  Dr. Eiseley happens to be an archaeologist, an anthropologist, and

a naturalist, but, if I have understood him rightly, the first point he wishes to make is that in order to be a scientist, an artist, a doctor, a lawyer, or what-have-you, one has first to be a human being. No member of any other species can have a special "field." One question his book raises is: "What differences have recent scientific discoveries, in physics, astronomy, biology, etc., made to man's conception, individually or collectively, of himself?" The answer is, I believe, very little.

We did not have to wait for Darwin to tell us that, as physical creatures, we are akin to other animals. Like them, we breathe, eat, digest, excrete, copulate, are viviparously born, and, whatever views we may have about an "afterlife," must certainly suffer physical death in this. Indeed, one result of urbanization has been that, despite what we now know about our ancestry, we feel far less akin and grateful to the animal kingdom than did primitive tribes, with their totem systems and animal folktales.

Speaking of the recognition of Odysseus by his dog Argos, Dr. Eiseley says:

"The magic that gleams an instant between Argos and Odysseus is both the recognition of diversity and the need for affection across the illusions of form. It is nature's cry to homeless, far-wandering, insatiable man: 'Do not forget your brethren, nor the green wood from which you sprang. To do so is to invite disaster. . . . One does not meet oneself until one catches the reflection from an eye other than human.'"

Before Descartes, such a warning would have been unnecessary. On the other hand, nothing Darwin and the geneticists have to tell us can alter the fact that, as self-conscious beings who speak (that is to say, give Proper Names to other beings), who laugh, who pray, and who, as creators of history and culture, continue to change after our biological evolution is complete, we are unique among all the creatures we know of. All attempts to account for our behavior on the basis of our pre-human ancestors are myths, and usually invented to justify base behavior. As Karl Kraus wrote:

"When a man is treated like a beast, he says, 'After all, I'm human.' When he behaves like a beast, he says, 'After all, I'm only human.'"

# INTRODUCTION

No; as Dr. Eiseley says, "There is no definition or description of man possible by reducing him to ape or tree-shrew. Once, it is true, the shrew contained him, but he is gone." Or, as G. K. Chesterton said, "If it is not true that a divine being fell, then one can only say that one of the animals went completely off its head."

What modern science has profoundly changed is our way of thinking about the non-human universe. We have always been aware that human beings are characters in a story in which we can know more or less what has happened but can never predict what is going to happen; what we never realized until recently is that the same is true of the universe. But, of course, its story is even more mysterious to us than our own. When we act, we do know something about our motives for action, but it is rarely possible for us to say why anything novel happens in the universe. All the same, I do not personally believe there is such a thing as a "random" event. "Unpredictable" is a factual description; "random" contains, without having the honesty to admit it, a philosophical bias typical of persons who have forgotten how to pray. Though he does use the term once, I don't think Dr. Eiseley believes in it, either:

"The earth's atmosphere of oxygen appears to be the product of a biological invention, photosynthesis, another random event that took place in Archeozoic times. That single 'invention,' for such it was, determined the entire nature of life on this planet, and there is no possibility at present of calling it preordained. Similarly, the stepped-up manipulation of chance, in the shape of both mutation and recombination of genetic factors, which is one result of the sexual mechanism, would have been unprophesiable."

I must now openly state my own bias and say that I do not believe in Chance; I believe in Providence and Miracles. If photosynthesis was invented by chance, then I can only say it was a damned lucky chance for us. If, biologically speaking, it is a "statistical impossibility" that I should be walking the earth instead of a million other possible people, I can only think of it as a miracle which I must do my best to deserve. Natural Selection as a negative force is comprehensible. It is obvious that a drastic change in the environment, like an ice age, will destroy a large number of species adapted to a warm climate. What I cannot swallow is the assertion that "chance"

17

mutations can explain the fact that whenever an ecological niche is free, some species evolves to fit it, especially when one thinks how peculiar some such niches—the one occupied by the liver fluke, for example—can be. Dr. Eiseley quotes George Gaylord Simpson as saying:

"The association of unusual physical conditions with a crisis in evolution is not likely to be pure coincidence. Life and its environment are interdependent and evolve together."

Dr. Eiseley has excellent things to say about the myth of the Survival of the Fittest:

"A major portion of the world's story appears to be that of fumbling little creatures of seemingly no great potential, falling, like the helpless little girl Alice, down a rabbit hole or an unexpected crevice into some new and topsy-turvy realm. . . . The first land-walking fish was, by modern standards, an ungainly and inefficient vertebrate. Figuratively, he was a water failure who had managed to climb ashore on a continent where no vertebrates existed. In a time of crisis he had escaped his enemies. . . . The wet fish gasping in the harsh air on the shore, the warm-blooded mammal roving unchecked through the torpor of the reptilian night, the lizard-bird launching into a moment of ill-aimed flight, shatter all purely competitive assumptions. These singular events reveal escapes through the living screen, penetrated, one would have to say in retrospect, by the 'overspecialized' and the seemingly 'inefficient,' the creatures driven to the wall."

The main theme of *The Unexpected Universe* is Man as the Quest Hero, the wanderer, the voyager, the seeker after adventure, knowledge, power, meaning, and righteousness. The Quest is dangerous (he may suffer shipwreck or ambush) and unpredictable (he never knows what will happen to him next). The Quest is not of his own choosing—often, in weariness, he wishes he had never set out on it —but is enjoined upon him by his nature as a human being:

"No longer, as with the animal, can the world be accepted as given. It has to be perceived and consciously thought about, abstracted, and considered. The moment one does so, one is outside of the natural; objects are each one surrounded with an aura radiating meaning to man alone.

# INTRODUCTION

"Mostly the animals understand their roles, but man, by comparison, seems troubled by a message that, it is often said, he cannot quite remember or has gotten wrong. . . . Bereft of instinct, he must search continually for meanings. . . . Man was a reader before he became a writer, a reader of what Coleridge once called the mighty alphabet of the universe."

For illustrations of his thesis, Dr. Eiseley begins with an imaginary voyage—Homer's epic the *Odyssey*—and goes on to two famous historical voyages, that of Captain Cook in the *Resolution,* during which he discovered not the Terra Incognita he was sent to find— a rich and habitable continent south and westward of South America —but what he described as "an inexpressibly horrid Antarctica," and Darwin's voyage in the *Beagle,* during which he found the data which led him to doubt the Fixity of Species. Lastly, Dr. Eiseley tells us many anecdotes from his own life voyage, and these are to me the most fascinating passages in the book. Of the *Odyssey* he says:

"Odysseus' passage through the haunted waters of the eastern Mediterranean symbolizes, at the start of the Western intellectual tradition, the sufferings that the universe and his own nature impose upon homeward-yearning man. In the restless atmosphere of today all the psychological elements of the Odyssey are present to excess: the driving will toward achievement, the technological cleverness crudely manifest in the blinding of Cyclops, the fierce rejection of the sleepy Lotus Isles, the violence between man and man. Yet, significantly, the ancient hero cries out in desperation, 'There is nothing worse for men than wandering.' "

Dr. Eiseley's autobiographical passages are, most of them, descriptions of numinous encounters—some joyful, some terrifying. After reading them, I get the impression of a wanderer who is often in danger of being shipwrecked on the shores of Dejection—it can hardly be an accident that three of his encounters take place in cemeteries—and a solitary who feels more easily at home with animals than with his fellow human beings. Aside from figures in his childhood, the human beings who have "messages" for him are all total strangers—someone tending a rubbish dump, a mysterious figure throwing stranded starfish back into the sea, a vagrant scientist with a horrid parasitic worm in a bottle, a girl in the Wild West with Neanderthal features. As a rule, though, his numinous encounters are with non-human objects—a spider, the eye of a dead octopus, his own shepherd dog, a starving jackrabbit, a young fox. It is also clear that he is a deeply compassionate man who, in his own words, "loves the lost ones, the failures of the world." It is typical of him that, on recovering consciousness after a bad fall to find himself bleeding profusely, he should, quite unself-consciously, apologize to his now doomed blood cells—phagocytes and platelets—"Oh, don't go. I'm sorry, I've done for you." More importantly, he reveals himself as a man unusually well trained in the habit of prayer, by which I mean the habit of listening. The petitionary aspect of prayer is its most trivial because it is involuntary. We cannot help asking that our wishes may be granted, though all too many of them are like wishing that two and two may make five, and cannot and should not be granted. But the serious part of prayer begins when we have got our begging over with and listen for the Voice of what I would call the Holy Spirit, though if others prefer to say the Voice of Oz or the Dreamer or Conscience, I shan't quarrel, so long as they don't call it the Voice of the Super-Ego, for that "entity" can only tell us what we know already, whereas the Voice I am talking about always says something new and unpredictable—an unexpected demand, obedience to which involves a change of self, however painful.

At this point, a digression. Last September, I attended a symposium in Stockholm on "The Place of Value in a World of Fact." Most of those present were scientists, some of them very distinguished indeed. To my shock and amazement, they kept saying that what we need today is a set of *Ethical Axioms* (italics mine). I can only say that to me the phrase is gibberish. An axiom is stated in the indicative and addressed to the intellect. From one set of axioms one kind of mathematics will follow, from another set another, but it would be nonsense to call one of them "better" than the other. All ethical statements are addressed to the will, usually a reluctant will, and must therefore appear in the imperative. "Thou shalt love thy neighbor as thyself" and "A straight line is the shortest distance between two points" belong to two totally different realms of discourse.

# INTRODUCTION

But to return to Dr. Eiseley. As a rule, the Voice speaks to him not directly but through messengers who are unaware of the message they bear. In the following dream, however, he is spoken to without intermediaries:

"The dream was of a great blurred bearlike shape emerging from the snow against the window. It pounded on the glass and beckoned importunately toward the forest. I caught the urgency of a message as uncouth and indecipherable as the shape of its huge bearer in the snow. In the immense terror of my dream I struggled against the import of that message as I struggled also to resist the impatient pounding of the frost-enveloped beast at the window.

"Suddenly I lifted the telephone beside my bed, and through the receiver came a message as cryptic as the message from the snow, but far more miraculous in origin. For I knew intuitively, in the still snowfall of my dream, that the voice I heard, a long way off, was my own voice in childhood. Pure and sweet, incredibly refined and beautiful beyond the things of earth, yet somehow inexorable and not to be stayed, the voice was already terminating its message. 'I am sorry to have troubled you,' the clear faint syllables of the child persisted. They seemed to come across a thinning wire that lengthened far away into the years of my past. 'I am sorry, I am sorry to have troubled you at all.' The voice faded before I could speak. I was awake now, trembling in the cold."

I have said that I suspect Dr. Eiseley of being a melancholic. He recognizes that man is the only creature who speaks personally, works, and prays, but nowhere does he overtly say that man is the only creature who laughs. True laughter is not to be confused with the superior titter of the intellect, though we are capable, alas, of that, too: when we truly laugh, we laugh simultaneously *with* and *at*. True laughter (belly laughter) I would define as the spirit of Carnival.

Again a digression, on the meaning of Carnival as it was known in the Middle Ages and persisted in a few places, like Rome, where Goethe witnessed and described it in February of 1788. Carnival celebrates the unity of our human race as mortal creatures, who come into this world and depart from it without our consent, who must eat, drink, defecate, belch, and break wind in order to live, and procreate if our species is to survive. Our feelings about this are ambiguous. To us as individuals, it is a cause for rejoicing to know that we are not alone, that all of us, irrespective of age or sex or rank or talent, are in the same boat. As unique persons, on the other hand, all of us are resentful that an exception cannot be made in our own case. We oscillate between wishing we were unreflective animals and wishing we were disembodied spirits, for in either case we should not be problematic to ourselves. The Carnival solution of this ambiguity is to laugh, for laughter is simultaneously a protest and an acceptance. During Carnival, all social distinctions are suspended, even that of sex. Young men dress up as girls, young girls as boys. The escape from social personality is symbolized by the wearing of masks. The oddity of the human animal expresses itself through the grotesque—false noses, huge bellies and buttocks, farcical imitations of childbirth and copulation. The protest element in laughter takes the form of mock aggression: people pelt each other with small, harmless objects, draw cardboard daggers, and abuse each other verbally, like the small boy Goethe heard screaming at his father, *"Sia ammazzato il Signore Padre!"* Traditionally, Carnival, the days of feasting and fun, immediately precedes Lent, the days of fasting and prayer. In medieval carnivals, parodies of the rituals of the Church were common, but what Lewis Carroll said of literary parody—"One can only parody a poem one admires"—is true of all parody. One can only blaspheme if one believes. The world of Laughter is much more closely related to the world of Worship and Prayer than either is to the everyday, secular world of Work, for both are worlds in which we are all equal, in the first as individual members of our species, in the latter as unique persons. In the world of Work, on the other hand, we are not and cannot be equal, only diverse and interdependent: each of us, whether as scientist, artist, cook, cabdriver, or whatever, has to do "our thing." So long as we thought of Nature in polytheistic terms as the abode of gods, our efficiency and success as workers were hampered by a false humility which tried to make Nature responsible for us. But, according to Genesis, God made Adam responsible for looking after the Garden of Eden on His behalf, and it now seems as if He expects us to be responsible for

INTRODUCTION

the whole natural universe, which means that, as workers, we have to regard the universe *etsi deus non daretur*: God must be a hidden deity, veiled by His creation.

A satisfactory human life, individually or collectively, is possible only if proper respect is paid to all three worlds. Without Prayer and Work, the Carnival laughter turns ugly, the comic obscenities grubby and pornographic, the mock aggression into real hatred and cruelty. (The hippies, it appears to me, are trying to recover the sense of Carnival which is so conspicuously absent in this age, but so long as they reject Work they are unlikely to succeed.) Without Laughter and Work, Prayer turns Gnostic, cranky, Pharisaic, while those who try to live by Work alone, without Laughter or Prayer, turn into insane lovers of power, tyrants who would enslave Nature to their immediate desires—an attempt which can only end in utter catastrophe, shipwreck on the Isle of the Sirens.

Carnival in its traditional forms is not, I think, for Dr. Eiseley any more than it is for me. Neither of us can enjoy crowds and loud noises. But even introverted intellectuals can share the Carnival experience if they are prepared to forget their dignity, as Dr. Eiseley did when he unexpectedly encountered a fox cub:

"The creature was very young. He was alone in a dread universe. I crept on my knees around the prow and crouched beside him. It was a small fox pup from a den under the timbers who looked up at me. God knows what had become of his brothers and sisters. His parent must not have been home from hunting.

"He innocently selected what I think was a chicken bone from an untidy pile of splintered rubbish and shook it at me invitingly. There was a vast and playful humor in his face. . . . Here was the thing in the midst of the bones, the wide-eyed, innocent fox inviting me to play, with the innate courtesy of its two forepaws placed appealingly together, along with a mock shake of the head. The universe was swinging in some fantastic fashion around to present its face, and the face was so small that the universe itself was laughing.

"It was not a time for human dignity. It was a time only for the careful observance of amenities written behind the stars. Gravely I arranged my forepaws while the puppy whimpered with ill-concealed excitement. I drew the breath of a fox's den into my nostrils. On impulse, I picked up clumsily a whiter bone and shook it in teeth that had not entirely forgotten their original purpose. Round and round we tumbled for one ecstatic moment. . . . For just a moment I had held the universe at bay by the simple expedient of sitting on my haunches before a fox den and tumbling about with a chicken bone. It is the gravest, most meaningful act I shall ever accomplish, but, as Thoreau once remarked of some peculiar errand of his own, there is no use reporting it to the Royal Society."

Thank God, though, Dr. Eiseley has reported it to me. *Bravo!* say I.

W. H. Auden

# I
# Nature and Autobiography

# The Judgment
# of the Birds

It is a commonplace of all religious thought, even the most primitive, that the man seeking visions and insight must go apart from his fellows and live for a time in the wilderness. If he is of the proper sort, he will return with a message. It may not be a message from the god he set out to seek, but even if he has failed in that particular, he will have had a vision or seen a marvel, and these are always worth listening to and thinking about.

The world, I have come to believe, is a very queer place, but we have been part of this queerness for so long that we tend to take it for granted. We rush to and fro like Mad Hatters upon our peculiar errands, all the time imagining our surroundings to be dull and ourselves quite ordinary creatures. Actually, there is nothing in the world to encourage this idea, but such is the mind of man, and this is why he finds it necessary from time to time to send emissaries into the wilderness in the hope of learning of great events, or plans in store for him, that will resuscitate his waning taste for life. His great news services, his worldwide radio network, he knows with a last remnant of healthy distrust will be of no use to him in this matter. No miracle can withstand a radio broadcast, and it is certain that it would be no miracle if it could. One must seek, then, what only the solitary approach can give—a natural revelation.

Let it be understood that I am not the sort of man to whom is entrusted direct knowledge of great events or prophecies. A naturalist, however, spends much of his life alone, and my life is no exception. Even in New York City there are patches of wilderness, and a man by himself is bound to undergo certain experiences falling into the class of which I speak. I set mine down, therefore: a matter of pigeons, a flight of chemicals, and a judgment of birds, in the hope that they will come to the eye of those who have retained a true taste for the marvelous, and who are capable of discerning in the flow of ordinary events the point at which the mundane world gives way to quite another dimension.

New York is not, on the whole, the best place to enjoy the downright miraculous nature of the planet. There are, I do not doubt, many remarkable stories to be heard there and many strange sights to be seen, but to grasp a marvel fully it must be savored from all aspects. This cannot be done while one is being jostled and hustled along a crowded street. Nevertheless, in any city there are true wildernesses where a man can be alone. It can happen in a hotel room, or on the high roofs at dawn.

One night on the twentieth floor of a midtown hotel I awoke in the dark and grew restless. On an impulse I climbed upon the broad old-fashioned window sill, opened the curtains, and peered out. It was the hour just before dawn, the hour when men sigh in their sleep or, if awake, strive to focus their wavering eyesight upon a world emerging from the shadows. I leaned out sleepily through the open window. I had expected depths, but not the sight I saw.

I found I was looking down from that great height into a series of curious cupolas or lofts that I could just barely make out in the darkness. As I looked, the outlines of these lofts became more distinct because the light was being reflected from the wings of pigeons who, in utter silence, were beginning to float outward upon the city. In and out through the open slits in the cupolas passed the white-winged birds on their mysterious errands. At this hour the city was theirs, and quietly, without the brush of a single wing tip against stone in that high, eerie place, they were taking over the spires of Manhattan. They were pouring upward in a light that was not yet perceptible to human eyes, while far down in the black darkness of the alleys it was still midnight.

As I crouched half-asleep across the sill, I had a moment's illusion that the world had changed in the night, as in some immense snowfall, and that, if I were to leave, it would have to be as these other inhabitants were doing, by the window. I should have to launch out into that great bottomless void with the simple confidence of young birds reared high up there among the familiar chimney pots and interposed horrors of the abyss.

I leaned farther out. To and fro went the white wings, to and fro. There were no sounds from any of them. They knew man was asleep and this light for a little while was theirs. Or perhaps I had only dreamed about man in this city of wings—which he could surely never have built. Perhaps I, myself, was one of these birds dreaming unpleasantly a moment of old dangers far below as I teetered on a window ledge.

Around and around went the wings. It needed only a little courage, only a little shove from the window ledge, to enter that city of light. The muscles of my hands were already making little premonitory lunges. I wanted to enter that city and go away over the roofs in the first dawn. I wanted to enter it so badly that I drew back carefully into the room and opened the hall door. I found my coat on the chair, and it slowly became clear to me that there was a way down through the floors, that I was, after all, only a man.

I dressed then and went back to my own kind, and I have been rather more than usually careful ever since not to look into the city of light. I had seen, just once, man's greatest creation from a strange inverted angle, and it was not really his at all. I will never forget how those wings went round and round, and how, by the merest pressure of the fingers and a feeling for air, one might go away over the roofs. It is a knowledge, however, that is better kept to oneself. I think of it sometimes in such a way that the wings, beginning far down in the black depths of the mind, begin to rise and whirl till all the mind is lit by their spinning, and there is a sense of things passing away, but lightly, as a wing might veer over an obstacle.

To see from an inverted angle, however, is not a gift allotted merely to the human imagination. I have come to suspect that within their degree it is sensed by animals, though perhaps as rarely as among men. The time has to be right; one has to be, by chance or intention, upon the border of two worlds. And sometimes these two borders may shift or interpenetrate and one sees the miraculous.

I once saw this happen to a crow.

This crow lives near my house, and though I have never injured him, he takes good care to stay up in the very highest trees and, in general, to avoid humanity. His world begins at about the limit of my eyesight.

On the particular morning when this episode occurred, the whole countryside was buried in one of the thickest fogs in years. The ceiling was absolutely zero. All planes were grounded, and even a pedestrian could hardly see his outstretched hand before him.

I was groping across a field in the general direction of the railroad station, following a dimly outlined path. Suddenly out of the fog, at about the level of my eyes, and so closely that I flinched, there flashed a pair of immense black wings and a huge beak. The whole bird rushed over my head with a frantic cawing outcry of such hideous terror as I have never heard in a crow's voice before and never expect to hear again.

He was lost and startled, I thought, as I recovered my poise. He ought not to have flown out in this fog. He'd knock his silly brains out.

All afternoon that great awkward cry rang in my head. Merely being lost in a fog seemed scarcely to account for it—especially in a tough, intelligent old bandit such as I knew that particular crow to be. I even looked once in the mirror to see what it might be about me that had so revolted him that he had cried out in protest to the very stones.

Finally, as I worked my way homeward along the path, the solution came to me. It should have been clear before. The borders of our worlds had shifted. It was the fog that had done it. That crow, and I knew him well, never under normal circumstances flew low near men. He had been lost all right, but it was more than that. He had thought he was high up, and when he encountered me looming gigantically through the fog, he had perceived a ghastly and, to the crow mind, unnatural sight. He had seen a man walking on air, desecrating the very heart of the crow kingdom, a harbinger of the most profound evil a crow mind could conceive of—air-walking men. The encounter, he must have thought, had taken place a hundred feet over the roofs.

He caws now when he sees me leaving for the station in the

morning, and I fancy that in that note I catch the uncertainty of a mind that has come to know things are not always what they seem. He has seen a marvel in his heights of air and is no longer as other crows. He has experienced the human world from an unlikely perspective. He and I share a viewpoint in common: our worlds have interpenetrated, and we both have faith in the miraculous.

It is a faith that in my own case has been augmented by two remarkable sights. I once saw some very odd chemicals fly across a waste so dead it might have been upon the moon, and once, by an even more fantastic piece of luck, I was present when a group of birds passed a judgment upon life.

On the maps of the old voyageurs it is called *Mauvaises Terres*, the evil lands, and, slurred a little with the passage through many minds, it has come down to us anglicized as the badlands. The soft shuffle of moccasins has passed through its canyons on the grim business of war and flight, but the last of those slight disturbances of immemorial silences died out almost a century ago. The land, if one can call it a land, is a waste as lifeless as that valley in which lie the kings of Egypt. Like the Valley of the Kings, it is a mausoleum, a place of dry bones in what once was a place of life. Now it has silences as deep as those in the moon's airless chasms.

Nothing grows among its pinnacles; there is no shade except under great toadstools of sandstone whose bases have been eaten to the shape of wine glasses by the wind. Everything is flaking, cracking, disintegrating, wearing away in the long, imperceptible weather of time. The ash of ancient volcanic outbursts still sterilizes its soil, and its colors in that waste are the colors that flame in the lonely sunsets on dead planets. Men come there but rarely, and for one purpose only, the collection of bones.

It was a late hour on a cold, wind-bitten autumn day when I climbed a great hill spined like a dinosaur's back and tried to take my bearings. The tumbled waste fell away in waves in all directions. Blue air was darkening into purple along the bases of the hills. I shifted my knapsack, heavy with the petrified bones of long-vanished creatures, and studied my compass. I wanted to be out of there by nightfall, and already the sun was going sullenly down in the west.

It was then that I saw the flight coming on. It was moving like a little close-knit body of black specks that danced and darted and closed again. It was pouring from the north and heading toward me with the undeviating relentlessness of a compass needle. It streamed through the shadows rising out of monstrous gorges. It rushed over towering pinnacles in the red light of the sun or momentarily sank from sight within their shade. Across that desert of eroding clay and wind-worn stone they came with a faint wild twittering that filled all the air about me as those tiny living bullets hurtled past into the night.

It may not strike you as a marvel. It would not, perhaps, unless you stood in the middle of a dead world at sunset, but that was where I stood. Fifty million years lay under my feet, fifty million years of bellowing monsters moving in a green world now gone so utterly that its very light was traveling on the farther edge of space. The chemicals of all that vanished age lay about me in the ground. Around me still lay the shearing molars of dead titanotheres, the delicate sabers of soft-stepping cats, the hollow sockets that had held the eyes of many a strange, outmoded beast. Those eyes had looked out upon a world as real as ours; dark, savage brains had roamed and roared their challenges into the steaming night.

Now they were still here, or, put it as you will, the chemicals that made them were here about me in the ground. The carbon that had driven them ran blackly in the eroding stone. The stain of iron was in the clays. The iron did not remember the blood it had once moved within, the phosphorus had forgot the savage brain. The little individual moment had ebbed from all those strange combinations of chemicals as it would ebb from our living bodies into the sinks and runnels of oncoming time.

I had lifted up a fistful of that ground. I held it while that wild flight of south-bound warblers hurtled over me into the oncoming dark. There went phosphorus, there went iron, there went carbon, there beat the calcium in those hurrying wings. Alone on a dead planet I watched that incredible miracle speeding past. It ran by some true compass over field and waste land. It cried its individual ecstasies into the air until the gullies rang. It swerved like a single body, it knew itself, and, lonely, it bunched close in the racing darkness, its individual entities feeling about them the rising night.

And so, crying to each other their identity, they passed away out of my view.

I dropped my fistful of earth. I heard it roll inanimate back into the gully at the base of the hill: iron, carbon, the chemicals of life. Like men from those wild tribes who had haunted these hills before me seeking visions, I made my sign to the great darkness. It was not a mocking sign, and I was not mocked. As I walked into my camp late that night, one man, rousing from his blankets beside the fire, asked sleepily, "What did you see?"

"I think, a miracle," I said softly, but I said it to myself. Behind me that vast waste began to glow under the rising moon.

I have said that I saw a judgment upon life, and that it was not passed by men. Those who stare at birds in cages or who test minds by their closeness to our own may not care for it. It comes from far away out of my past, in a place of pouring waters and green leaves. I shall never see an episode like it again if I live to be a hundred, nor do I think that one man in a million has ever seen it, because man is an intruder into such silences. The light must be right, and the observer must remain unseen. No man sets up such an experiment. What he sees, he sees by chance.

You may put it that I had come over a mountain, that I had slogged through fern and pine needles for half a long day, and that on the edge of a little glade with one long, crooked branch extending across it, I had sat down to rest with my back against a stump. Through accident I was concealed from the glade, although I could see into it perfectly.

The sun was warm there, and the murmurs of forest life blurred softly away into my sleep. When I awoke, dimly aware of some commotion and outcry in the clearing, the light was slanting down through the pines in such a way that the glade was lit like some vast cathedral. I could see the dust motes of wood pollen in the long shaft of light, and there on the extended branch sat an enormous raven with a red and squirming nestling in his beak.

The sound that awoke me was the outraged cries of the nestling's parents, who flew helplessly in circles about the clearing. The sleek black monster was indifferent to them. He gulped, whetted his beak on the dead branch a moment, and sat still. Up to that point the little tragedy had followed the usual pattern. But suddenly, out of all that area of woodland, a soft sound of complaint began to rise. Into the glade fluttered small birds of half a dozen varieties drawn by the anguished outcries of the tiny parents.

No one dared to attack the raven. But they cried there in some instinctive common misery, the bereaved and the unbereaved. The glade filled with their soft rustling and their cries. They fluttered as though to point their wings at the murderer. There was a dim intangible ethic he had violated, that they knew. He was a bird of death.

And he, the murderer, the black bird at the heart of life, sat on there, glistening in the common light, formidable, unmoving, unperturbed, untouchable.

The sighing died. It was then I saw the judgment. It was the judgment of life against death. I will never see it again so forcefully presented. I will never hear it again in notes so tragically prolonged. For in the midst of protest, they forgot the violence. There, in that clearing, the crystal note of a song sparrow lifted hesitantly in the hush. And finally, after painful fluttering, another took the song, and then another, the song passing from one bird to another, doubtfully at first, as though some evil thing were being slowly forgotten. Till suddenly they took heart and sang from many throats joyously together as birds are known to sing. They sang because life is sweet and sunlight beautiful. They sang under the brooding shadow of the raven. In simple truth they had forgotten the raven, for they were the singers of life, and not of death.

I was not of that airy company. My limbs were the heavy limbs of an earthbound creature who could climb mountains, even the mountains of the mind, only by a great effort of will. I knew I had seen a marvel and observed a judgment, but the mind which was my human endowment was sure to question it and to be at me day by day with its heresies until I grew to doubt the meaning of what I had seen. Eventually darkness and subtleties would ring me round once more.

And so it proved until, on the top of a stepladder, I made one more observation upon life. It was cold that autumn evening, and, standing under a suburban street light in a spate of leaves and beginning snow, I was suddenly conscious of some huge and hairy shadows dancing over the pavement. They seemed attached to an odd, globular shape that was magnified above me. There was no mistaking it. I was standing under the shadow of an orb-weaving spider. Gigantically projected against the street, she was about her spinning when everything was going underground. Even her cables were magnified upon the sidewalk and already I was half-entangled in their shadows.

"Good Lord," I thought, "she has found herself a kind of minor sun and is going to upset the course of nature."

I procured a ladder from my yard and climbed up to inspect the situation. There she was, the universe running down around her, warmly arranged among her guy ropes attached to the lamp supports —a great black and yellow embodiment of the life force, not giving up to either frost or stepladders. She ignored me and went on tightening and improving her web.

I stood over her on the ladder, a faint snow touching my cheeks, and surveyed her universe. There were a couple of iridescent green beetle cases turning slowly on a loose strand of web, a fragment of luminescent eye from a moth's wing and a large indeterminable object, perhaps a cicada, that had struggled and been wrapped in silk. There were also little bits and slivers, little red and blue flashes from the scales of anonymous wings that had crashed there.

Some days, I thought, they will be dull and gray and the shine will be out of them; then the dew will polish them again and drops hang on the silk until everything is gleaming and turning in the light. It is like a mind, really, where everything changes but remains, and in the end you have these eaten-out bits of experience like beetle wings.

I stood over her a moment longer, comprehending somewhat reluctantly that her adventure against the great blind forces of winter, her seizure of this warming globe of light, would come to nothing and was hopeless. Nevertheless it brought the birds back into my mind, and that faraway song which had traveled with growing strength around a forest clearing years ago—a kind of heroism, a world where even a spider refuses to lie down and die if a rope can still be spun on to a star. Maybe man himself will fight like this in the end, I thought, slowly realizing that the web and its threatening yellow occupant had been added to some luminous store of experience, shining for a moment in the fogbound reaches of my brain.

The mind, it came to me as I slowly descended the ladder, is a very remarkable thing; it has gotten itself a kind of courage by looking at a spider in a street lamp. Here was something that ought to be passed on to those who will fight our final freezing battle with the void. I thought of setting it down carefully as a message to the future: *In the days of the frost seek a minor sun.*

But as I hesitated, it became plain that something was wrong. The marvel was escaping—a sense of bigness beyond man's power to grasp, the essence of life in its great dealings with the universe. It was better, I decided, for the emissaries returning from the wilderness, even if they were merely descending from a stepladder, to record their marvel, not to define its meaning. In that way it would go echoing on through the minds of men, each grasping at that beyond out of which the miracles emerge, and which, once defined, ceases to satisfy the human need for symbols.

In the end I merely made a mental note: One specimen of Epeira observed building a web in a street light. Late autumn and cold for spiders. Cold for men, too. I shivered and left the lamp glowing there in my mind. The last I saw of Epeira she was hauling steadily on a cable. I stepped carefully over her shadow as I walked away.

# The Long
# Loneliness

There is nothing more alone in the universe than man. He is alone because he has the intellectual capacity to know that he is separated by a vast gulf of social memory and experiment from the lives of his animal associates. He has entered into the strange world of history, of social and intellectual change, while his brothers of the field and forest remain subject to the invisible laws of biological evolution. Animals are molded by natural forces they do not comprehend. To their minds there is no past and no future. There is only the everlasting present of a single generation—its trails in the forest, its hidden pathways of the air and in the sea.

Man, by contrast, is alone with the knowledge of his history until the day of his death. When we were children we wanted to talk to animals and struggled to understand why this was impossible. Slowly we gave up the attempt as we grew into the solitary world of human adulthood; the rabbit was left on the lawn, the dog was relegated to his kennel. Only in acts of inarticulate compassion, in rare and hidden moments of communion with nature, does man briefly escape his solitary destiny. Frequently in science fiction he dreams of worlds with creatures whose communicative power is the equivalent of his own.

It is with a feeling of startlement, therefore, and eager interest touching the lost child in every one of us, that the public has received the recent accounts of naval research upon the intelligence of one of our brother mammals—the sea-dwelling bottle-nosed porpoise or dolphin.

These small whales who left the land millions of years ago to return to the great mother element of life, the sea, are now being regarded by researchers as perhaps the most intelligent form of life on our planet next to man. Dr. John Lilly of the Communications Research Institute in the Virgin Islands reports that the brain of the porpoise is 40 per cent larger than man's and is just as complex in its functional units. Amazed by the rapidity with which captive porpoises solved problems that even monkeys found difficult, Dr. Lilly is quoted as expressing the view that "man's position at the top of the hierarchy [of intelligence] begins to be questioned."

Dr. Lilly found that his captives communicated in a series of underwater whistles and that, in addition, they showed an amazing "verbalizing" ability in copying certain sounds heard in the laboratory. The experimental animal obviously hoped to elicit by this means a reproduction of the pleasurable sensations he had been made to experience under laboratory conditions. It is reported that in spite of living in a medium different from the one that man inhabits, and therefore having quite a different throat structure, one of the porpoises even uttered in a Donald-Duckish voice a short number series it had heard spoken by one of the laboratory investigators.

The import of these discoveries is tremendous and may not be adequately known for a long time. An animal from a little-explored medium, which places great barriers in the way of the psychologist, has been found to have not only a strong social organization but to show a degree of initiative in experimental communicative activity unmatched by man's closest relatives, the great apes. The porpoises reveal, moreover, a touching altruism and friendliness in their attempts to aid injured companions. Can it be, one inevitably wonders, that man is so locked in his own type of intelligence—an intelligence that is linked to a prehensile, grasping hand giving him power over his environment—that he is unable to comprehend the intellectual life of a highly endowed creature from another domain such as the sea?

Perhaps the water barrier has shut us away from a potentially communicative and jolly companion. Perhaps we have some things still to learn from the natural world around us before we turn to the far shores of space and whatever creatures may await us there. After all, the porpoise is a mammal. He shares with us an ancient way of birth and affectionate motherhood. His blood is warm, he breathes air as we do. We both bear in our bodies the remnants of a common skeleton torn asunder for divergent purposes far back in the dim dawn of mammalian life. The porpoise has been superficially stream-lined like a fish.

His are not, however, the cold-blooded ways of the true fishes. Far higher on the tree of life than fishes, the dolphin's paddles are made-over paws, rather than fins. He is an ever-constant reminder of the versatility of life and its willingness to pass through strange dimensions of experience. There are environmental worlds on earth every bit as weird as what we may imagine to revolve by far-off suns. It is our superficial familiarity with this planet that inhibits our appreciation of the unknown until a porpoise, rearing from a tank to say Three-Two-Three, re-creates for us the utter wonder of child-hood.

Unless we are specialists in the study of communication and its relation to intelligence, however, we are apt to oversimplify or define poorly what intelligence is, what communication and language are, and thus confuse and mystify both ourselves and others. The myster-ies surrounding the behavior of the bottle-nosed porpoise, and even of man himself, are not things to be probed simply by the dissector's scalpel. They lie deeper. They involve the whole nature of the mind and its role in the universe.

We are forced to ask ourselves whether native intelligence in another form than man's might be as high as or even higher than his own, yet be marked by no such material monuments as man has placed upon the earth. At first glance we are alien to this idea, because man is particularly a creature who has turned the tables on his environment so that he is now engrossed in shaping it, rather than being shaped by it. Man expresses himself upon his environ-ment through the use of tools. We therefore tend to equate the use of tools in a one-to-one relationship with intelligence.

The question we must now ask ourselves, however, is whether this involves an unconsciously man-centered way of looking at intelli-gence. Let us try for a moment to enter the dolphin's kingdom and the dolphin's body, retaining, at the same time, our human intelligence. In this imaginative act, it may be possible to divest ourselves of certain human preconceptions about our kind of intelligence and at the same time to see more clearly why mind, even advanced mind, may have manifestations other than the tools and railroad tracks and laboratories that we regard as evidence of intellect. If we are particularly adept in escaping from our own bodies, we may even learn to discount a little the kind of world of rockets and death that our type of busy human curiosity, linked to a hand noted for its ability to open assorted Pandora's boxes, has succeeded in foisting upon the world as a symbol of universal intelligence.

We have now sacrificed, in our imagination, our hands for flippers and our familiar land environment for the ocean. We will go down into the deep waters as naked of possessions as when we entered life itself. We will take with us one thing alone that exists among porpoises as among men: an ingrained biological gregariousness—a sociality that in our new world will permit us to run in schools, just as early man ran in the packs that were his ancient anthropoid heritage. We will assume in the light of Dr. Lilly's researches that our native intelligence, as distinguished from our culturally transmitted habits, is very high. The waters have closed finally over us, our paws have been sacrificed for the necessary flippers with which to navigate.

The result is immediately evident and quite clear: No matter how well we communicate with our fellows through the water medium we will never build drowned empires in the coral; we will never inscribe on palace walls the victorious boasts of porpoise kings. We will know only water and the wastes of water beyond the power of man to describe. We will be secret visitors in hidden canyons beneath the mouths of torrential rivers. We will survey in innocent astonishment the flotsam that pours from the veins of continents— dead men, great serpents, giant trees—or perhaps the little toy boat of a child loosed far upstream will come floating past. Bottles with winking green lights will plunge by us into the all-embracing ooze. Meaningless appearances and disappearances will comprise our philosophies. We will hear the earth's heart ticking in its thin granitic shell. Volcanic fires will growl ominously in steam-filled crevices. Vapor, bird cries, and sea wrack will compose our memories. We will see death in many forms and, on occasion, the slow majestic fall of battleships through the green light that comes from beyond our domain.

Over all that region of wondrous beauty we will exercise no more control than the simplest mollusk. Even the octopus with flexible arms will build little shelters that we cannot imitate. Without hands we will have only the freedom to follow the untrammeled sea winds across the planet.

Perhaps if those whistling sounds that porpoises make are truly symbolic and capable of manipulation in our brains, we will wonder about the world in which we find ourselves—but it will be a world not susceptible to experiment. At best we may nuzzle in curiosity a passing shipbottom and be harpooned for our pains. Our thoughts, in other words, will be as limited as those of the first men who roved in little bands in the times before fire and the writing that was to open to man the great doorway of his past.

Man without writing cannot long retain his history in his head. His intelligence permits him to grasp some kind of succession of generations; but without writing, the tale of the past rapidly degenerates into fumbling myth and fable. Man's greatest epic, his four long battles with the advancing ice of the great continental glaciers, has vanished from human memory without a trace. Our illiterate fathers disappeared and with them, in a few scant generations, died one of the great stories of all time. This episode has nothing to do with the biological quality of a brain as between then and now. It has to do instead with a device, an invention made possible by the hand. That invention came too late in time to record eyewitness accounts of the years of the Giant Frost.

Primitives of our own species, even today, are historically shallow in their knowledge of the past. Only the poet who writes speaks his message across the millennia to other hearts. Only in writing can the cry from the great cross on Golgotha still be heard in the minds of men. The thinker of perceptive insight, even if we allow him for the moment to be a porpoise rather than a man, has only his individual glimpse of the universe until such time as he can impose that insight upon unnumbered generations. In centuries of pondering, man has come upon but one answer to this problem: speech translated into writing that passes beyond human mortality.

Writing, and later printing, is the product of our adaptable many-purposed hands. It is thus, through writing, with no increase in genetic, inborn capacity since the last ice advance, that modern man carries in his mind the intellectual triumphs of all his predecessors who were able to inscribe their thoughts for posterity.

All animals which man has reason to believe are more than usually intelligent—our relatives the great apes, the elephant, the raccoon, the wolverine, among others—are problem solvers, and in at least a small way manipulators of their environment. Save for the instinctive calls of their species, however, they cannot communicate except by direct imitation. They cannot invent words for new situations nor get their fellows to use such words. No matter how high the individual intelligence, its private world remains a private possession locked forever within a single, perishable brain. It is this fact that finally balks our hunger to communicate even with the sensitive dog who shares our fireside.

Dr. Lilly insists, however, that the porpoises communicate in high-pitched, underwater whistles that seem to transmit their wishes and problems. The question then becomes one of ascertaining whether these sounds represent true language—in the sense of symbolic meanings, additive, learned elements—or whether they are simply the instinctive signals of a pack animal. To this there is as yet no clear answer, but the eagerness with which laboratory sounds and voices were copied by captive porpoises suggests a vocalizing ability extending perhaps to or beyond the threshold of speech.

Most of the intelligent land animals have prehensile, grasping organs for exploring their environment—hands in man and his anthropoid relatives, the sensitive inquiring trunk in the elephant. One of the surprising things about the porpoise is that his superior brain is unaccompanied by any type of manipulative organ. He has, however, a remarkable range-finding ability involving some sort of echo-sounding. Perhaps this acute sense—far more accurate than any man has been able to devise artificially—brings him greater knowledge of his watery surroundings than might at first seem possible. Human beings think of intelligence as geared to things. The hand and the tool are to us the unconscious symbols of our intellectual achievement. It is difficult for us to visualize another kind of lonely, almost disembodied intelligence floating in the wavering green fairyland of the sea—an intelligence possibly near or comparable to our own but without hands to build, to transmit knowledge by writing, or to alter by one hairsbreadth the planet's surface. Yet at the same time there are indications that this is a warm, friendly and eager intelligence quite capable of coming to the assistance of injured companions and striving to rescue them from drowning. Porpoises left the land when mammalian brains were still small and primitive. Without the stimulus provided by agile exploring fingers, these great sea mammals have yet taken a divergent road toward intelligence of a high order. Hidden in their sleek bodies is an impressively elaborated instrument, the reason for whose appearance is a complete enigma. It is as though both man and porpoise were each part of some great eye which yearned to look both outward on eternity and inward to the sea's heart—that fertile entity so like the mind in its swarming and grotesque life.

Perhaps man has something to learn after all from fellow creatures without the ability to drive harpoons through living flesh, or poison with strontium the planetary winds. One is reminded of those watery blue vaults in which, as in some idyllic eternity, Herman Melville once saw the sperm whales nurse their young. And as Melville wrote of the sperm whale, so we might now paraphrase his words in speaking of the porpoise. "Genius in the porpoise? Has the porpoise ever written a book, spoken a speech? No, his great genius is declared in his doing nothing particular to prove it. It is declared in his pyramidical silence." If man had sacrificed his hands for flukes, the moral might run, he would still be a philosopher, but there would have been taken from him the devastating power to wreak his thought upon the body of the world. Instead he would have lived and wandered, like the porpoise, homeless across currents and winds and oceans, intelligent, but forever the lonely and curious observer of unknown wreckage falling through the blue light of eternity. This role would now be a deserved penitence for man. Perhaps such a transformation would bring him once more into that mood of childhood innocence in which he talked successfully to all things living but had no power and no urge to harm. It is worth at least a wistful thought that someday the porpoise may talk to us and we to him. It would break, perhaps, the long loneliness that has made man a frequent terror and abomination even to himself.

# Man the
# Firemaker

Man, it is well to remember, is the discoverer but not the inventor of fire. Long before this meddling little Prometheus took to experimenting with flints, then matches, and finally (we hope not too finally) hydrogen bombs, fires had burned on this planet. Volcanoes had belched molten lava, lightning had struck in dry grass, winds had rubbed dead branches against each other until they burst into flame. There are evidences of fire in ancient fossil beds that lie deep below the time of man.

Man did not invent fire but he did make it one of the giant powers on the earth. He began this experiment long ago in the red morning of the human mind. Today he continues it in the midst of coruscating heat that is capable of rending the very fabric of his universe. Man's long adventure with knowledge has, to a very marked degree, been a climb up the heat ladder, for heat alone enables man to mold metals and glassware, to create his great chemical industries, to drive his swift machines. It is my intention here to trace man's manipulation of this force far back into its ice-age beginnings and to observe the part that fire has played in the human journey across the planet. The torch has been carried smoking through the ages of glacial advance. As we follow man on this journey, we shall learn another aspect of his nature: that he is himself a consuming fire.

At just what level in his intellectual development man mastered the art of making fire is still unknown. Neanderthal man of 50,000 years ago certainly knew the art. Traces of the use of fire have turned up in a cave of Peking man, the primitive human being of at least 250,000 years ago who had a brain only about two-thirds the size of modern man's. And in 1947 Raymond Dart of Witwatersrand University announced the discovery in South Africa of *Australopithecus prometheus*, a man-ape cranium recovered from deposits which he believed showed traces of burned bone.

This startling announcement of the possible use of fire by a subhuman creature raised a considerable storm in anthropological circles. The chemical identifications purporting to indicate evidence of fire are now considered highly questionable. It has also been intimated that the evidence may represent only traces of a natural brush fire. Certainly, so long as the South African man-apes have not been clearly shown to be tool users, wide doubts about their use of fire will remain. There are later sites of tool-using human beings which do not show traces of fire.

Until there is proof to the contrary, it would seem wise to date the earliest use of fire to Peking man—*Sinanthropus*. Other human sites of the same antiquity have not yielded evidence of ash, but this is not surprising, for as a new discovery the use of fire would have taken time to diffuse from one group to another. Whether it was discovered once or several times we have no way of knowing. The fact that fire was in worldwide use at the beginning of man's civilized history enables us to infer that it is an old human culture trait—doubtless one of the earliest. Furthermore, it is likely that man used fire long before he became sophisticated enough to produce it himself.

In 1865 Sir John Lubbock, a British banker who made a hobby of popular writing on science, observed: "There can be no doubt that man originally crept over the earth's surface, little by little, year by year, just, for instance, as the weeds of Europe are now gradually but surely creeping over the surface of Australia." This remark was, in its time, a very shrewd and sensible observation. We know today, however, that there have been times when man suddenly made great strides across the face of the earth. I want to review one of those startling expansions—a lost episode in which fire played a tremendous part. To make its outlines clear we shall have to review the human drama in three acts.

The earliest humanlike animals we can discern are the man-apes of South Africa. Perhaps walking upright on two feet, this creature seems to have been roaming the East African grasslands about one million years ago. Our ancestor, proto-man, probably emerged from the tropics and diffused over the region of warm climate in Eurasia and North Africa. He must have been dependent upon small game, insects, wild seeds, and fruits. His life was hard, his search for food incessant, his numbers were small.

The second stage in human history is represented by the first true men. Paleoanthropic man is clearly a tool user, a worker in stone and bone, but there is still something of the isolated tinkerer and fumbler about him. His numbers are still sparse, judging from the paucity of skeletal remains. Short, stocky, and powerful, he spread over the most temperate portions of the Afro-Eurasiatic land mass but never attempted the passage through the high Arctic to America. Through scores of millennia he drifted with the seasons, seemingly content with his troglodyte existence, making little serious change in his array of flint tools. It is quite clear that some of these men knew the use of fire, but many may not have.

The third act begins some 15,000 or 20,000 years ago. The last great ice sheet still lies across northern Europe and North America. Roving on the open tundra and grasslands below those ice sheets is the best-fed and most varied assemblage of grass-eating animals the world has ever seen. Giant long-horned bison, the huge wild cattle of the Pleistocene, graze on both continents. Mammoth and mastodon wander about in such numbers that their bones are later to astonish the first American colonists. Suddenly, into this late paradise of game, there erupts our own species of man—*Homo sapiens*. Just where he came from we do not know. Tall, lithe, long-limbed, he is destined to overrun the continents in the blink of a geological eye. He has an excellent projectile weapon in the shape of the spear thrower. His flint work is meticulous and sharp. And the most aggressive carnivore the world has ever seen comes at a time made for his success: the grasslands are alive with seemingly inexhaustible herds of game.

Yet fire as much as flesh was the magic that opened the way for the supremacy of *Homo sapiens*. We know that he was already the master of fire, for the track of it runs from camp to buried camp:

the blackened bones of the animals he killed, mute testimony to the relentless step of man across the continents, lie in hundreds of sites in the Old and the New Worlds. Meat, more precious than the gold for which men later struggled, supplied the energy that carried man across the world. Had it not been for fire, however, all that enormous source of life would have been denied to him: he would have gone on drinking the blood from small kills, chewing wearily at uncooked bone ends or masticating the crackling bodies of grasshoppers.

Fire shortens the digestive process. It breaks down tough masses of flesh into food that the human stomach can easily assimilate. Fire made the difference that enabled man to expand his numbers rapidly and to press on from hunting to more advanced cultures. Yet we take fire so much for granted that this first great upswing in human numbers, this first real gain in the seizure of vast quantities of free energy, has to a remarkable degree eluded our attention.

With fire primitive man did more than cook his meat. He extended the pasture for grazing herds. A considerable school of thought, represented by such men as the geographer Carl Sauer and the anthropologist Omer Stewart, believes that the early use of fire by the aborigines of the New World greatly expanded the grassland areas. Stewart says: "The number of tribes reported using fire leads one to the conclusion that burning of vegetation was a universal culture pattern among the Indians of the U.S. Furthermore, the amount of burning leads to the deduction that nearly all vegetation in America at the time of discovery and exploration was what ecologists would call fire vegetation. That is to say, fire was a major factor, along with soil, moisture, temperature, wind, animals, and so forth, in determining the types of plants occurring in any region. It follows then, that the vegetation of the Great Plains was a fire vegetation." In short, the so-called primeval wilderness which awed our forefathers had already felt the fire of the Indian hunter. Here, as in many other regions, man's fire altered the ecology of the earth.

It had its effect not only on the flora but also on the fauna. Of the great herds of grazing animals that flourished in America in the last Ice Age, not a single trace remains—the American elephants, camels, long-horned bison are all gone. Not all of them were struck down by the hunters' weapons. Sauer argues that a major explanation of the extinction of the great American mammals may be fire. He says that the aborigines used fire drives to stampede game, and he contends that this weapon would have worked with peculiar effectiveness to exterminate such lumbering creatures as the mammoth. I have stood in a gully in western Kansas and seen outlined in the earth the fragmented black bones of scores of bison who had perished in what was probably a man-made conflagration. If, at the end of Pleistocene times, vast ecological changes occurred, if climates shifted, if lakes dried and in other places forests sprang up, and if, in this uncertain and unsteady time, man came with flint and fire upon the animal world about him, he may well have triggered a catastrophic decline and extinction. Five thousand years of man and his smoking weapon rolling down the wind may have finished the story for many a slow-witted animal species. In the great scale of geological time this act of destruction amounts to but one brief hunt.

Man, as I have said, is himself a flame. He has burned through the animal world and appropriated its vast stores of protein for his own. When the great herds failed over many areas, he had to devise new ways to feed his increase or drop back himself into a precarious balance with nature. Here and there on the world's margins there have survived into modern times men who were forced into just such local adjustments. Simple hunters and collectors of small game in impoverished areas, they maintain themselves with difficulty. Their numbers remain the same through generations. Their economy permits no bursts of energy beyond what is necessary for the simple age-old struggle with nature. Perhaps, as we view the looming shadow of atomic disaster, this way of life takes on a certain dignity today.

Nevertheless there is no road back; the primitive way is no longer our way. We are the inheritors of an aggressive culture which, when the great herds disappeared, turned to agriculture. Here again the magic of fire fed the great human wave and built up man's numbers and civilization.

Man's first chemical experiment involving the use of heat was to make foods digestible. He had cooked his meat; now he used fire to crack his grain. In the process of adopting the agricultural way of life he made his second chemical experiment with heat: baking pottery.

Ceramics may have sprung in part from the need for storage vessels to protect harvested grain from the incursions of rats and mice and moisture. At any rate, the potter's art spread with the revolutionary shift in food production in early Neolithic times.

People who have only played with mud pies or made little sun-dried vessels of clay are apt to think of ceramics as a simple art. Actually it is not. The sundried vessels of our childhood experiments would melt in the first rain that struck them. To produce true pottery one must destroy the elasticity of clay through a chemical process which can be induced only by subjecting the clay to an intense baking at a temperature of at least 400 or 500 degrees centigrade. The baking drives out the so-called water of constitution from the aluminum silicate in the clay. Thereafter the clay will no longer dissolve in water; a truly fired vessel will survive in the ground for centuries. This is why pottery is so important to the archaeologist. It is impervious to the decay that overtakes many other substances, and, since it was manufactured in quantity, it may tell tales of the past when other clues fail us.

Pottery can be hardened in an open campfire, but the results can never be so excellent as those achieved in a kiln. At some point the early potter must have learned that he could concentrate and conserve heat by covering his fire—perhaps making it in a hole or trench. From this it was a step to the true closed kiln, in which there was a lower chamber for the fire and an upper one for the pottery. Most of the earthenware of simple cultures was fired at temperatures around 500 degrees centigrade, but really thorough firing demands temperatures in the neighborhood of 900 degrees.

After man had learned to change the chemical nature of clay, he began to use fire to transform other raw materials—ores into metals, for instance. One measure of civilization is the number of materials manipulated. The savage contents himself with a few raw materials which can be shaped without the application of high temperatures. Civilized man uses fire to extract, alter, or synthesize a multitude of substances.

By the time metals came into extended use, the precious flame no longer burned in the open campfire, radiating its heat away into the dark or flickering on the bronzed faces of the hunters. Instead it roared in confined furnaces and was fed oxygen through crude bellows. One of the by-products of more intensified experiments with heat was glass—the strange, impassive substance which, in the form of the chemist's flask, the astronomer's telescope, the biologist's microscope, and the mirror, has contributed so vastly to our knowledge of ourselves and the universe.

We hear a good deal about the Iron Age, or age of metals, as a great jump forward in man's history; actually the metals themselves played a comparatively small part in the rise of the first great civilizations. While men learned to use bronze, which demands little more heat than is necessary to produce good ceramics, and later iron, for tools and ornaments, the use of metal did not make a really massive change in civilization for well over 1,500 years. It was what Leslie White of the University of Michigan calls the "Fuel Revolution" that brought the metals into their own. Coal, oil, and gas, new sources of energy, combined with the invention of the steam and combustion engines, ushered in the new age. It was not metals as tools, but metals combined with heat in new furnaces and power machinery that took human society off its thousand-year plateau and made possible another enormous upswing in human numbers, with all the social repercussions.

Today the flames grow hotter in the furnaces. Man has come far up the heat ladder. The creature that crept furred through the glitter of blue glacial nights lives surrounded by the hiss of steam, the roar of engines, and the bubbling of vats. Like a long-armed crab, he manipulates the tongs in dangerous atomic furnaces. In asbestos suits he plunges into the flaming debris of hideous accidents. With intricate heat-measuring instruments he investigates the secrets of the stars, and he has already found heat-resistant alloys that have enabled him to hurl himself into space.

How far will he go? Three hundred years of the scientific method have built the great sky-touching buildings and nourished the incalculable fertility of the human species. But man is also *Homo duplex*, as they knew in the darker ages. He partakes of evil and of good, of god and of man. Both struggle in him perpetually. And he is himself a flame—a great, roaring, wasteful furnace devouring irreplaceable substances of the earth. Before this century is out, either *Homo duplex* must learn that knowledge without greatness of spirit is not enough for man, or there will remain only his calcined cities and the little charcoal of his bones.

# The Innocent Fox

Only to a magician is the world forever fluid, infinitely mutable
and eternally new. Only he knows the secret of change, only
he knows truly that all things are crouched in eagerness to
become something else, and it is from this universal tension
that he draws his power.

—Peter Beagle

## I

Since man first saw an impossible visage staring upward from a still
pool, he has been haunted by meanings—meanings felt even in the
wood, where the trees leaned over him, manifesting a vast and living
presence. The image in the pool vanished at the touch of his finger,
but he went home and created a legend. The great trees never spoke,
but man knew that dryads slipped among their boles. Since the red
morning of time it has been so, and the compulsive reading of such
manuscripts will continue to occupy man's attention long after the
books that contain his inmost thoughts have been sealed away by the
indefatigable spider.

Some men are daylight readers, who peruse the ambiguous word-
ing of clouds or the individual letter shapes of wandering birds.
Some, like myself, are librarians of the night, whose ephemeral
documents consist of root-inscribed bones or whatever rustles in
thickets upon solitary walks. Man, for all his daylight activities, is,
at best, an evening creature. Our very addiction to the day and our
compulsion, manifest through the ages, to invent and use illuminat-
ing devices, to contest with midnight, to cast off sleep as we would
death, suggest that we know more of the shadows than we are willing
to recognize. We have come from the dark wood of the past, and

our bodies carry the scars and unhealed wounds of that transition. Our minds are haunted by night terrors that arise from the subterranean domain of racial and private memories.

Lastly, we inhabit a spiritual twilight on this planet. It is perhaps the most poignant of all the deprivations to which man has been exposed by nature. I have said *deprivation,* but perhaps I should rather maintain that this feeling of loss is an unrealized anticipation. We imagine we are day creatures, but we grope in a lawless and smoky realm toward an exit that eludes us. We appear to know instinctively that such an exit exists.

I am not the first man to have lost his way only to find, if not a gate, a mysterious hole in a hedge that a child would know at once led to some other dimension at the world's end. Such passageways exist, or man would not be here. Not for nothing did Santayana once contend that life is a movement from the forgotten into the unexpected.

As adults, we are preoccupied with living. As a consequence, we see little. At the approach of age some men look about them at last and discover the hole in the hedge leading to the unforeseen. By then, there is frequently no child companion to lead them safely through. After one or two experiences of getting impaled on thorns, the most persistent individual is apt to withdraw and to assert angrily that no such opening exists.

My experience has been quite the opposite, but I have been fortunate. After several unsuccessful but tantalizing trials, which I intend to disclose, I had the help, not of a child, but of a creature —a creature who, appropriately, came out of a quite unremarkable and prosaic den. There was nothing, in retrospect, at all mysterious or unreal about him. Nevertheless, the creature was baffling, just as, I suppose, to animals, man himself is baffling.

II

An autumn midnight in 1967 caught me staring idly from my study window at the attic cupola of an old Victorian house that loomed far above a neighboring grove of trees. I suppose the episode happened just as I had grown dimly aware, amidst my encasing cocoon of books and papers, that something was missing from my life. This feeling had brought me from my desk to peer hopelessly upon the relentless advance of suburban housing. For years, I had not seen anything from that particular window that did not spell the death of something I loved.

Finally, in blundering, good-natured confidence, the last land tortoise had fallen a victim to the new expressway. None of his kind any longer came to replace him. A chipmunk that had held out valiantly in a drainpipe on the lawn had been forced to flee from the usurping rats that had come with the new supermarket. A parking lot now occupied most of the view from the window. I was a man trapped in the despair once alluded to as the utterly hopeless fear confined to moderns—that no miracles can ever happen. I considered, as I tried to will myself away into the attic room far above the trees, the wisdom of a search, a search unlikely to yield tangible results.

Since boyhood I have been charmed by the unexpected and the beautiful. This was what had led me originally into science, but now I felt instinctively that something more was needed—though what I needed verged on a miracle. As a scientist, I did not believe in miracles, though I willingly granted the word broad latitudes of definition.

My whole life had been unconsciously a search, and the search had not been restricted to the bones and stones of my visible profession. Moreover, my age could allow me folly; indeed, it demanded a boldness that the young frequently cannot afford. All I needed to do was to set forth either mentally or physically, but to where escaped me.

At that instant the high dormer window beyond the trees blazed as blue as a lightning flash. As I have remarked, it was midnight. There was no possibility of reflection from a street lamp. A giant bolt of artificial lightning was playing from a condenser, leaping at intervals across the interior of the black pane in the distance. It was the artificial lightning that only one of several engineers with unusual equipment could produce.

Now the old house was plebeian enough. Rooms were rented. People of modest middle-class means lived there, as I was to learn later. But still, in the midmost of the night, somebody or some group was engaged in that attic room upon a fantastic experiment. For, you see, I spied. I spied for nights in succession. I was bored, I was sleepless, and it pleased me to think that the mad scientists, as I came to call them, were engaged, in their hidden room, upon some remarkable and unheard-of adventure.

Why else would they be active at midnight, why else would they be engaged for a brief hour and then extinguish the spark? In the next few days I trained high-powered field glasses upon the window, but the blue bolt defeated me, as did the wavering of autumn boughs across the distant roof. I could only believe that science still possessed some of its old, mad fascination for a mind outside the professional circle of the great laboratories. Perhaps, I thought eagerly, there was a fresh intelligence groping after some secret beyond pure technology. I thought of the dreams of Emerson and others when evolution was first anticipated but its mechanisms remained a mystery entangled with the first galvanic batteries. Night after night, while the leaves thinned and the bolt leaped at its appointed hour, I dreamed, staring from my window, of that coruscating arc revivifying flesh or leaping sentient beyond it into some unguessed state of being. Only for such purposes, I thought, would a man toil in an attic room at midnight.

I began unconsciously to hang more and more upon that work of which, in reality, I knew nothing. It sustained me in my waking hours when the old house, amidst its yellowing leaves, assumed a sleepy and inconsequential air. For me, it had restored wonder and lifted my dreams to the height they had once had when, as a young student, I had peeped through the glass door of a famous experimenter's laboratory. I no longer read. I sat in the darkened study and watched and waited for the unforeseen. It came in a way I had not expected.

One night the window remained dark. My powerful glasses revealed only birds flying across the face of the moon. A bat fluttered about the tessellated chimney. A few remaining leaves fell into the dark below the roofs.

I waited expectantly for the experiment to be resumed. It was not.

The next night it rained violently. The window did not glow. Leaves yellowed the wet walks below the street lamps. It was the same the next night and the next. The episode, I came to feel, peering ruefully from my window, was altogether too much like science itself— science with its lightning bolts, its bubbling retorts, its elusive promises of perfection. All too frequently the dream ended in a downpour of rain and leaves upon wet walks. The men involved had a way, like my mysterious neighbors, of vanishing silently and leaving, if anything at all, corroding bits of metal out of which no one could make sense.

I had once stood in a graveyard that was a great fallen city. It was not hard to imagine another. After watching fruitlessly at intervals until winter was imminent, I promised myself a journey. After all, there was nothing to explain my disappointment. I had not known for what I was searching.

Or perhaps I did know, secretly, and would not admit it to myself: I wanted a miracle. Miracles, by definition, are without continuity, and perhaps my rooftop scientist had nudged me in that direction by the uncertainty of his departure. The only thing that characterizes a miracle, to my mind, is its sudden appearance and disappearance within the natural order, although, strangely, this loose definition would include each individual person. Miracles, in fact, momentarily dissolve the natural order or place themselves in opposition to it. My first experience had been only a tantalizing expectation, a hint that I must look elsewhere than in retorts or coiled wire, however formidable the powers that could be coerced to inhabit them. There was magic, but it was an autumnal, sad magic. I had a growing feeling that miracles were particularly concerned with life, with the animal aspect of things.

Just at this time, and with my thoughts in a receptive mood, a summons came that made it necessary for me to make a long night drive over poor roads through a dense forest. As a subjective experience, which it turned out to be, I would call it a near approach to what I was seeking. There was no doubt I was working further toward the heart of the problem. The common man thinks a miracle can just be "seen" to be reported. Quite the contrary. One has to be, I was discovering, reasonably sophisticated even to *perceive* the miraculous. It takes experience; otherwise, more miracles would be encountered.

One has, in short, to refine one's perceptions. Lightning bolts observed in attics, I now knew, were simply raw material, a lurking extravagant potential in the cosmos. In themselves, they were merely powers summoned up and released by the human mind. Wishing would never make them anything else and might make them worse. Nuclear fission was a ready example. No, a miracle was definitely something else, but that I would have to discover in my own good time.

Preoccupied with such thoughts, I started my journey of descent through the mountains. For a long time I was alone. I followed a road of unexpectedly twisting curves and abrupt descents. I bumped over ruts, where I occasionally caught the earthly starshine of eyes under leaves. Or I plunged at intervals into an impenetrable gloom buttressed by the trunks of huge pines.

After hours of arduous concentration and the sudden crimping of the wheel, my eyes were playing tricks with me. It was time to stop, but I could not afford to stop. I shook my head to clear it and blundered on. For a long time, in this confined glen among the mountains, I had been dimly aware that something beyond the reach of my headlights, but at times momentarily caught in their flicker, was accompanying me.

Whatever the creature might be, it was amazingly fleet. I never really saw its true outline. It seemed, at times, to my weary and much-rubbed eyes, to be running upright like a man, or, again, its color appeared to shift in a multiform illusion. Sometimes it seemed to be bounding forward. Sometimes it seemed to present a face to me and dance backward. From weary consciousness of an animal I grew slowly aware that the being caught momentarily in my flickering headlights was as much a shapeshifter as the wolf in a folk tale. It was not an animal; it was a gliding, leaping mythology. I felt the skin crawl on the back of my neck, for this was still the forest of the windigo and the floating heads commemorated so vividly in the masks of the Iroquois. I was lost, but I understood the forest. The blood that ran in me was not urban. I almost said not human. It had come from other times and a far place.

I slowed the car and silently fought to contain the horror that even animals feel before the disruption of the natural order. But was there a natural order? As I coaxed my lights to a fuller blaze I suddenly realized the absurdity of the question. Why should life tremble before the unexpected if it had not already anticipated the answer? There was no order. Or, better, what order there might be was far wilder and more formidable than that conjured up by human effort.

It did not help in the least to make out finally that the creature who had assigned himself to me was an absurdly spotted dog of dubious affinities—nor did it help that his coat had the curious properties generally attributable to a magician. For how, after all, could I assert with surety what shape this dog had originally possessed a half-mile down the road? There was no way of securing his word for it.

The dog was, in actuality, an illusory succession of forms finally, but momentarily, frozen into the shape "dog" by me. A word, no more. But as it turned away into the night how was I to know it would remain "dog"? By experience? No, it had been picked by me out of a running weave of colors and faces into which it would lapse once more as it bounded silently into the inhuman, unpopulated wood. We deceive ourselves if we think our self-drawn categories exist there. The dog would simply become once more an endless running series of forms, which would not, the instant I might vanish, any longer know themselves as "dog."

By a mental effort peculiar to man, I had wrenched a leaping phantom into the flesh "dog," but the shape could not be held, neither his nor my own. We were contradictions and unreal. A nerve net and the lens of an eye had created us. Like the dog, I was destined to leap away at last into the unknown wood. My flesh, my own seemingly unique individuality, was already slipping like flying mist, like the colors of the dog, away from the little parcel of my bones. If there was order in us, it was the order of change. I started the car again, but I drove on chastened and unsure. Somewhere something was running and changing in the haunted wood. I knew

59

no more than that. In a similar way, my mind was leaping and also changing as it sped. That was how the true miracle, my own miracle, came to me in its own time and fashion.

## III

The episode occurred upon an unengaging and unfrequented shore. It began in the late afternoon of a day devoted at the start to ordinary scientific purposes. There was the broken prow of a beached boat subsiding in heavy sand, left by the whim of ancient currents a long way distant from the shifting coast. Somewhere on the horizon wavered the tenuous outlines of a misplaced building, growing increasingly insubstantial in the autumn light.

After my companions had taken their photographs and departed, their persistent voices were immediately seized upon and absorbed by the extending immensity of an incoming fog. The fog trailed in wisps over the upthrust ribs of the boat. For a time I could see it fingering the tracks of some small animal, as though engaged in a belated dialogue with the creature's mind. The tracks crisscrossed a dune, and there the fog hesitated, as though puzzled. Finally, it approached and enwrapped me, as though to peer into my face. I was not frightened, but I also realized with a slight shock that I was not intended immediately to leave.

I sat down then and rested with my back against the overturned boat. All around me the stillness intensified and the wandering tendrils of the fog continued their search. Nothing escaped them.

The broken cup of a wild bird's egg was touched tentatively, as if with meaning, for the first time. I saw a sand-colored ghost crab, hitherto hidden and immobile, begin to sidle amidst the beach grass as though imbued suddenly with a will derived ultimately from the fog. A gull passed high overhead, but its cry took on the plaint of something other than itself.

I began dimly to remember a primitive dialogue as to whether God is a mist or merely a mist maker. Since a great deal of my thought has been spent amidst such early human and, to my mind, not outworn speculations, the idea did not seem particularly irrational or blasphemous. How else would so great a being, assuming his existence, be able thoroughly to investigate his world, or, perhaps, merely a world that he had come upon, than as he was now proceeding to do?

I closed my eyes and let the tiny diffused droplets of the fog gently palpate my face. At the same time, by some unexplained affinity, I felt my mind drawn inland, to pour, smoking and gigantic as the fog itself, through the gorges of a neighboring mountain range.

In a little shaft of falling light my consciousness swirled dimly over the tombstones of a fallen cemetery. Something within me touched half-obliterated names and dates before sliding imperceptibly onward toward an errand in the city. That errand, whatever its purpose, perhaps because I was mercifully guided away from the future, was denied me.

As suddenly as I had been dispersed I found myself back among the boat timbers and the broken shell of something that had not achieved existence. "I am the thing that lives in the midst of the bones"—a line from the dead poet Charles Williams persisted obstinately in my head. It was true. I was merely condensed from that greater fog to a smaller congelation of droplets. Vague and smoky wisplets of thought were my extensions.

From a rack of bone no more substantial than the broken boat ribs on the beach, I was moving like that larger, all-investigating fog through the doorways of the past. Somewhere far away in an inland city the fog was transformed into a blizzard. Nineteen twenty-nine was a meaningless date that whipped by upon a flying newspaper. The blizzard was beating upon a great gate marked St. Elizabeth's. I was no longer the blizzard. I was hurrying, a small dark shadow, up a stairway beyond which came a labored and importunate breathing.

The man lay back among the pillows, wracked, yellow, and cadaverous. Though I was his son he knew me only as one lamp is briefly lit from another in the windy night. He was beyond speech, but a question was there, occupying the dying mind, excluding the living, something before which all remaining thought had to be mustered. At the time I was too young to understand. Only now could the hurrying shadow drawn from the wrecked boat interpret and relive the question. The starving figure on the bed was held back from death only by a magnificent heart that would not die.

I, the insubstantial substance of memory, the dispersed droplets of the ranging fog, saw the man lift his hands for the last time. Strangely, in all that ravished body, they alone had remained unchanged. They were strong hands, the hands of a craftsman who had played many roles in his life: actor, laborer, professional runner. They were the hands of a man, indirectly of all men, for such had been the nature of his life. Now, in a last lucid moment, he had lifted them up and, curiously, as though they belonged to another being, he had turned and flexed them, gazed upon them unbelievingly, and dropped them once more.

He, too, the shadow, the mist in the gaping bones, had seen these seemingly untouched deathless instruments rally as though with one last purpose before the demanding will. And I, also a shadow, come back across forty years, could hear the question at last. "Why are you, my hands, so separate from me at death, yet still to be commanded? Why have you served me, you who are alive and ingeniously clever?" For here he turned and contemplated them with his old superb steadiness. "What has been our partnership, for I, the shadow, am going, yet you of all of me are alive and persist?"

I could have sworn that his last thought was not of himself but of the fate of the instruments. He was outside, he was trying to look into the secret purposes of things, and the hands, the masterful hands, were the only purpose remaining, while he, increasingly without center, was vanishing. It was the hands that contained his last conscious act. They had been formidable in life. In death they had become strangers who had denied their master's last question.

Suddenly I was back under the overhang of the foundered boat. I had sat there stiff with cold for many hours. I was no longer the extension of a blizzard beating against immovable gates. The year of the locusts was done. It was, instead, the year of the mist maker that some obscure Macusi witch doctor had chosen to call god. But the mist maker had gone over the long-abandoned beach, touching for his inscrutable purposes only the broken shell of the nonexistent, only the tracks of a wayward fox, only a man who, serving the mist maker, could be made to stream wispily through the interstices of time.

# THE INNOCENT FOX

I was a biologist, but I chose not to examine my hands. The fog and the night were lifting. I had been far away for hours. Crouched in my heavy sheepskin I waited without thought as the witch doctor might have waited for the morning dispersion of his god. Finally, the dawn began to touch the sea, and then the worn timbers of the hulk beside which I sheltered reddened just a little. It was then I began to glimpse the world from a different perspective.

I had watched for nights the great bolts leaping across the pane of an attic window, the bolts Emerson had dreamed in the first scientific days might be the force that hurled reptile into mammal. I had watched at midnight the mad scientists intent upon their own creation. But in the end, those fantastic flashes of the lightning had ceased without issue, at least for me. The pane, the inscrutable pane, had darkened at last; the scientists, if scientists they were, had departed, carrying their secret with them. I sighed, remembering. It was then I saw the miracle. I saw it because I was hunched at ground level smelling rank of fox, and no longer gazing with upright human arrogance upon the things of this world.

I did not realize at first what it was that I looked upon. As my wandering attention centered, I saw nothing but two small projecting ears lit by the morning sun. Beneath them, a small neat face looked shyly up at me. The ears moved at every sound, drank in a gull's cry and the far horn of a ship. They crinkled, I began to realize, only with curiosity; they had not learned to fear. The creature was very young. He was alone in a dread universe. I crept on my knees around the prow and crouched beside him. It was a small fox pup from a den under the timbers who looked up at me. God knows what had become of his brothers and sisters. His parent must not have been home from hunting.

He innocently selected what I think was a chicken bone from an untidy pile of splintered rubbish and shook it at me invitingly. There was a vast and playful humor in his face. "If there was only one fox in the world and I could kill him, I would do." The words of a British poacher in a pub rasped in my ears. I dropped even further and painfully away from human stature. It has been said repeatedly that one can never, try as he will, get around to the front of the universe. Man is destined to see only its far side, to realize nature only in retreat.

Yet here was the thing in the midst of the bones, the wide-eyed, innocent fox inviting me to play, with the innate courtesy of its two forepaws placed appealingly together, along with a mock shake of the head. The universe was swinging in some fantastic fashion around to present its face, and the face was so small that the universe itself was laughing.

It was not a time for human dignity. It was a time only for the careful observance of amenities written behind the stars. Gravely I arranged my forepaws while the puppy whimpered with ill-concealed excitement. I drew the breath of a fox's den into my nostrils. On impulse, I picked up clumsily a whiter bone and shook it in teeth that had not entirely forgotten their original purpose. Round and round we tumbled for one ecstatic moment. We were the innocent thing in the midst of the bones, born in the egg, born in the den, born in the dark cave with the stone ax close to hand, born at last in human guise to grow coldly remote in the room with the rifle rack upon the wall.

But I had seen my miracle. I had seen the universe as it begins for all things. It was, in reality, a child's universe, a tiny and laughing universe. I rolled the pup on his back and ran, literally ran for the nearest ridge. The sun was half out of the sea, and the world was swinging back to normal. The adult foxes would be already trotting home.

A little farther on, I passed one on a ridge who knew well I had no gun, for it swung by quite close, stepping delicately with brush and head held high. Its face was watchful but averted. It did not matter. It was what I had experienced and the fox had experienced, what we had all experienced in adulthood. We passed carefully on our separate ways into the morning, eyes not meeting.

But to me the mist had come, and the mere chance of two lifted sunlit ears at morning. I knew at last why the man on the bed had smiled finally before he dropped his hands. He, too, had worked around to the front of things in his death agony. The hands were playthings and had to be cast aside at last like a little cherished toy. There was a meaning and there was not a meaning, and therein lay the agony.

The meaning was all in the beginning, as though time was awry.

# THE INNOCENT FOX

It was a little beautiful meaning that did not stay, and the sixty-year-old man on the hospital bed had traveled briefly toward it through the dark at the end of the universe. There was something in the desperate nature of the world that had to be reversed, but he had been too weak to tell me, and the hands had dropped helplessly away.

After forty years I had been just his own age when the fog had come groping for my face. I think I can safely put it down that I had been allowed my miracle. It was very small, as is the way of great things. I had been permitted to correct time's arrow for a space of perhaps five minutes—and that is a boon not granted to all men. If I were to render a report upon this episode, I would say that men must find a way to run the arrow backward. Doubtless it is impossible in the physical world, but in the memory and the will man might achieve the deed if he would try.

For just a moment I had held the universe at bay by the simple expedient of sitting on my haunches before a fox den and tumbling about with a chicken bone. It is the gravest, most meaningful act I shall ever accomplish, but, as Thoreau once remarked of some peculiar errand of his own, there is no use reporting it to the Royal Society.

# How Flowers Changed
# the World

If it had been possible to observe the earth from the far side of the
solar system over the long course of geological epochs, the watchers
might have been able to discern a subtle change in the light emanat-
ing from our planet. That world of long ago would, like the red
deserts of Mars, have reflected light from vast drifts of stone and
gravel, the sands of wandering wastes, the blackness of naked basalt,
the yellow dust of endlessly moving storms. Only the ceaseless
marching of the clouds and the intermittent flashes from the restless
surface of the sea would have told a different story, but still essen-
tially a barren one. Then, as the millennia rolled away and age
followed age, a new and greener light would, by degrees, have come
to twinkle across those endless miles.

This is the only difference those far watchers, by the use of subtle
instruments, might have perceived in the whole history of the planet
Earth. Yet that slowly growing green twinkle would have contained
the epic march of life from the tidal oozes upward across the raw
and unclothed continents. Out of the vast chemical bath of the sea
—not from the deeps, but from the element-rich, light-exposed
platforms of the continental shelves—wandering fingers of green
had crept upward along the meanderings of river systems and fringed
the gravels of forgotten lakes.

In those first ages plants clung of necessity to swamps and
watercourses. Their reproductive processes demanded direct ac-
cess to water. Beyond the primitive ferns and mosses that en-

66

closed the borders of swamps and streams the rocks still lay vast and bare, the winds still swirled the dust of a naked planet. The grass cover that holds our world secure in place was still millions of years in the future. The green marchers had gained a soggy foothold upon the land, but that was all. They did not reproduce by seeds but by microscopic swimming sperm that had to wriggle their way through water to fertilize the female cell. Such plants in their higher forms had clever adaptations for the use of rain water in their sexual phases and survived with increasing success in a wet land environment. They now seem part of man's normal environment. The truth is, however, that there is nothing very "normal" about nature. Once upon a time there were no flowers at all.

A little while ago—about one hundred million years, as the geologist estimates time in the history of our four-billion-year-old planet —flowers were not to be found anywhere on the five continents. Wherever one might have looked, from the poles to the equator, one would have seen only the cold dark monotonous green of a world whose plant life possessed no other color.

Somewhere, just a short time before the close of the Age of Reptiles, there occurred a soundless, violent explosion. It lasted millions of years, but it was an explosion, nevertheless. It marked the emergence of the angiosperms—the flowering plants. Even the great evolutionist Charles Darwin called them "an abominable mystery," because they appeared so suddenly and spread so fast.

Flowers changed the face of the planet. Without them, the world we know—even man himself—would never have existed. Francis Thompson, the English poet, once wrote that one could not pluck a flower without troubling a star. Intuitively he had sensed like a naturalist the enormous interlinked complexity of life. Today we know that the appearance of the flowers contained also the equally mystifying emergence of man.

If we were to go back into the Age of Reptiles, its drowned swamps and birdless forests would reveal to us a warmer but, on the whole, a sleepier world than that of today. Here and there, it is true, the serpent heads of bottom-feeding dinosaurs might be upreared in suspicion of their huge flesh-eating compatriots. Tyrannosaurs, enormous bipedal caricatures of men, would stalk mindlessly across the sites of future cities and go their slow way down into the dark of geologic time.

In all that world of living things nothing saw save with the intense concentration of the hunt, nothing moved except with the grave sleepwalking intentness of the instinct-driven brain. Judged by modern standards, it was a world in slow motion, a cold-blooded world whose occupants were most active at noonday but torpid on chill nights, their brains damped by a slower metabolism than any known to even the most primitive of warm-blooded animals today.

A high metabolic rate and the maintenance of a constant body temperature are supreme achievements in the evolution of life. They enable an animal to escape, within broad limits, from the overheating or the chilling of its immediate surroundings, and at the same time to maintain a peak mental efficiency. Creatures without a high metabolic rate are slaves to weather. Insects in the first frosts of autumn all run down like little clocks. Yet if you pick one up and breathe warmly upon it, it will begin to move about once more.

In a sheltered spot such creatures may sleep away the winter, but they are hopelessly immobilized. Though a few warm-blooded mammals, such as the woodchuck of our day, have evolved a way of reducing their metabolic rate in order to undergo winter hibernation, it is a survival mechanism with drawbacks, for it leaves the animal helplessly exposed if enemies discover him during his period of suspended animation. Thus bear or woodchuck, big animal or small, must seek, in this time of descending sleep, a safe refuge in some hidden den or burrow. Hibernation is, therefore, primarily a winter refuge of small, easily concealed animals rather than of large ones.

A high metabolic rate, however, means a heavy intake of energy in order to sustain body warmth and efficiency. It is for this reason that even some of these later warm-blooded mammals existing in our day have learned to descend into a slower, unconscious rate of living during the winter months when food may be difficult to obtain. On a slightly higher plane they are following the procedure of the cold-blooded frog sleeping in the mud at the bottom of a frozen pond.

The agile brain of the warm-blooded birds and mammals demands a high oxygen consumption and food in concentrated forms, or the creatures cannot long sustain themselves. It was the rise of the flowering plants that provided that energy and changed the nature of the living world. Their appearance parallels in a quite surprising manner the rise of the birds and mammals.

Slowly, toward the dawn of the Age of Reptiles, something over two hundred and fifty million years ago, the little naked sperm cells wriggling their way through dew and raindrops had given way to a kind of pollen carried by the wind. Our present-day pine forests represent plants of a pollen-disseminating variety. Once fertilization was no longer dependent on exterior water, the march over drier regions could be extended. Instead of spores, simple primitive seeds carrying some nourishment for the young plant had developed, but true flowers were still scores of millions of years away. After a long period of hesitant evolutionary groping, they exploded upon the world with truly revolutionary violence.

The event occurred in Cretaceous times in the close of the Age of Reptiles. Before the coming of the flowering plants our own ancestral stock, the warm-blooded mammals, consisted of a few mousy little creatures hidden in trees and underbrush. A few lizard-like birds with carnivorous teeth flapped awkwardly on ill-aimed flights among archaic shrubbery. None of these insignificant creatures gave evidence of any remarkable talents. The mammals in particular had been around for some millions of years but had remained well lost in the shadow of the mighty reptiles. Truth to tell, man was still, like the genie in the bottle, encased in the body of a creature about the size of a rat.

As for the birds, their reptilian cousins the Pterodactyls flew farther and better. There was just one thing about the birds that paralleled the physiology of the mammals. They, too, had evolved warm blood and its accompanying temperature control. Nevertheless, if one had been seen stripped of his feathers, he would still have seemed a slightly uncanny and unsightly lizard.

Neither the birds nor the mammals, however, were quite what they seemed. They were waiting for the Age of Flowers. They were waiting for what flowers, and with them the true encased seed, would bring. Fish-eating, gigantic, leather-winged reptiles, twenty-eight feet from wing tip to wing tip, hovered over the coasts that one day would be swarming with gulls.

Inland the monotonous green of the pine and spruce forests with their primitive wooden cone flowers stretched everywhere. No grass hindered the fall of the naked seeds to earth. Great sequoias towered to the skies. The world of that time has a certain appeal but it is a giant's world, a world moving slowly like the reptiles who stalked magnificently among the boles of its trees.

The trees themselves are ancient, slow-growing, and immense, like the redwood groves that have survived to our day on the California coast. All is stiff, formal, upright and green, monotonously green. There is no grass as yet; there are no wide plains rolling in the sun, no tiny daisies dotting the meadows underfoot. There is little versatility about this scene; it is, in truth, a giant's world.

A few nights ago it was brought home vividly to me that the world has changed since that far epoch. I was awakened out of sleep by an unknown sound in my living room. Not a small sound—not a creaking timber or a mouse's scurry—but a sharp, rending explosion as though an unwary foot had been put down upon a wine glass. I had come instantly out of sleep and lay tense, unbreathing. I listened for another step. There was none.

Unable to stand the suspense any longer, I turned on the light and passed from room to room glancing uneasily behind chairs and into closets. Nothing seemed disturbed, and I stood puzzled in the center of the living room floor. Then a small button-shaped object upon the rug caught my eye. It was hard and polished and glistening. Scattered over the length of the room were several more, shining up at me like wary little eyes. A pine cone that had been lying in a dish had been blown the length of the coffee table. The dish itself could hardly have been the source of the explosion. Beside it I found two ribbonlike strips of a velvety-green. I tried to place the two strips together to make a pod. They twisted resolutely away from each other and would no longer fit.

I relaxed in a chair, then, for I had reached a solution of the midnight disturbance. The twisted strips were wistaria pods that I had brought in a day or two previously and placed in the dish. They had chosen midnight to explode and distribute their multiplying fund of life down the length of the room. A plant, a fixed, rooted thing, immobilized in a single spot, had devised a way of propelling its offspring across open space. Immediately there passed before my eyes the million airy troopers of the milkweed pod and the clutching hooks of the sandburs. Seeds on the coyote's tail, seeds on the hunter's coat, thistledown mounting on the winds—all were somehow triumphing over life's limitations. Yet the ability to do this had not been with them at the beginning. It was the product of endless effort and experiment.

The seeds on my carpet were not going to lie stiffly where they had dropped like their antiquated cousins, the naked seeds on the pine-cone scales. They were travelers. Struck by the thought, I went out next day and collected several other varieties. I line them up now in a row on my desk—so many little capsules of life, winged, hooked or spiked. Every one is an angiosperm, a product of the true flowering plants. Contained in these little boxes is the secret of that far-off Cretaceous explosion of a hundred million years ago that changed the face of the planet. And somewhere in here, I think, as I poke seriously at one particularly resistant seedcase of a wild grass, was once man himself.

When the first simple flower bloomed on some raw upland late in the Dinosaur Age, it was wind-pollinated, just like its early pine-cone relatives. It was a very inconspicuous flower because it had not yet evolved the idea of using the surer attraction of birds and insects to achieve the transportation of pollen. It sowed its own pollen and received the pollen of other flowers by the simple vagaries of the wind. Many plants in regions where insect life is scant still follow this principle today. Nevertheless, the true flower—and the seed that it produced—was a profound innovation in the world of life.

In a way, this event parallels, in the plant world, what happened among animals. Consider the relative chance for survival of the exteriorly deposited egg of a fish in contrast with the fertilized egg of a mammal, carefully retained for months in the mother's body until the young animal (or human being) is developed to a point where it may survive. The biological wastage is less—and so it is with the flowering plants. The primitive spore, a single cell fertilized in the beginning by a swimming sperm, did not promote rapid distribution, and the young plant, moreover, had to struggle up from nothing. No one had left it any food except what it could get by its own unaided efforts.

By contrast, the true flowering plants (angiosperm itself means "encased seed") grew a seed in the heart of a flower, a seed whose development was initiated by a fertilizing pollen grain independent of outside moisture. But the seed, unlike the developing spore, is already a fully equipped *embryonic plant* packed in a little enclosed box stuffed full of nutritious food. Moreover, by featherdown attachments, as in dandelion or milkweed seed, it can be wafted upward on gusts and ride the wind for miles; or with hooks it can cling to a bear's or a rabbit's hide; or like some of the berries, it can be covered with a juicy, attractive fruit to lure birds, pass undigested through their intestinal tracts, and be voided miles away.

The ramifications of this biological invention were endless. Plants traveled as they had never traveled before. They got into strange environments heretofore never entered by the old spore plants or stiff pine-cone-seed plants. The well-fed, carefully cherished little embryos raised their heads everywhere. Many of the older plants with more primitive reproductive mechanisms began to fade away under this unequal contest. They contracted their range into secluded environments. Some, like the giant redwoods, lingered on as relics; many vanished entirely.

The world of the giants was a dying world. These fantastic little seeds skipping and hopping and flying about the woods and valleys brought with them an amazing adaptability. If our whole lives had not been spent in the midst of it, it would astound us. The old, stiff, sky-reaching wooden world had changed into something that glowed here and there with strange colors, put out queer, unheard-of fruits and little intricately carved seed cases, and, most important of all, produced concentrated foods in a way that the land had never seen before, or dreamed of back in the fish-eating, leaf-crunching days of the dinosaurs.

That food came from three sources, all produced by the reproductive system of the flowering plants. There were the tantalizing nectars and pollens intended to draw insects for pollenizing purposes, and which are responsible also for that wonderful jeweled creation, the hummingbird. There were the juicy and enticing fruits to attract larger animals, and in which tough-coated seeds were concealed, as in the tomato, for example. Then, as if this were not enough, there was the food in the actual seed itself, the food intended to nourish the embryo. All over the world, like hot corn in a popper, these incredible elaborations of the flowering plants kept exploding. In a movement that was almost instantaneous, geologically speaking, the angiosperms had taken over the world. Grass was beginning to cover the bare earth until, today, there are over six thousand species. All kinds of vines and bushes squirmed and writhed under new trees with flying seeds.

The explosion was having its effect on animal life also. Specialized groups of insects were arising to feed on the new sources of food and, incidentally and unknowingly, to pollinate the plant. The flowers bloomed and bloomed in ever larger and more spectacular varieties. Some were pale unearthly night flowers intended to lure moths in the evening twilight, some among the orchids even took the shape of female spiders in order to attract wandering males, some flamed redly in the light of noon or twinkled modestly in the meadow grasses. Intricate mechanisms splashed pollen on the breasts of hummingbirds or stamped it on the bellies of black, grumbling bees droning assiduously from blossom to blossom. Honey ran, insects multiplied, and even the descendants of that toothed and ancient lizard-bird had become strangely altered. Equipped with prodding beaks instead of biting teeth they pecked the seeds and gobbled the insects that were really converted nectar.

Across the planet grasslands were now spreading. A slow continental upthrust which had been a part of the early Age of Flowers had cooled the world's climates. The stalking reptiles and the leather-winged black imps of the seashore cliffs had vanished. Only birds roamed the air now, hot-blooded and high-speed metabolic machines.

The mammals, too, had survived and were venturing into new domains, staring about perhaps a bit bewildered at their sudden eminence now that the thunder lizards were gone. Many of them, beginning as small browsers upon leaves in the forest, began to venture out upon this new sunlit world of the grass. Grass has a high silica content and demands a new type of very tough and resistant tooth enamel, but the seeds taken incidentally in the cropping of the grass are highly nutritious. A new world had opened out for the warm-blooded mammals. Great herbivores like the mammoths, horses, and bisons appeared. Skulking about them had arisen savage flesh-feeding carnivores like the now extinct dire wolves and the saber-toothed tiger.

Flesh eaters though these creatures were, they were being sustained on nutritious grasses one step removed. Their fierce energy was being maintained on a high, effective level, through hot days and frosty nights, by the concentrated energy of the angiosperms. That energy, thirty per cent or more of the weight of the entire plant among some of the cereal grasses, was being accumulated and concentrated in the rich proteins and fats of the enormous game herds of the grasslands.

On the edge of the forest, a strange, old-fashioned animal still hesitated. His body was the body of a tree dweller, and though tough and knotty by human standards, he was, in terms of that world into which he gazed, a weakling. His teeth, though strong for chewing on the tough fruits of the forest, or for crunching an occasional unwary bird caught with his prehensile hands, were not the tearing sabers of the great cats. He had a passion for lifting himself up to see about, in his restless, roving curiosity. He would run, a little stiffly and uncertainly perhaps, on his hind legs, but only in those rare moments when he ventured out upon the ground. All this was the legacy of his climbing days; he had a hand with flexible fingers and no fine specialized hoofs upon which to gallop like the wind.

If he had any idea of competing in that new world, he had better forget it; teeth or hooves, he was much too late for either. He was a ne'er-do-well, an in-betweener. Nature had not done well by him. It was as if she had hesitated and never quite made up her mind. Perhaps as a consequence he had a malicious gleam in his eye, the gleam of an outcast who has been left nothing and knows he is going to have to take what he gets. One day a little band of these odd apes —for apes they were—shambled out upon the grass; the human story had begun.

# HOW FLOWERS CHANGED THE WORLD

Apes were to become men, in the inscrutable wisdom of nature, because flowers had produced seeds and fruits in such tremendous quantities that a new and totally different store of energy had become available in concentrated form. Impressive as the slow-moving, dim-brained dinosaurs had been, it is doubtful if their age had supported anything like the diversity of life that now rioted across the planet or flashed in and out among the trees. Down on the grass by a streamside, one of those apes with inquisitive fingers turned over a stone and hefted it vaguely. The group clucked together in a throaty tongue and moved off through the tall grass foraging for seeds and insects. The one still held, sniffed, and hefted the stone he had found. He liked the feel of it in his fingers. The attack on the animal world was about to begin.

If one could run the story of that first human group like a speeded-up motion picture through a million years of time, one might see the stone in the hand change to the flint ax and the torch. All that swarming grassland world with its giant bison and trumpeting mammoths would go down in ruin to feed the insatiable and growing numbers of a carnivore who, like the great cats before him, was taking his energy indirectly from the grass. Later he found fire and it altered the tough meats and drained their energy even faster into a stomach ill adapted for the ferocious turn man's habits had taken.

His limbs grew longer, he strode more purposefully over the grass. The stolen energy that would take man across the continents would fail him at last. The great Ice Age herds were destined to vanish. When they did so, another hand like the hand that grasped the stone by the river long ago would pluck a handful of grass seed and hold it contemplatively.

In that moment, the golden towers of man, his swarming millions, his turning wheels, the vast learning of his packed libraries, would glimmer dimly there in the ancestor of wheat, a few seeds held in a muddy hand. Without the gift of flowers and the infinite diversity of their fruits, man and bird, if they had continued to exist at all, would be today unrecognizable. Archaeopteryx, the lizard-bird, might still be snapping at beetles on a sequoia limb; man might still be a nocturnal insectivore gnawing a roach in the dark. The weight of a petal has changed the face of the world and made it ours.

75

# The Ghostly
# Guardian

There is an animal that is followed everywhere by a ghost. The ghost floats uncannily a little above and just back of the animal's head. Whether the creature is clambering up the bars of a cage in the zoo or ascending trees in the dense rain forests of the Amazon or the Orinoco, the ghost is always there, sensitive, exploring, shrinking back or protruding forward as the occasion may demand.

The animal is a skinny creature in a funereal black dress. Its legs, arms, and tail are so elongated in proportion to its body that, seen obscurely through a curtain of leaves, it often appears like a huge and repulsive spider as it sidles about in the forest. As a result it has earned the name of "spider monkey," and the ghost that accompanies it is its tremendously lengthy tail. This tail is one of the most remarkable organs to be found anywhere among a group of animals, the monkeys, noted for their addiction to quite varied styles in posterior adornment.

The spider monkey's tail is prehensile—that is, it is capable of grasping objects and transferring them to its owner's mouth, or of holding him safe while he is seated on a waving branch, or its almost preternatural grasping power may save his life as he hurtles headlong from some lofty spot in the forest attic. The muscles and nerves of such tails are of so extraordinary a character that even in death they may hold their owner to his aerial refuge after he has been slain by rifles from the ground.

The spider monkey's tail, however, is not the strangest part of the

76

story. He lives in an area where a great variety of animals of quite unrelated ancestry have tails of this general type, although the spider monkey's is perhaps the most clever and appears to have almost literally taken on an independent life of its own. It is, in very truth, a guardian ghost, but the tail itself is not nearly so mysterious as the way in which numerous diverse creatures in one particular area of forest have acquired these hovering appendages.

These contemporaneous animals, all of one time and place but of widely different origins and habits, share in common one thing: the prehensile grasping tail. In a living world regarded by many scientists as the creation of chance mutations in animals acted upon by selective forces in the environment, they present a strange spectacle. These dangling creatures with their uncanny third hand suggest, inescapably, that nature, somewhere in the vast intricacies with which she complicates the world of life, has here been playing with loaded dice.

On the basis of pure chance it is hard to see why the mysterious evolutionary forces behind the universe should have bestowed this gift with such incredible profusion in only one area of the world, the Amazon basin. It is as though all human beings had spun coins at a particular moment but only those who tossed in San Francisco came up with "tails." This is an obvious simplification, but it makes the issue clear. We would regard such an event as outside the known laws of mathematics. We would feel a hair-raising chill down our spines and demand an explanation.

That is the way one feels when one looks at the ghostly guardian hovering behind a spider monkey, particularly when one walks to the next cage of the mammal house and sees *Coendou,* the prehensile-tailed porcupine of South America; or *Disactylus,* the pygmy anteater, "note the strongly prehensile tail." At such times, though I am supposed to be a naturalist and adjusted to such matters, I get the chill to which I referred. I slink out, almost as if I were followed by a tail myself, and go and sit on a bench to meditate upon the inscrutable way of tails in nature. Of six whole genera—not species, but genera—of South American monkeys, only one lacks a grasping tail.

If you are not a student of these matters you may think indifferently, So what? All monkeys, you see cartoons of them everywhere, hang by their tails. It's the way of monkeys. But the "way of things" is a cover-up for our ignorance. As a matter of simple fact, there isn't a single solitary monkey on the continent of Africa who possesses a true prehensile tail. Yet many monkeys live lives in the high green attic of Africa that, so far as we can tell, are the precise equivalent of those lived by their relatives in the South American forests. But the monkeys of Africa climb without the help of their adorning tails, and as for other African animals only an obscure lizard and a peculiar scaled anteater, the pangolin, seem to be endowed with this helpful little secondary personality.

No, there is something else to be seen here than the "way of things," or, at least, the way of things turns out to be unaccountably marvelous whenever we turn sharply and begin to scrutinize it instead of using the phrase as an opiate. Involved in this matter of tails are some strange factors of inheritance and change which still trouble the modern scientist and over which philosophers have puzzled in vain. Only by climbing ourselves into that lofty world hung on the unstable rafters of strangling vines or by peering down at the wandering and uncertain waters that drench the forest floor in the season of floods can we expect to learn anything of the dark forces that created the grotesque little appendage which, in the spider monkey, may affectionately caress his fellows or faithfully sustain his broken body beyond the hour of death.

The basins of the Amazon and Orinoco rivers contain the largest untouched tropical rain forest left anywhere in the world. Here is the world of the past as it existed over much of the globe before the crawling continent-wide glaciers of the Age of Ice met and forced back, in million-year-long battles, the forces of the green. Now, harried by the fires and axes of man, forests are everywhere in the process of disappearance. Their last strongholds lie in the damp hot lands along the equator in Africa, in South America, in a few South Sea Islands, and in the remoter confines of Asia. In these areas, and particularly in the state of Amazonas in Brazil, man can move only along the waterways that pour under the great archways of the forest. He is still a puny shadow who, a few feet from the protecting river, may vanish without a trace. If he flies above that endless green expanse and falls, he will be as soundlessly engulfed as though he had gone down into the sea itself. For this world *is* a sea, a sea over whose swaying green billows pass the wind and the birds. Below, the depths are still. Nevertheless, there is life there, scampering wildly through orchid gardens high in the dim green forest garret, just as, below the waves of the sea, there is also life among the forests of the coral.

The forest floor of the great jungles can almost be compared to the abyssal depths of the sea. It is barren and dark and it receives the dead that fall from above. Few higher forms of life haunt its dim recesses. The real life of the rain forest lives among the rafters of a thousand-mile attic more than one hundred feet above the ground. Here, safely elevated above the floods that swirl over hundreds of miles of forest during the rainy season, the monkeys pass on their trembling pathways, serpents creep through networks of vines, brilliantly colored parrots shriek discordantly, and even frogs are born in aerial ponds and never go beneath their floor of leaves. In short, this is a world whose life needs the help of a friendly ghost, and among all the animals who creep and climb on rickety stairs and crumbling balustrades, tails are much in evidence. Not just any old tail, but tails that creep along behind and hold one safe. Tails with naked sensitive tips furrowed like fingers with nonskid whorls of skin.

In a place where death lurks frequently on either side of some quivering patchwork of cables it is no great marvel that everything from porcupines to arboreal anteaters should have a second life in their tails. The real mystery, to the student of tails, lies in another direction. It is the problem of how so many totally unrelated animals have acquired these tails in the Amazonian basin while in the great forests along the Congo scarcely a single aerial performer makes use of a prehensile tail. This is an uncanny situation. The dice of chance have fallen in a certain way all in one place.

The student of animal evolution is accustomed to the assumption that a series of chance changes in the heredity of an animal—"mutations," the biologist calls them—happen to promote the animal's welfare in a given way of life. Slowly, by infinitesimal degrees, such advantageous mutations may be followed by others until an animal is equipped with some highly improved organ such as a grasping tail or other useful character. All of this, as far as present-day experimentation can tell us, is the result of chance adaptations which are very infrequent compared with poor or disadvantageous variations that lead to an animal's destruction. Chance adaptation, in other words, might have readily explained the appearance of one species of monkey with a prehensile tail. It might even explain the occurrence of a grasping tail in two closely related forms, because closely related forms, possibly because of similarities in their body chemistry, may show a tendency to produce similar mutations and hence to evolve along the same pathway, particularly if their environment is such as to similarly select them. But here, in a single great jungle, numerous quite unrelated animals have all chosen to pull out of the grab bag of chance a single useful organ: the grasping tail. Within a reasonably limited period of geological time, they have drawn from the mysterious little packets of the genes, the hereditary substance, an identical solution to a similar problem, and supposedly it has been done by chance variation and selection.

"Easy," runs one solution. "Tails all tend to vary in this direction. It's one of the few useful ways they can vary. Nothing to it."

If one says this, one is forced to look at the arboreal life of Africa. The minute one does so the ease of this solution slips away. There are many tails; among the African mammals there are no prehensile ones save that of the scaled and ancient pangolin. If the grasping tail has been so easy to produce by chance, why is it so scarce in Africa and so common in South America?

One writer, confining himself discreetly to monkeys, argues that the South American forms like the spider monkey are thumbless; as a consequence they have developed the prehensile tail as a compensation for this absence of a digit. Very well, but the colobus monkeys of Africa are thumbless and they do not possess a grasping tail. The correlation does not seem to hold, and in any case it does not explain why certain arboreal opossums, kinkajous, and other queer Amazonian beasts with paws and no missing digits should go in for grasping tails.

Another suggestion is that the Amazonian lowlands, being frequently inundated by floods, have stimulated the selection of prehensile tails more vigorously than the African forests. In this connection one must consider the Uakari monkey. He is a queer little fellow with an absolutely bald head and a choleric, equally bald face. Uncannily human in facial appearance, he looks, in his coat of moth-eaten brown fur, as though he were a human being who had been playing an orangutang at a masked ball and had just removed his head mask. He has a nonprehensile, stumpy, rudimentary, and almost useless tail, but he continues to flourish happily among the Amazonian floods.

In any case it is to be noticed that while these varied theories attempt to explain the selection of mutations leading to the development of grasping tails, none of them really comes to grips with the more formidable problem of why these apt variations were all conveniently at hand in this one place. The difficulty is enhanced by the presence of such a diverse array of creatures all showing the same characteristic, which comprises several lesser adaptations such as suitably flattened vertebrae, muscular enhancement in the tail and lower back, a certain way of rolling up or manipulating the organ, and its control by the brain.

Darwin, always troubled by such problems, used to speak of the mysterious and unknown laws governing these matters. Unlike many of his followers he had no illusions that he had solved all the mysteries of life and evolution. Reading his works one is often made aware of how that great mind hesitated painfully over much that his followers take for granted.

Once he expressed himself to the effect that the independent duplication of a single animal form, if proven for two separate areas of the world, might force him to entertain the possibility of some other explanation for evolution than that offered by chance mutations acted upon by natural selection. Strangely enough, these monkeys of South America offer an evolutionary problem very close to, though admittedly not identical with, the hypothetical case proposed by Darwin. These monkeys, while not totally identical anatomically with those of the Old World, are remarkably similar to them. In fact, only the sophisticated observer can recognize the differences. Yet the separation of these two monkey groups from each other is ancient, and no ancestral monkey remains connecting the Old World with the New are known by fossil hunters.

Instead, it is believed by many authorities that the New World and Old World monkeys have arisen as parallel developments from older pre-monkey forms, the lemurs, which were once spread over the whole region from Asia to South America. In this case, creatures of very similar brain, face, habits, and general appearance would have come into being in separate parts of the world from ancestors far below the monkey level. Such a development might suggest latent evolutionary powers not entirely the simple product of what we, in our ignorance of a better word, call chance. We are not in a position as yet to verify absolutely this interpretation of the separate origins of the Old and New World monkeys, but it is the most reasonable theory that we possess.

There is no doubt that this mystery would have intrigued the brooding mind of Darwin, particularly since one of the South American monkeys involved has a brain which in proportion to its body weight is larger than man's. Perhaps fortunately for us, however, Chrysothrix, the squirrel monkey, stayed small and remained in the trees so that his large and elflike cranium presents no threat to us. Yet withal, these strange parallelisms leave one with an odd feeling about what the biologist means by chance.

Elusive, tantalizing, and remote in the green attic of the elder world one catches an occasional glimpse of faces hauntingly like one's own and yet different, as though one peered into a charmed mirror. And slowly, through the shifting endless greenery, crawl the multitudinous things with tails, the tails that curl and hold, or wave forward like slender ghosts. There is something, particularly in a spider monkey's tail, that is too bold and purposeful to be easily called the product of simple chance. It floats there like a complete little personality. At least it may cause the true philosopher to pause hesitantly and ponder before he dismisses the universe as totally a world of chance.

# The Bird and
# the Machine

I suppose their little bones have years ago been lost among the stones and winds of those high glacial pastures. I suppose their feathers blew eventually into the piles of tumbleweed beneath the straggling cattle fences and rotted there in the mountain snows, along with dead steers and all the other things that drift to an end in the corners of the wire. I do not quite know why I should be thinking of birds over the *New York Times* at breakfast, particularly the birds of my youth half a continent away. It is a funny thing what the brain will do with memories and how it will treasure them and finally bring them into odd juxtapositions with other things, as though it wanted to make a design, or get some meaning out of them, whether you want it or not, or even see it.

It used to seem marvelous to me, but I read now that there are machines that can do these things in a small way, machines that can crawl about like animals, and that it may not be long now until they do more things—maybe even make themselves—I saw that piece in the *Times* just now. And then they will, maybe—well, who knows —but you read about it more and more with no one making any protest, and already they can add better than we and reach up and hear things through the dark and finger the guns over the night sky.

This is the new world that I read about at breakfast. This is the world that confronts me in my biological books and journals, until there are times when I sit quietly in my chair and try to hear the little purr of the cogs in my head and the tubes flaring and dying as the messages go through them and the circuits snap shut or open. This is the great age, make no mistake about it; the robot has been born somewhat appropriately along with the atom bomb, and the brain they say now is just another type of more complicated feedback system. The engineers have its basic principles worked out; it's mechanical, you know; nothing to get superstitious about; and man can always improve on nature once he gets the idea. Well, he's got it all right and that's why, I guess, that I sit here in my chair, with the article crunched in my hand, remembering those two birds and that blue mountain sunlight. There is another magazine article on my desk that reads "Machines Are Getting Smarter Every Day." I don't deny it, but I'll still stick with the birds. It's life I believe in, not machines.

Maybe you don't believe there is any difference. A skeleton is all joints and pulleys, I'll admit. And when man was in his simpler stages of machine building in the eighteenth century, he quickly saw the resemblances. "What," wrote Hobbes, "is the heart but a spring, and the nerves but so many strings, and the joints but so many wheels, giving motion to the whole body?" Tinkering about in their shops it was inevitable in the end that men would see the world as a huge machine "subdivided into an infinite number of lesser machines."

The idea took on with a vengeance. Little automatons toured the country—dolls controlled by clockwork. Clocks described as little worlds were taken on tours by their designers. They were made up of moving figures, shifting scenes, and other remarkable devices. The life of the cell was unknown. Man, whether he was conceived as possessing a soul or not, moved and jerked about like these tiny puppets. A human being thought of himself in terms of his own tools and implements. He had been fashioned like the puppets he produced and was only a more clever model made by a greater designer.

Then in the nineteenth century, the cell was discovered, and the single machine in its turn was found to be the product of millions of infinitesimal machines—the cells. Now, finally, the cell itself dissolves away into an abstract chemical machine, and that into some intangible, inexpressible flow of energy. The secret seems to lurk all about, the wheels get smaller and smaller, and they turn more rapidly, but when you try to seize it the life is gone—and so, by popular definition, some would say that life was never there in the first place. The wheels and the cogs are the secret and we can make them better in time—machines that will run faster and more accurately than real mice to real cheese.

I have no doubt it can be done, though a mouse harvesting seeds on an autumn thistle is to me a fine sight and more complicated, I think, in his multiform activity than a machine "mouse" running a maze. Also, I like to think of the possible shape of the future brooding in mice, just as it brooded once in a rather ordinary mousy insectivore who became a man. It leaves a nice fine indeterminate sense of wonder that even an electronic brain hasn't got, because you know perfectly well that if the electronic brain changes, it will be because of something man has done to it. But what man will do to himself he doesn't really know. A certain scale of time and a ghostly intangible thing called change are ticking in him. Powers and potentialities like the oak in the seed, or a red and awful ruin. Either way, it's impressive; and the mouse has it, too. Or those birds, I'll never forget those birds—yet before I measured their significance, I learned the lesson of time first of all. I was young then and left alone in a great desert—part of an expedition that had scattered its men over several hundred miles in order to carry on research more effectively. I learned there that time is a series of planes existing superficially in the same universe. The tempo is a human illusion, a subjective clock ticking in our own kind of protoplasm.

As the long months passed, I began to live on the slower planes and to observe more readily what passed for life there. I sauntered, I passed more and more slowly up and down the canyons in the dry baking heat of midsummer. I slumbered for long hours in the shade of huge brown boulders that had gathered in tilted companies out on the flats. I had forgotten the world of men and the world had forgotten me. Now and then I found a skull in the canyons, and these justified my remaining there. I took a serene cold interest in these discoveries. I had come, like many a naturalist before me, to view life with a wary and subdued attention. I had grown to take pleasure in the divested bone.

I sat once on a high ridge that fell away before me into a waste of sand dunes. I sat through hours of a long afternoon. Finally, as I glanced beside my boot an indistinct configuration caught my eye. It was a coiled rattlesnake, a big one. How long he had sat with me I do not know. I had not frightened him. We were both locked in the sleep-walking tempo of the earlier world, baking in the same high air and sunshine. Perhaps he had been there when I came. He slept on as I left, his coils, so ill-discerned by me, dissolving once more among the stones and gravel from which I had barely made him out.

Another time I got on a higher ridge, among some tough little wind-warped pines half covered over with sand in a basinlike depression that caught everything carried by the air up to those heights. There were a few thin bones of birds, some cracked shells of indeterminable age, and the knotty fingers of pine roots bulged out of shape from their long and agonizing grasp upon the crevices of the rock. I lay under the pines in the sparse shade and went to sleep once more.

It grew cold finally, for autumn was in the air by then, and the few things that lived thereabouts were sinking down into an even chillier scale of time. In the moments between sleeping and waking I saw the roots about me and slowly, slowly, a foot in what seemed many centuries, I moved my sleep-stiffened hands over the scaling bark and lifted my numbed face after the vanishing sun. I was a great awkward thing of knots and aching limbs, trapped up there in some long, patient endurance that involved the necessity of putting living fingers into rock and by slow, aching expansion bursting those rocks asunder. I suppose, so thin and slow was the time of my pulse by then, that I might have stayed on to drift still deeper into the lower cadences of the frost, or the crystalline life that glistens pebbles, or shines in a snowflake, or dreams in the meteoric iron between the worlds.

It was a dim descent, but time was present in it. Somewhere far down in that scale the notion struck me that one might come the other way. Not many months thereafter I joined some colleagues heading higher into a remote windy tableland where huge bones were reputed to protrude like boulders from the turf. I had drowsed with reptiles and moved with the century-long pulse of trees; now, lethargically, I was climbing back up some invisible ladder of quickening hours. There had been talk of birds in connection with my duties. Birds are intense, fast-living creatures—reptiles, I suppose one might say, that have escaped out of the heavy sleep of time, transformed fairy creatures dancing over sunlit meadows. It is a youthful fancy, no doubt, but because of something that happened up there among the escarpments of that range, it remains with me a lifelong impression. I can never bear to see a bird imprisoned.

We came into that valley through the trailing mists of a spring night. It was a place that looked as though it might never have known the foot of man, but our scouts had been ahead of us and we knew all about the abandoned cabin of stone that lay far up on one hillside. It had been built in the land rush of the last century and then lost to the cattlemen again as the marginal soils failed to take to the plow.

There were spots like this all over that country. Lost graves marked by unlettered stones and old corroding rim-fire cartridge cases lying where somebody had made a stand among the boulders that rimmed the valley. They are all that remain of the range wars; the men are under the stones now. I could see our cavalcade winding in and out through the mist below us: torches, the reflection of the truck lights on our collecting tins, and the far-off bumping of a loose dinosaur thigh bone in the bottom of a trailer. I stood on a rock a moment looking down and thinking what it cost in money and equipment to capture the past.

We had, in addition, instructions to lay hands on the present. The word had come through to get them alive—birds, reptiles, anything. A zoo somewhere abroad needed restocking. It was one of those reciprocal matters in which science involves itself. Maybe our museum needed a stray ostrich egg and this was the payoff. Anyhow, my job was to help capture some birds and that was why I was there before the trucks.

The cabin had not been occupied for years. We intended to clean it out and live in it, but there were holes in the roof and the birds had come in and were roosting in the rafters. You could depend on it in a place like this where everything blew away, and even a bird needed some place out of the weather and away from coyotes. A cabin going back to nature in a wild place draws them till they come in, listening at the eaves, I imagine, pecking softly among the shingles till they find a hole, and then suddenly the place is theirs and man is forgotten.

Sometimes of late years I find myself thinking the most beautiful sight in the world might be the birds taking over New York after the last man has run away to the hills. I will never live to see it, of course, but I know just how it will sound because I've lived up high and I know the sort of watch birds keep on us. I've listened to sparrows tapping tentatively on the outside of air conditioners when they thought no one was listening, and I know how other birds test the vibrations that come up to them through the television aerials.

"Is he gone?" they ask, and the vibrations come up from below, "Not yet, not yet."

Well, to come back, I got the door open softly and I had the spotlight all ready to turn on and blind whatever birds there were so they couldn't see to get out through the roof. I had a short piece of ladder to put against the far wall where there was a shelf on which I expected to make the biggest haul. I had all the information I needed, just like any skilled assassin. I pushed the door open, the hinges squeaking only a little. A bird or two stirred—I could hear them—but nothing flew and there was a faint starlight through the holes in the roof.

I padded across the floor, got the ladder up and the light ready, and slithered up the ladder till my head and arms were over the shelf. Everything was dark as pitch except for the starlight at the little place back of the shelf near the eaves. With the light to blind them, they'd never make it. I had them. I reached my arm carefully over in order to be ready to seize whatever was there and I put the flash on the edge of the shelf where it would stand by itself when I turned it on. That way I'd be able to use both hands.

Everything worked perfectly except for one detail—I didn't know what kind of birds were there. I never thought about it at all, and it wouldn't have mattered if I had. My orders were to get something interesting. I snapped on the flash and sure enough there was a great beating and feathers flying, but instead of my having them, they, or rather he, had me. He had my hand, that is, and for a small hawk not much bigger than my fist he was doing all right. I heard him give one short metallic cry when the light went on and my hand descended on the bird beside him; after that he was busy with his claws and his beak was sunk in my thumb. In the struggle I knocked the lamp over on the shelf, and his mate got her sight back and whisked neatly through the hole in the roof and off among the stars outside. It all happened in fifteen seconds and you might think I would have fallen down the ladder, but no, I had a professional assassin's reputation to keep up, and the bird, of course, made the mistake of thinking the hand was the enemy and not the eyes behind it. He chewed my thumb up pretty effectively and lacerated my hand with his claws, but in the end I got him, having two hands to work with.

He was a sparrow hawk and a fine young male in the prime of life. I was sorry not to catch the pair of them, but as I dripped blood and folded his wings carefully, holding him by the back so that he couldn't strike again, I had to admit the two of them might have been more than I could have handled under the circumstances. The little fellow had saved his mate by diverting me, and that was that. He was born to it and made no outcry now, resting in my hand hopelessly but peering toward me in the shadows behind the lamp with a fierce, almost indifferent glance. He neither gave nor expected mercy and something out of the high air passed from him to me, stirring a faint embarrassment.

I quit looking into that eye and managed to get my huge carcass with its fist full of prey back down the ladder. I put the bird in a box too small to allow him to injure himself by struggle and walked out to welcome the arriving trucks. It had been a long day, and camp still to make in the darkness. In the morning that bird would be just another episode. He would go back with the bones in the truck to a small cage in a city where he would spend the rest of his life. And a good thing, too. I sucked my aching thumb and spat out some blood. An assassin has to get used to these things. I had a professional reputation to keep up.

In the morning, with the change that comes on suddenly in that high country, the mist that had hovered below us in the valley was gone. The sky was a deep blue, and one could see for miles over the high outcroppings of stone. I was up early and brought the box in which the little hawk was imprisoned out onto the grass where I was building a cage. A wind as cool as a mountain spring ran over the grass and stirred my hair. It was a fine day to be alive. I looked up and all around and at the hole in the cabin roof out of which the other little hawk had fled. There was no sign of her anywhere that I could see.

"Probably in the next county by now," I thought cynically, but before beginning work I decided I'd have a look at my last night's capture.

Secretively, I looked again all around the camp and up and down and opened the box. I got him right out in my hand with his wings folded properly and I was careful not to startle him. He lay limp in my grasp and I could feel his heart pound under the feathers but he only looked beyond me and up.

I saw him look that last look away beyond me into a sky so full of light that I could not follow his gaze. The little breeze flowed over me again, and nearby a mountain aspen shook all its tiny leaves. I suppose I must have had an idea then of what I was going to do, but I never let it come up into consciousness. I just reached over and laid the hawk on the grass.

He lay there a long minute without hope, unmoving, his eyes still fixed on that blue vault above him. It must have been that he was already so far away in heart that he never felt the release from my hand. He never even stood. He just lay with his breast against the grass.

In the next second after that long minute he was gone. Like a flicker of light, he had vanished with my eyes full on him but without actually seeing even a premonitory wing beat. He was gone straight into that towering emptiness of light and crystal that my eyes could scarcely bear to penetrate. For another long moment there was silence. I could not see him. The light was too intense. Then from far up somewhere a cry came ringing down.

I was young then and had seen little of the world, but when I heard that cry my heart turned over. It was not the cry of the hawk I had captured; for, by shifting my position against the sun, I was now seeing farther up. Straight out of the sun's eye, where she must have been soaring restlessly above us for untold hours, hurtled his mate. And from far up, ringing from peak to peak of the summits over us, came a cry of such unutterable and ecstatic joy that it sounds down across the years and tingles among the cups on my quiet breakfast table.

I saw them both now. He was rising fast to meet her. They met in a great soaring gyre that turned to a whirling circle and a dance of wings. Once more, just once, their two voices, joined in a harsh wild medley of question and response, struck and echoed against the pinnacles of the valley. Then they were gone forever somewhere into those upper regions beyond the eyes of men.

I am older now, and sleep less, and have seen most of what there is to see and am not very much impressed any more, I suppose, by anything. "What Next in the Attributes of Machines?" my morning headline runs. "It Might Be the Power to Reproduce Themselves."

I lay the paper down and across my mind a phrase floats insinuatingly: "It does not seem that there is anything in the construction, constituents, or behavior of the human being which it is essentially impossible for science to duplicate and synthesize. On the other hand . . ."

All over the city the cogs in the hard, bright mechanisms have begun to turn. Figures move through computers, names are spelled out, a thoughtful machine selects the fingerprints of a wanted criminal from an array of thousands. In the laboratory an electronic mouse runs swiftly through a maze toward the cheese it can neither taste nor enjoy. On the second run it does better than a living mouse.

"On the other hand . . ." Ah, my mind takes up, on the other hand the machine does not bleed, ache, hang for hours in the empty sky in a torment of hope to learn the fate of another machine, nor does it cry out with joy nor dance in the air with the fierce passion of a bird. Far off, over a distance greater than space, that remote cry from the heart of heaven makes a faint buzzing among my breakfast dishes and passes on and away.

# The Fire Apes

## (EXCERPT)

I was the only man in the world who saw him do it. Everybody else was hurrying. Everybody else around that hospital was busy, or flat on his back and beyond seeing. I had a smashed ankle and was using a crutch, so I couldn't hurry. That was the only reason I was on the grounds and allowed to sit on a bench. If it hadn't been for that I would have missed it. I saw what it meant, too. I had the perspective, you see, and the time to think about it. In the end I hardly knew whether to be glad or sorry, but it was a frightening experience, perhaps not so much frightening as weird because I suddenly and preternaturally saw very close to the end—the end of all of us—and it happened because of that squirrel.

The bird-feeding station stood on the lawn before my bench. Whoever had erected it was a bird-lover, not a squirrel enthusiast, that much was certain. It was on top of a section of thin pipe stuck upright in the ground, and over the end of the pipe half of a bread can had been inverted. The thin, smooth pipe and the bread can were to keep squirrels from the little wooden platform and roof where the birds congregated to feed. The feeding platform was attached just above the tin shield that protected it from the squirrels. I could see that considerable thought had gone into the production of this apparatus and that it was carefully placed so that no squirrel could spring across from a nearby tree.

In the space of the morning I watched five squirrels lope easily across the lawn and try their wits on the puzzle. It was clear that they knew the bread was there—the problem was to reach it. Five squirrels in succession clawed their way up the thin pipe only to discover they were foiled by the tin umbrella around which they could not pass. Each squirrel in turn slid slowly and protestingly back to earth, flinched at my distant chuckle, and went away with a careful appearance of total disinterest that preserved his dignity.

There was a sixth squirrel that came after a time, but I was bored by then, and only half watching. God knows how many things a man misses by becoming smug and assuming that matters will take their natural course. I almost drowsed enough to miss it, and if I had, I might have gone away from there still believing in the fixity of species, or the inviolability of the human plane of existence. I might even have died believing some crass anthropocentric dogma about the uniqueness of the human brain.

As it was, I had just one sleepy eye half open, and it was through that that I saw the end of humanity. It was really a very little episode, and if it hadn't been for the squirrel I wouldn't have seen it at all. The thing was: he stopped to think. He stopped right there at the bottom of the pole and looked up and I knew he was thinking. Then he went up.

He went up with a bound that swayed the thin pipe slightly and teetered the loose shield. In practically the next second he had caught the tilted rim of the shield with an outstretched paw, flicked his body on to and over it, and was sitting on the platform where only birds were supposed to be. He dined well there and daintily, and went away in due time in the neat quick fashion by which he had arrived. I clucked at him and he stopped a moment in his leisurely sweep over the grass, holding up one paw and looking at me with the small shrewd glance of the wood people. There are times now when I think it was a momentous meeting and that for just a second in that sunlit glade, the present and the future measured each other, half conscious in some strange way of their destinies. Then he was loping away with the autumn sunlight flickering on his fur, to a tree where I could not follow him. I turned away and limped back to the shadow of my bench.

He's a smart squirrel, all right, I tried to reassure myself. He's a super-smart squirrel, but just the same he's only a squirrel. Besides, there are monkeys that can solve better problems than that. A nice bit of natural history, an insight into a one-ounce brain at its best, but what's the significance of—

It was just then I got it. The chill that had been slowly crawling up my back as I faced that squirrel. You have to remember what I said about perspective. I have been steeped in geological eras; my mind is filled with the osseous debris of a hundred graveyards. Up till now I had dealt with the past. I was one of the planet's undisputed masters. But that squirrel had busy fingers. He was loping away from me into the future.

The chill came with the pictures, and those pictures rose dim and vast, as though evoked from my subconscious memory by that small uplifted paw. They were not pleasant pictures. They had to do with times far off and alien. There was one, I remember, of gasping amphibian heads on the shores of marshes, with all about them the birdless silence of a land into which no vertebrate life had ever penetrated because it could not leave the water. There was another in which great brainless monsters bellowed in the steaming hollows of a fern forest, while tiny wraithlike mammals eyed them from the underbrush. There was a vast lonely stretch of air, through which occasionally skittered the ill-aimed flight of lizardlike birds. And finally there was a small gibbonlike primate teetering along through a great open parkland, upright on his two hind feet. Once he turned, and I seemed to see something familiar about him, but he passed into the shade.

There were more pictures, but always they seemed to depict great empty corridors, corridors in the sense of a planet's spaces, first empty and then filled with life. Always along those corridors as they filled were eager watchers, watching from the leaves, watching from the grasses, watching from the woods' edge. Sometimes the watchers ventured out a little way and retreated. Sometimes they emerged and strange changes overtook the corridor.

It was somewhere there at the last on the edge of a dying city that I thought I recognized my squirrel. He was farther out of the woods now, bolder, and a bit more insolent, but he was still a squirrel. The city was dying, that was plain, but the cause was undiscernible. I saw with a slight shock that nothing seemed very important about it. It was dying slowly, in the length of centuries, and all about it the little eyes under the leaves were closing in. It was then that I understood, finally, and no longer felt particularly glad or sorry. The city was forfeit to those little shining brains at the woods' edge. I knew how long they had waited. And we, too, had been at the woods' edge in our time. We could afford to go now. Our vast intellectual corridor might stretch empty for a million years. It did not matter. My squirrel would attend to it. And if not he, then the wood rats. They were all there waiting under the leaves. . . .

# Easter: The Isle
of Faces

Easter Island, twelve miles long by seven broad, juts up from the Pacific waters like the triconodont tooth of some primeval mammal. Volcanic cones like cusps mark the corners of the island. On the slopes that fall toward the sea lie great stone platforms cut and fitted from volcanic rock. Standing here and there on the slopes or lying unmoved in the old quarries are the huge stone faces which, like the island itself, hint of a distant and unimaginable past. Once the isle must have been forested by whatever trees could be wafted over the desolate mid-Pacific waters before man came. Today it is clothed sparsely by bushes, grazed by cattle, and supports a few hundred people. It has been known since the Dutch navigator Roggeveen discovered it on Easter day in 1772. Other great Pacific captains such as James Cook and Jean François de la Perouse touched there a few years later and recorded a flourishing population of 2000 to 3000 people. The story of how they came there is lost.

We know only that here man engaged in an incalculable frenzy of creative efforts which apparently ended as suddenly as it began. More than 600 figures lie in the quarries or on the slopes—figures weighing many tons. On the heads of the erect completed torsos were placed huge hats made of reddish stone from separate quarries. Dropped tools and unfinished efforts suggest a hasty and perhaps tragic ending to an unknown religious cult whose purpose is lost. Did a wearied, god-enslaved populace destroy its priesthood? There are suggestions of this in island legends, but these are as misty as modern ideas of how the great statues were transported from their quarries and erected. Even small populations imbued with religious fervor can achieve remarkable feats. The story which we shall never read and which will forever intrigue mankind lies in the meaning of this fantastic performance. It is as though some mad sculptor had bent an entire people to his will—as though a collective will to expend all one's days in the creation of men in stone had spread throughout Easter society. There was an intent, judging from the remains in the quarries, to populate the entire island with gods—if gods they were. Even today the remains are so inspiring in terms of the effort they represent that one can be sure of just one thing: only a tremendous religious stimulus could have incited such labors. Only man, the seer of visions, could have produced such work.

The distances in Polynesia are enormous. Beyond Easter Island the waves run sheer for 2000 miles to the South American shore. In this waste of waters the venturesome canoes that had always found land in the low archipelagoes must have drifted into oblivion with their parched occupants. Easter was the last isle, the outpost on the edge of desolation. Easter was the end. When primitive man found Easter he had finally encompassed the world. He had proved that courage, a stone ax, and an outrigger canoe could take man anywhere on the planet.

The great Pacific triangle known as Polynesia is drawn on the maps through Hawaii, Easter, and New Zealand. It was the last livable area in the world to be settled by man and in some ways the strangest: mostly it was water, but the little groups of islands scattered in the endless seas were fertile. For 3000 years before the dawn of the modern era man had been learning the keys to that vast region. Floating, drifting, paddling, through typhoons and unknown breakers, he had passed from one isle to another farther into the illimitable reaches of the Pacific. After a time, as from a living brain beneath the water, strange psychological worlds had thrust up. Cannibalism on one isle, great mysterious faces on another. Here man lived alone, as he has lived in no other place. Here in the great waters he was free to indulge his cultural fantasies without the visible contradictions presented by too-close neighbors. As in Robert Louis Stevenson's story of "The Isle of Voices" with its unseen population of sorcerers and little fires, so the Polynesian until the eighteenth century remained invisible to the rest of mankind. The water dwellers from the mid-Pacific are, in their history, bodiless and without substance. They make maps of strangely assembled sticks, they steer by the stars and know the secrets of clouds that hover over islands. Their legends are all of lands dragged up from the primeval waters or of lands sunken again into the abyss. Like all history-less people they attract history. The sea vapors that have concealed their passage seem to hint of sunken continents, lost cities, and forgotten arts. Who are these people? From whence did they come? And why at Easter Island, at the very edge of nowhere, did they carve the great sad faces whose eyes look into distances too remote for man? Romantics have linked them to the lost cities of Asia, the cities lying beneath desert sands or crumbling in the green depths of tropical jungles. Others have reversed these wanderings of the Polynesians and seen them as drifting originally westward from Peru. Many of these tales and carefully spun theories are fantastic, but so also is the life of man. Easter Island since the early nineteenth century has become a symbol in Western literature, a symbol of human aspiration to an alien people—ourselves. These seaward-gazing stone faces, transmuted out of their time and place, have played an undying role in a great human drama whose end it is perhaps only now possible to express.

In 1885 Stevenson dreamed a strange dream of transformation which resulted in a story known the world over as "Dr. Jekyll and Mr. Hyde." In it the ill-fated Dr. Jekyll made the horrifying discovery that man is not one but two; that the human consciousness is racked by opposing forces. Stevenson was epitomizing one of the great preoccupations of the Victorians—the struggle between good and evil. The philosophy of this subject is as old as man. What marked the Victorian approach to the problem was the emergence of a new conception of man's mind which had arisen along with the Darwinian discovery of the evolution of man's body.

Darwin and his followers had seen man as arising from the struggle of beast against beast and as therefore inevitably dragging with him out of his midnight experiences a vestigial ferocity only slowly eroding away under conditions of civilized enlightenment. The intricacies of the human mind had not yet been touched by the penetrating scalpel of Freud, but it was becoming plain that, if man's way had come upward from the beast, then the myth of the deathless Garden and the moral fall which occurred there would have to be abandoned. Ascending ape or fallen angel—man would have to make his choice. Oddly enough, it was by the circumstances of this theological quarrel in England that the giant faces upon Easter Island reentered history and have occupied scientific attention ever since.

Legend has it that in some remote castle on the Continent two intertwined stairs run upward in a tower. So clever was the architect, so remarkable was his design of the stairway, that although the steps twine and intertwine in their ascent, a man ascending gets no glimpse at any point of his counterpart coming down. Both are private pathways. In a similar fashion the moral imperfections of man can be seen as a corrupt descent from a state of perfection and absolute innocence, or the flaws of a creature wearily dragging with him up a dark stairwell the imperfections of the slime from which he rose. The two themes circle about each other but are not one.

This was the dilemma that confronted western Europe after the rise of the evolutionary philosophy. The ancestors of genteel Englishmen appeared in the Ice Age past to have chewed knucklebones by open fires and to have shaped and battered common stones for tools. For a proud people at the height of world empire this was a distasteful notion. As always in such cases a school of thought arose to combat the heresy. It was in this connection that men's thoughts returned to Easter Island. Man has never accepted his low-born state. He dreams still. All over the world he dreams, amid the wreckage of great palaces, about the road he has come down. Only in the west where life was young had he devised this other dream —the belief that he had crept outward into the sunlight long ago from the boughs of a dark forest. In the England of Darwin's day these two ideas met and mingled. To many intellectuals, after the publication of the *Origin of Species* and the finding of shaped implements in the earth, the enigma of man could be represented by the allegory of the two stairs. Either man had slowly and painfully made his way upward through the ages while his mind and his body changed, or, on the other hand, the crude remnants of early cultures found in the earth were those of a creature fallen from a state of grace, fallen from divine inspiration—a creature possessing no memory of his great past and dwelling barbarically amid the fallen monuments of his predecessors. Heated controversy echoed in the halls of scientific societies, and learned men debated the question with vigor. Primitive tools alone could not prove human evolution. This only fossils could achieve, and acceptable human "missing links" were not to be discovered for several decades. The "degenerationists," so far as man was concerned, had successfully inverted the archaeological argument for evolution. Man had not arisen from barbarism, they argued; instead he had sunk to it. "No simple tool," wrote one savant of the period, "of and by itself, would be sufficient to prove that there was a condition of mankind lying near that of animals." The foes of human evolution began to search for the evidences of man's coming down in the world.

Albert Mott, the president of the Philosophical Society of Liverpool, addressing that body in 1873 on "The Origin of Savage Life," publicized Easter Island and made much of the inferiority of the living inhabitants to their ancestors. Mott dwelt upon the great size and weight of the stone images scattered around the island, the terraces of fitted stone, the utter isolation of this little pinnacle thrust upward in the vast waste of waters. "If," Mott argued, "this island was first peopled by the accidental drifting of a canoe, it is incredible that the art of making these images and terraces should have developed there. To suppose that savages, under such circumstances, would spend their time and strength upon such labors is altogether past belief."

Instead of accepting a local origin for the sculptures, Mott contended that the islanders must have been an outpost colony of some maritime power long since vanished. Their descendants "though nearly white in colour have degenerated into ordinary savages." Turning from a consideration of Easter Island, Mott hinted that similar ancient ruins would be found in other unexplored islands of the Pacific. Passing to other parts of the world he brought forward additional arguments to prove his point that "savage life is the result of decay and degradation." Such examples as Easter Island, Mott concluded, make it unnecessary to believe "that the earth has been peopled through vast periods of time by the most brutish forms of humanity alone."

The degenerationist-evolutionist controversy, which I have allegorized in the legend of the two stairways, echoed for thirty years in the literature of America and Europe. It faded in importance only with the discovery of genuine human fossils and a better understanding of the archaeological past. The degenerationists, though mistaken in their main theme, contributed many astute observations upon human culture. Mott, for example, profoundly influenced Darwin's great compatriot and fellow scholar Alfred Russel Wallace. Easter Island, lifted out of its Pacific obscurity and attached to a great epoch in human thinking, became known all over the civilized world as a place of mystery. Just as the shadowy continent of Atlantis seemed for a time to haunt the mists of the Atlantic, so Easter Island contributed to romantic theories which involved a similar continental submergence in the mid-Pacific.

Long after the argument of the degenerationists had been forgotten, Easter Island and its inscrutable stone faces continued to be a source of literary dissension which has persisted right down to the present day. Hardly a year passes that some scholar, eccentric or otherwise, does not publish a volume or a special theory about Easter Island. Mott's published lecture, it is now clear, struck some universal chord in the make-up of the human mind. It touched the love of mystery that lies in us all. We are caught in the spell of the dreaming faces and of the three-coned volcanic isle without history. The whole vast sweep of Polynesia and its people take on significance in many minds merely as a clue to the unknown tragedy of which Easter is the heart. Has a continent vanished, has a high civilization foundered and gone down forever into the depths? Was Polynesia populated from Asia or from America? And what of the Polynesians themselves—those near-whites of whom Mott spoke? Of what race are they and from where? What is the lesson of their wanderings? Eternally these questions repeat themselves.

The story even in careful scientific terms is an enthralling one. It has to be pieced together from such debris as litters the shores of a hundred sea-pounded isles. Here it may be a greenstone adze blade dropped on a coral strand which contains no such stone. There it may be an outrigger canoe rotting on an uninhabited beach. From the cargo of the canoe a few coconut palms have sprouted and wave in the light-filled Pacific air. The bleached skeleton of a man is subsiding into the sand a little way up the shore. A few rats that survived the journey have scuttled away into the underbrush. Or one learns of an atoll upon which marooned men without their women survived for years, scanning, until they grew old, the endless sea-glint of the far horizon. One by one they died and were buried until the last survivor went mad with loneliness among the graves. Or men and women on genial trading visits to nearby islands vanished behind a screen of rain never to be seen again, unless, if they were fortunate, some uninhabited island, hundreds of miles removed, received them. If not, they vanished like the insubstantial vapors of the sea itself. Mostly there was no way back from these adventures; no return for wandering Odysseus. The seas were too vast, the isles of home far too elusive. Yet the old chronicles tell that rescued men have been known, in nostalgic desperation, to launch their frail vessels once more in the hope of finding home or death in the waves of earth's greatest sea.

For us, the continent dwellers, this Pacific world will never be totally understandable. We look upon it from too great a height of security. We have mapped in the course of three centuries the entire world. The compass and chronometer and sextant take us through dark nights unerringly across thousands of miles of sea to a speck of land not much larger than a single farm. By contrast, only two peoples in the world have known what it is to be alone: the polar Eskimos of the nineteenth century who thought they were the only men in the world and that the explorers who came to them were ghosts, and those inhabitants of the more remote Pacific islets who learned in astonishment that theirs was not the only land above the water that stretched, as they thought, to infinity.

The people, the sturdy golden-brown people of whom Mott spoke as nearly white, are certainly from Asia, not America. They have ridden with the east wind rather than the west. Their domestic animals, such as the pig, are of the east. It is true that one or two plants in the islands, such as the sweet potato, come from America, but the cultural connection cannot have been sustained. At best it represents the single passage of some great lost voyager. The Polynesian racial strain contains, beside Mongoloid elements, forgotten Asiatic white components which were later drowned in the rising yellow tide. In Fiji in the far south an admixture of darker Melanesian blood is evident. The islands themselves have doubtless exerted a selective influence upon the people. Small islands promote inbreeding. In 3000 years a comparatively small number of families can multiply and spread over a great area; such a development may well have added to the homogeneity of the original population of Polynesia. It is not necessary to postulate great planned migrations. The steady drift of an increasing population into regions of uninhabited land is sufficient to explain the peopling of the mid-Pacific. Except for the poles, it was the last open region of the earth. Each isle was a small paradise until crowding produced war. Local differences of culture and language arose, but these are minor. The basic linguistic stock is the same over the whole vast Pacific triangle.

These archipelagoes in which even the gods traveled in coconut shells or on the backs of fishes contain no trace or rumor of a vanished continent. The islands reveal no signs of animals or plants which could be called continental in type. The vegetation, the animal life, is all such as the sea in long ages brings by chance to island shores: the seeds that survive immersion in salt water, the plant and animal life that travels with primitive man. Yet man's pigs, dogs, and chickens, as well as his food plants, reveal clearly that Polynesia has seen many undirected comings and goings. The vagaries of voyaging without compass have dropped humanly transported plants and animals upon islands where man did not survive, or by contrast men have survived in circumstances where the full complement of his cultural items was not present.

Men forgot, in the island world, much they had learned on the continents, but they learned new things as well. The low coral islands limited man. They constricted his use of stone and forced him into greater reliance upon shells for tools. The high volcanic isles like Easter offered another environment. The superficial similarities of an island existence conceal cultural differences. In an archipelago of closely related islets, voyaging and sea craft may be encouraged. On the distant edge of nowhere, as at lonely Easter Island, sea skills may lapse because the venturesome disappear. The whole of Polynesia, containing perhaps a few hundred thousand souls at the time of discovery, has been populated at an enormous cost in human lives over something like 3000 years in time. Skilled seamen though the islanders were, the lack of navigating instruments must have led to innumerable tragedies at the same time that it resulted in movement farther and farther into the central Pacific.

Great voyaging canoes carrying scores of people and their chattels were used in some regions, and there is evidence that mounting population pressure led to searches for new land. Nevertheless there can be no doubt that these deliberate efforts have been exaggerated by later writers. Captain Cook, who saw the natives in their own untouched environment, felt that chance rather than deliberate intention had populated most of Polynesia. Even in the eighteenth century there was evidence of accidental voyages in which men, women, and children had survived storms and distances of over a thousand miles. They reached, if they survived at all, lands from which they could not return. In this lay the secret of man's trek to the end of the infinite waters. Each generation carried its seed farther. Whether by chance or intent the result was the same at last. If anthropological investigations have produced no traces of a lost continent they have revealed an unwritten epic of man's courage. The populating of Polynesia cost infinitely more in lives than the taking of a continent. Perhaps our star ships may someday search frantically in the great dark for planets as desperately as those lost canoemen sought for a mile-long atoll in thousands of square miles of sea.

Thus there was no lost continent after all, the scholar is forced to conclude. Whatever was carved here or inscribed hieroglyphically on wooden tablets or carried as a seed in the wind from island to island was shaped by the men whom the Pacific voyagers found. But perhaps these seeds of the wind, like those escaped from cultivated gardens, grew wild in strange places, mounted perhaps some strange and effervescing growth where conditions were ripe. Perhaps at that far spot where the stone faces lie in the great quarries horizon-searching man had come at last upon some inexpressible thought to which he gave all his labor. Indeed, at the edge of the world perhaps there was nothing further he could do. The stone was there to be worked, and the deep loneliness for contemplation.

Easter Island shows linguistic differences from the rest of Polynesia that indicate, not lack of relationship, but long isolation from the rest of the Polynesian world. The people's limited traditional memory is partly the result of the raids of South American slavers who descended upon the island in 1863 and carried the greater part of the men away into exile. Yet it is not without significance that the statues and stone platforms are not unique, even though they show local peculiarities and monstrous enhancement. Rather they appear to reflect a cultural trait which flickered sporadically across the Pacific as time and appropriate stone gave opportunities. Man has always been a builder. Perhaps he has built best in loneliness. At least this appears to be the case in the isles of Polynesia.

As sunset falls on the inscrutable stylized faces, one thinks again how appropriately, in the event of man's passing, they would symbolize the end of this age. For the faces are formless, nameless; they represent no living style. They are therefore all men and no man, and they stare indifferently upon that rolling waste which has seen man come and will see him fade once more into the primal elements from which he came. No tears are marked upon the faces, and when at last the waves close over them in the red light of some later sun than ours, the secret of mankind, if indeed man has a secret, will go with them, and all will be upon that waste as it has been before. A flight of sea birds will wind away into the west like smoke. The stars will come out. There will be no one to ask where we, or the stones on which men tried to inscribe their immortality, have gone. There will linger momentarily only a dim sense of something too tragic and too powerful to endure imprisonment in matter or long suffer itself to be reproduced in stone. This is the message from the transcendent heart of man—the seafarer and spacefarer, the figure always beckoning through the mist.

# The Dance of
# the Frogs

## I

He was a member of the Explorers Club, and he had never been outside the state of Pennsylvania. Some of us who were world travelers used to smile a little about that, even though we knew his scientific reputation had been, at one time, great. It is always the way of youth to smile. I used to think of myself as something of an adventurer, but the time came when I realized that old Albert Dreyer, huddling with his drink in the shadows close to the fire, had journeyed farther into the Country of Terror than any of us would ever go, God willing, and emerge alive.

He was a morose and aging man, without family and without intimates. His membership in the club dated back into the decades when he was a zoologist famous for his remarkable experiments upon amphibians—he had recovered and actually produced the adult stage of the Mexican axolotl, as well as achieving remarkable tissue transplants in salamanders. The club had been flattered to have him then, travel or no travel, but the end was not fortunate. The brilliant scientist had become the misanthrope; the achievement lay all in the past, and Albert Dreyer kept to his solitary room, his solitary drink, and his accustomed spot by the fire.

The reason I came to hear his story was an odd one. I had been north that year, and the club had asked me to give a little talk on the religious beliefs of the Indians of the northern forest, the Naskapi of Labrador. I had long been a student of the strange mélange of superstition and woodland wisdom that makes up the religious life of the nature peoples. Moreover, I had come to know something of the strange similarities of the "shaking tent rite" to the phenomena of the modern medium's cabinet.

"The special tent with its entranced occupant is no different from the cabinet," I contended. "The only difference is the type of voices that emerge. Many of the physical phenomena are identical—the movement of powerful forces shaking the conical hut, objects thrown, all this is familiar to Western psychical science. What is different are the voices projected. Here they are the cries of animals, the voices from the swamp and the mountain—the solitary elementals before whom the primitive man stands in awe, and from whom he begs sustenance. Here the game lords reign supreme; man himself is voiceless."

A low, halting query reached me from the back of the room. I was startled, even in the midst of my discussion, to note that it was Dreyer.

"And the game lords, what are they?"

"Each species of animal is supposed to have gigantic leaders of more than normal size," I explained. "These beings are the immaterial controllers of that particular type of animal. Legend about them is confused. Sometimes they partake of human qualities, will and intelligence, but they are of animal shape. They control the movements of game, and thus their favor may mean life or death to man."

"Are they visible?" Again Dreyer's low, troubled voice came from the back of the room.

"Native belief has it that they can be seen on rare occasions," I answered. "In a sense they remind one of the concept of the archetypes, the originals behind the petty show of our small, transitory existence. They are the immortal renewers of substance—the force behind and above animate nature."

"Do they dance?" persisted Dreyer.

At this I grew nettled. Old Dreyer in a heckling mood was something new. "I cannot answer that question," I said acidly. "My informants failed to elaborate upon it. But they believe implicitly in these monstrous beings, talk to and propitiate them. It is their voices that emerge from the shaking tent."

"The Indians believe it," pursued old Dreyer relentlessly, "but do *you* believe it?"

"My dear fellow—I shrugged and glanced at the smiling audience —"I have seen many strange things, many puzzling things, but I am a scientist." Dreyer made a contemptuous sound in his throat and went back to the shadow out of which he had crept in his interest. The talk was over. I headed for the bar.

## II

The evening passed. Men drifted homeward or went to their rooms. I had been a year in the woods and hungered for voices and companionship. Finally, however, I sat alone with my glass, a little mellow, perhaps, enjoying the warmth of the fire and remembering the blue snowfields of the North as they should be remembered—in the comfort of warm rooms.

I think an hour must have passed. The club was silent except for the ticking of an antiquated clock on the mantel and small night noises from the street. I must have drowsed. At all events it was some time before I grew aware that a chair had been drawn up opposite me. I started.

"A damp night," I said.

"Foggy," said the man in the shadow musingly. "But not too foggy. They like it that way."

"Eh?" I said. I knew immediately it was Dreyer speaking. Maybe I had missed something; on second thought, maybe not.

"And spring," he said. "Spring. That's part of it. God knows why, of course, but we feel it, why shouldn't they? And more intensely."

"Look—" I said. "I guess—" The old man was more human than I thought. He reached out and touched my knee with the hand that he always kept a glove over—burn, we used to speculate—and smiled softly.

"You don't know what I'm talking about," he finished for me. "And, besides, I ruffled your feelings earlier in the evening. You must forgive me. You touched on an interest of mine, and I was perhaps overeager. I did not intend to give the appearance of heck-ling. It was only that . . ."

"Of course," I said. "Of course." Such a confession from Dreyer was astounding. The man might be ill. I rang for a drink and decided to shift the conversation to a safer topic, more appropriate to a scholar.

"Frogs," I said desperately, like any young ass in a china shop. "Always admired your experiments. Frogs. Yes."

I give the old man credit. He took the drink and held it up and looked at me across the rim. There was a faint stir of sardonic humor in his eyes.

"Frogs, no," he said, "or maybe yes. I've never been quite sure. Maybe yes. But there was no time to decide properly." The humor faded out of his eyes. "Maybe I should have let go," he said. "It was what they wanted. There's no doubting that at all, but it came too quick for me. What would you have done?"

"I don't know," I said honestly enough and pinched myself.

"You had better know," said Albert Dreyer severely, "if you're planning to become an investigator of primitive religions. Or even not. I wasn't, you know, and the things came to me just when I least suspected—But I forget, you don't believe in them."

He shrugged and half rose, and for the first time, really, I saw the black-gloved hand and the haunted face of Albert Dreyer and knew in my heart the things he had stood for in science. I got up then, as a young man in the presence of his betters should get up, and I said, and I meant it, every word: "Please, Dr. Dreyer, sit down and tell me. I'm too young to be saying what I believe or don't believe in at all. I'd be obliged if you'd tell me."

Just at that moment a strange, wonderful dignity shone out of the countenance of Albert Dreyer, and I knew the man he was. He bowed and sat down, and there were no longer the barriers of age and youthful ego between us. There were just two men under a lamp, and around them a great waiting silence. Out to the ends of the universe, I thought fleetingly, that's the way with man and his lamps. One has to huddle in, there's so little light and so much space. One——

## III

"It could happen to anyone," said Albert Dreyer. "And especially in the spring. Remember that. And all I did was to skip. Just a few feet, mark you, but I skipped. Remember that, too.

"You wouldn't remember the place at all. At least not as it was then." He paused and shook the ice in his glass and spoke more easily.

"It was a road that came out finally in a marsh along the Schuykill River. Probably all industrial now. But I had a little house out there with a laboratory thrown in. It was convenient to the marsh, and that helped me with my studies of amphibia. Moreover, it was a wild, lonely road, and I wanted solitude. It is always the demand of the naturalist. You understand that?"

"Of course," I said. I knew he had gone there, after the death of his young wife, in grief and loneliness and despair. He was not a man to mention such things. "It is best for the naturalist," I agreed.

"Exactly. My best work was done there." He held up his black-gloved hand and glanced at it meditatively. "The work on the axolotl, newt neoteny. I worked hard. I had—" he hesitated— "things to forget. There were times when I worked all night. Or diverted myself, while waiting the result of an experiment, by mid-night walks. It was a strange road. Wild all right, but paved and close enough to the city that there were occasional street lamps. All uphill and downhill, with bits of forest leaning in over it, till you walked in a tunnel of trees. Then suddenly you were in the marsh, and the road ended at an old, unused wharf.

"A place to be alone. A place to walk and think. A place for shadows to stretch ahead of you from one dim lamp to another and spring back as you reached the next. I have seen them get tall, tall, but never like that night. It was like a road into space."

"Cold?" I asked.

"No. I shouldn't have said 'space.' It gives the wrong effect. Not cold. Spring. Frog time. The first warmth, and the leaves coming. A little fog in the hollows. The way they like it then in the wet leaves and bogs. No moon, though; secretive and dark, with just those street lamps wandered out from the town. I often wondered what graft had brought them there. They shone on nothing—except my walks at midnight and the journeys of toads, but still . . ."

"Yes?" I prompted, as he paused.

"I was just thinking. The web of things. A politician in town gets a rake-off for selling useless lights on a useless road. If it hadn't been for that, I might not have seen them. I might not even have skipped. Or, if I had, the effect—How can you tell about such things afterwards? Was the effect heightened? Did it magnify their power? Who is to say?"

"The skip?" I said, trying to keep things casual. "I don't understand. You mean, just skipping? Jumping?"

Something like a twinkle came into his eyes for a moment. "Just that," he said. "No more. You are a young man. Impulsive? You should understand."

"I'm afraid—" I began to counter.

"But of course," he cried pleasantly. "I forget. You were not there. So how could I expect you to feel or know about this skipping. Look, look at me now. A sober man, eh?"

I nodded. "Dignified," I said cautiously.

"Very well. But, young man, there is a time to skip. On country roads in the spring. It is not necessary that there be girls. You will skip without them. You will skip because something within you knows the time—frog time. Then you will skip."

"Then I will skip," I repeated, hypnotized. Mad or not, there was a force in Albert Dreyer. Even there under the club lights, the night damp of an unused road began to gather.

## IV

"It was a late spring," he said. "Fog and mist in those hollows in a way I had never seen before. And frogs, of course. Thousands of them, and twenty species, trilling, gurgling, and grunting in as many keys. The beautiful keen silver piping of spring peepers arousing as the last ice leaves the ponds—if you have heard that after a long winter alone, you will never forget it." He paused and leaned forward, listening with such an intent inner ear that one could almost hear that far-off silver piping from the wet meadows of the man's forgotten years.

I rattled my glass uneasily, and his eyes came back to me.

"They come out then," he said more calmly. "All amphibia have to return to the water for mating and egg laying. Even toads will hop miles across country to streams and waterways. You don't see them unless you go out at night in the right places as I did, but that night——

"Well, it was unusual, put it that way, as an understatement. It was late, and the creatures seemed to know it. You could feel the forces of mighty and archaic life welling up from the very ground. The water was pulling them—not water as we know it, but the mother, the ancient life force, the thing that made us in the days of creation, and that lurks around us still, unnoticed in our sterile cities.

"I was no different from any other young fool coming home on a spring night, except that as a student of life, and of amphibia in particular, I was, shall we say, more aware of the creatures. I had performed experiments"—the black glove gestured before my eyes. "I was, as it proved, susceptible.

"It began on that lost stretch of roadway leading to the river, and it began simply enough. All around, under the street lamps, I saw little frogs and big frogs hopping steadily toward the river. They were going in my direction.

"At that time I had my whimsies, and I was spry enough to feel the tug of that great movement. I joined them. There was no mystery about it. I simply began to skip, to skip gaily, and enjoy the great bobbing shadow I created as I passed onward with that leaping host all headed for the river.

"Now skipping along a wet pavement in spring is infectious, particularly going downhill, as we were. The impulse to take mightier leaps, to soar farther, increases progressively. The madness worked into me. I bounded till my lungs labored, and my shadow, at first my own shadow, bounded and labored with me.

"It was only midway in my flight that I began to grow conscious that I was not alone. The feeling was not strong at first. Normally a sober pedestrian, I was ecstatically preoccupied with the discovery of latent stores of energy and agility which I had not suspected in my subdued existence.

"It was only as we passed under a street lamp that I noticed, beside my own bobbing shadow, another great, leaping grotesquerie that had an uncanny suggestion of the frog world about it. The shocking aspect of the thing lay in its size, and the fact that, judging from the shadow, it was soaring higher and more gaily than myself.

" 'Very well,' you will say"—and here Dreyer paused and looked at me tolerantly—" 'Why didn't you turn around? That would be the scientific thing to do.'

"It would be the scientific thing to do, young man, but let me tell you it is not done—not on an empty road at midnight—not when the shadow is already beside your shadow and is joined by another, and then another.

"No, you do not pause. You look neither to left nor right, for fear of what you might see there. Instead, you dance on madly, hopelessly. Plunging higher, higher, in the hope the shadows will be left behind, or prove to be only leaves dancing, when you reach the next street light. Or that whatever had joined you in this midnight bacchanal will take some other pathway and depart.

"You do not look—you cannot look—because to do so is to destroy the universe in which we move and exist and have our transient being. You dare not look, because, beside the shadows, there now comes to your ears the loose-limbed slap of giant batrachian feet, not loud, not loud at all, but there, definitely there, behind you at your shoulder, plunging with the utter madness of spring, their rhythm entering your bones until you too are hurtling upward in some gigantic ecstasy that it is not given to mere flesh and blood to long endure.

"I was part of it, part of some mad dance of the elementals behind the show of things. Perhaps in that night of archaic and elemental passion, that festival of the wetlands, my careless hopping passage under the street lights had called them, attracted their attention, brought them leaping down some fourth-dimensional roadway into the world of time.

"Do not suppose for a single moment I thought so coherently

then. My lungs were bursting, my physical self exhausted, but I sprang, I hurtled, I flung myself onward in a company I could not see, that never outpaced me, but that swept me with the mighty ecstasies of a thousand springs, and that bore me onward exultantly past my own doorstep, toward the river, toward some pathway long forgotten, toward some unforgettable destination in the wetlands and the spring.

"Even as I leaped, I was changing. It was this, I think, that stirred the last remnants of human fear and human caution that I still possessed. My will was in abeyance; I could not stop. Furthermore, certain sensations, hypnotic or otherwise, suggested to me that my own physical shape was modifying, or about to change. I was leaping with a growing ease. I was——

"It was just then that the wharf lights began to show. We were approaching the end of the road, and the road, as I have said, ended in the river. It was this, I suppose, that startled me back into some semblance of human terror. Man is a land animal. He does not willingly plunge off wharfs at midnight in the monstrous company of amphibious shadows.

"Nevertheless their power held me. We pounded madly toward the wharf, and under the light that hung above it, and the beam that made a cross. Part of me struggled to stop, and part of me hurtled on. But in that final frenzy of terror before the water below engulfed me I shrieked, *'Help! In the name of God, help me! In the name of Jesus, stop!'* "

Dreyer paused and drew in his chair a little closer under the light. Then he went on steadily.

"I was not, I suppose, a particularly religious man, and the cries merely revealed the extremity of my terror. Nevertheless this is a strange thing, and whether it involves the crossed beam, or the appeal to a Christian deity, I will not attempt to answer.

"In one electric instant, however, I was free. It was like the release from demoniac possession. One moment I was leaping in an inhuman company of elder things, and the next moment I was a badly shaken human being on a wharf. Strangest of all, perhaps, was the sudden silence of that midnight hour. I looked down in the circle of the arc light, and there by my feet hopped feebly some tiny froglets of the great migration. There was nothing impressive about them, but you will understand that I drew back in revulsion. I have never been able to handle them for research since. My work is in the past."

He paused and drank, and then, seeing perhaps some lingering doubt and confusion in my eyes, held up his black-gloved hand and deliberately pinched off the glove.

A man should not do that to another man without warning, but I suppose he felt I demanded some proof. I turned my eyes away. One does not like a webbed batrachian hand on a human being.

As I rose embarrassedly, his voice came up to me from the depths of the chair.

"It is not the hand," Dreyer said. "It is the question of choice. Perhaps I was a coward, and ill prepared. Perhaps"—his voice searched uneasily among his memories—"perhaps I should have taken them and that springtime without question. Perhaps I should have trusted them and hopped onward. Who knows? They were gay enough, at least."

He sighed and set down his glass and stared so intently into empty space that, seeing I was forgotten, I tiptoed quietly away.

# The Hidden Teacher

Sometimes the best teacher teaches only once to a single child
or to a grownup past hope.

—Anonymous

I

The putting of formidable riddles did not arise with today's philosophers. In fact, there is a sense in which the experimental method of science might be said merely to have widened the area of man's homelessness. Over two thousand years ago, a man named Job, crouching in the Judean desert, was moved to challenge what he felt to be the injustice of his God. The voice in the whirlwind, in turn, volleyed pitiless questions upon the supplicant—questions that have, in truth, precisely the ring of modern science. For the Lord asked of Job by whose wisdom the hawk soars, and who had fathered the rain, or entered the storehouses of the snow.

A youth standing by, one Elihu, also played a role in this drama, for he ventured diffidently to his protesting elder that it was not true that God failed to manifest Himself. He may speak in one way or another, though men do not perceive it. In consequence of this remark perhaps it would be well, whatever our individual beliefs, to consider what may be called the hidden teacher, lest we become too much concerned with the formalities of only one aspect of the education by which we learn.

We think we learn from teachers, and we sometimes do. But the teachers are not always to be found in school or in great laboratories. Sometimes what we learn depends upon our own powers of insight. Moreover, our teachers may be hidden, even the greatest teacher.

And it was the young man Elihu who observed that if the old are not always wise, neither can the teacher's way be ordered by the young whom he would teach.

For example, I once received an unexpected lesson from a spider.

It happened far away on a rainy morning in the West. I had come up a long gulch looking for fossils, and there, just at eye level, lurked a huge yellow-and-black orb spider, whose web was moored to the tall spears of buffalo grass at the edge of the arroyo. It was her universe, and her senses did not extend beyond the lines and spokes of the great wheel she inhabited. Her extended claws could feel every vibration throughout that delicate structure. She knew the tug of wind, the fall of a raindrop, the flutter of a trapped moth's wing. Down one spoke of the web ran a stout ribbon of gossamer on which she could hurry out to investigate her prey.

Curious, I took a pencil from my pocket and touched a strand of the web. Immediately there was a response. The web, plucked by its menacing occupant, began to vibrate until it was a blur. Anything that had brushed claw or wing against that amazing snare would be thoroughly entrapped. As the vibrations slowed, I could see the owner fingering her guidelines for signs of struggle. A pencil point was an intrusion into this universe for which no precedent existed. Spider was circumscribed by spider ideas; its universe was spider universe. All outside was irrational, extraneous, at best raw material for spider. As I proceeded on my way along the gully, like a vast impossible shadow, I realized that in the world of spider I did not exist.

Moreover, I considered, as I tramped along, that to the phago-cytes, the white blood cells, clambering even now with some kind of elementary intelligence amid the thin pipes and tubing of my body—creatures without whose ministrations I could not exist—the conscious "I" of which I was aware had no significance to these amoeboid beings. I was, instead, a kind of chemical web that brought meaningful messages to them, a natural environment seemingly immortal if they could have thought about it, since generations of them had lived and perished, and would continue to so live and die, in that odd fabric which contained my intelligence—a misty light that was beginning to seem floating and tenuous even to me.

# NATURE AND AUTOBIOGRAPHY

I began to see that, among the many universes in which the world of living creatures existed, some were large, some small, but that all, including man's, were in some way limited or finite. We were creatures of many different dimensions passing through each other's lives like ghosts through doors.

In the years since, my mind has many times returned to that far moment of my encounter with the orb spider. A message has arisen only now from the misty shreds of that webbed universe. What was it that had so troubled me about the incident? Was it that spidery indifference to the human triumph?

If so, that triumph was very real and could not be denied. I saw, had many times seen, both mentally and in the seams of exposed strata, the long backward stretch of time whose recovery is one of the great feats of modern science. I saw the drifting cells of the early seas from which all life, including our own, has arisen. The salt of those ancient seas is in our blood, its lime is in our bones. Every time we walk along a beach some ancient urge disturbs us so that we find ourselves shedding shoes and garments or scavenging among seaweed and whitened timbers like the homesick refugees of a long war.

And war it has been indeed—the long war of life against its inhospitable environment, a war that has lasted for perhaps three billion years. It began with strange chemicals seething under a sky lacking in oxygen; it was waged through long ages until the first green plants learned to harness the light of the nearest star, our sun. The human brain, so frail, so perishable, so full of inexhaustible dreams and hungers, burns by the power of the leaf.

The hurrying blood cells charged with oxygen carry more of that element to the human brain than to any other part of the body. A few moments' loss of vital air and the phenomenon we know as consciousness goes down into the black night of inorganic things. The human body is a magical vessel, but its life is linked with an element it cannot produce. Only the green plant knows the secret of transforming the light that comes to us across the far reaches of space. There is no better illustration of the intricacy of man's relationship with other living things.

The student of fossil life would be forced to tell us that if we take the past into consideration the vast majority of earth's creatures—

perhaps over 90 percent—have vanished. Forms that flourished for a far longer time than man has existed upon earth have become either extinct or so transformed that their descendants are scarcely recognizable. The specialized perish with the environment that created them, the tooth of the tiger fails at last, the lances of men strike down the last mammoth.

In three billion years of slow change and groping effort only one living creature has succeeded in escaping the trap of specialization that has led in time to so much death and wasted endeavor. It is man, but the word should be uttered softly, for his story is not yet done.

With the rise of the human brain, with the appearance of a creature whose upright body enabled two limbs to be freed for the exploration and manipulation of his environment, there had at last emerged a creature with a specialization—the brain—that, paradoxically, offered escape from specialization. Many animals driven into the nooks and crannies of nature have achieved momentary survival only at the cost of later extinction.

Was it this that troubled me and brought my mind back to a tiny universe among the grass blades, a spider's universe concerned with spider thought?

Perhaps.

The mind that once visualized animals on a cave wall is now engaged in a vast ramification of itself through time and space. Man has broken through the boundaries that control all other life. I saw, at last, the reason for my recollection of that great spider on the arroyo's rim, fingering its universe against the sky.

The spider was a symbol of man in miniature. The wheel of the web brought the analogy home clearly. Man, too, lies at the heart of a web, a web extending through the starry reaches of sidereal space, as well as backward into the dark realm of prehistory. His great eye upon Mount Palomar looks into a distance of millions of light-years, his radio ear hears the whisper of even more remote galaxies, he peers through the electron microscope upon the minute particles of his own being. It is a web no creature of earth has ever spun before. Like the orb spider, man lies at the heart of it, listening. Knowledge has given him the memory of earth's history beyond the time of his emergence. Like the spider's claw, a part of him touches a world he will never enter in the flesh. Even now, one can see him reaching forward into time with new machines, computing, analyzing, until elements of the shadowy future will also compose part of the invisible web he fingers.

Yet still my spider lingers in memory against the sunset sky. Spider thoughts in a spider universe—sensitive to raindrop and moth flutter, nothing beyond, nothing allowed for the unexpected, the inserted pencil from the world outside.

Is man at heart any different from the spider, I wonder: man thoughts, as limited as spider thoughts, contemplating now the nearest star with the threat of bringing with him the fungus rot from earth, wars, violence, the burden of a population he refuses to control, cherishing again his dream of the Adamic Eden he had pursued and lost in the green forests of America. Now it beckons again like a mirage from beyond the moon. Let man spin his web, I thought further; it is his nature. But I considered also the work of the phagocytes swarming in the rivers of my body, the unresting cells in their mortal universe. What is it we are a part of that we do not see, as the spider was not gifted to discern my face, or my little probe into her world?

We are too content with our sensory extensions, with the fulfillment of that Ice Age mind that began its journey amidst the cold of vast tundras and that pauses only briefly before its leap into space. It is no longer enough to see as a man sees—even to the ends of the universe. It is not enough to hold nuclear energy in one's hand like a spear, as a man would hold it, or to see the lightning, or times past, or time to come, as a man would see it. If we continue to do this, the great brain—the human brain—will be only a new version of the old trap, and nature is full of traps for the beast that cannot learn.

It is not sufficient any longer to listen at the end of a wire to the rustlings of galaxies; it is not enough even to examine the great coil of DNA in which is coded the very alphabet of life. These are our extended perceptions. But beyond lies the great darkness of the ultimate Dreamer, who dreamed the light and the galaxies. Before act was, or substance existed, imagination grew in the dark. Man partakes of that ultimate wonder and creativeness. As we turn from the galaxies to the swarming cells of our own being, which toil for something, some entity beyond their grasp, let us remember man, the self-fabricator who came across an ice age to look into the mirrors and the magic of science. Surely he did not come to see himself or his wild visage only. He came because he is at heart a listener and a searcher for some transcendent realm beyond himself. This he has worshiped by many names, even in the dismal caves of his beginning. Man, the self-fabricator, is so by reason of gifts he had no part in devising—and so he searches as the single living cell in the beginning must have sought the ghostly creature it was to serve.

## II

The young man Elihu, Job's counselor and critic, spoke simply of the "Teacher," and it is of this teacher I speak when I refer to gifts man had no part in devising. Perhaps—though it is purely a matter of emotional reactions to words—it is easier for us today to speak of this teacher as "nature," that omnipresent all which contained both the spider and my invisible intrusion into her carefully planned universe. But nature does not simply represent reality. In the shapes of life, it prepares the future; it offers alternatives. Nature teaches, though what it teaches is often hidden and obscure, just as the voice from the spinning dust cloud belittled Job's thought but gave back no answers to its own formidable interrogation.

A few months ago I encountered an amazing little creature on a windy corner of my local shopping center. It seemed, at first glance, some long-limbed, feathery spider teetering rapidly down the edge of a store front. Then it swung into the air and, as hesitantly as a spider on a thread, blew away into the parking lot. It returned in a moment on a gust of wind and ran toward me once more on its spindly legs with amazing rapidity.

With great difficulty I discovered the creature was actually a filamentous seed, seeking a hiding place and scurrying about with the uncanny surety of a conscious animal. In fact, it *did* escape me before I could secure it. Its flexible limbs were stiffer than milkweed down, and, propelled by the wind, it ran rapidly and evasively over the pavement. It was like a gnome scampering somewhere with a hidden packet—for all that I could tell, a totally new one: one of the jumbled alphabets of life.

A new one? So stable seem the years and all green leaves, a botanist might smile at my imaginings. Yet bear with me a moment. I would like to tell a tale, a genuine tale of childhood. Moreover, I was just old enough to know the average of my kind and to marvel at what I saw. And what I saw was straight from the hidden Teacher, whatever be his name.

It is told in the Orient of the Hindu god Krishna that his mother, wiping his mouth when he was a child, inadvertently peered in and beheld the universe, though the sight was mercifully and immediately veiled from her. In a sense, this is what happened to me. One day there arrived at our school a newcomer, who entered the grade above me. After some days this lad, whose look of sleepy-eyed arrogance is still before me as I write, was led into my mathematics classroom by the principal. Our class was informed severely that we should learn to work harder.

With this preliminary exhortation, great rows of figures were chalked upon the blackboard, such difficult mathematical problems as could be devised by adults. The class watched in helpless wonder. When the preparations had been completed, the young pupil sauntered forward and, with a glance of infinite boredom that swept from us to his fawning teachers, wrote the answers, as instantaneously as a modern computer, in their proper place upon the board. Then he strolled out with a carelessly exaggerated yawn.

Like some heavy-browed child at the wood's edge, clutching the last stone hand ax, I was witnessing the birth of a new type of humanity—one so beyond its teachers that it was being used for mean purposes while the intangible web of the universe in all its shimmering mathematical perfection glistened untaught in the mind of a chance little boy. The boy, by then grown self-centered and contemptuous, was being dragged from room to room to encourage us, the paleanthropes, to duplicate what, in reality, our teachers could not duplicate. He was too precious an object to be released upon the playground among us, and with reason. In a few months his parents took him away.

Long after, looking back from maturity, I realized that I had been exposed on that occasion, not to human teaching, but to the Teacher, toying with some sixteen billion nerve cells interlocked in ways past understanding. Or, if we do not like the anthropomorphism implied in the word teacher, then nature, the old voice from the whirlwind fumbling for the light. At all events, I had been the fortunate witness to life's unbounded creativity—a creativity seemingly still as unbalanced and chance-filled as in that far era when a black-scaled creature had broken from an egg and the age of the giant reptiles, the creatures of the prime, had tentatively begun.

Because form cannot be long sustained in the living, we collapse inward with age. We die. Our bodies, which were the product of a kind of hidden teaching by an alphabet we are only beginning dimly to discern, are dismissed into their elements. What is carried onward, assuming we have descendants, is the little capsule of instructions such as I encountered hastening by me in the shape of a running seed. We have learned the first biological lesson: that in each generation life passes through the eye of a needle. It exists for a time molecularly and in no recognizable semblance to its adult condition. It *instructs* its way again into man or reptile. As the ages pass, so do variants of the code. Occasionally, a species vanishes on a wind as unreturning as that which took the pterodactyls.

Or the code changes by subtle degrees through the statistical altering of individuals; until I, as the fading Neanderthals must once have done, have looked with still-living eyes upon the creature whose genotype was quite possibly to replace me. The genetic alphabets, like genuine languages, ramify and evolve along unreturning pathways.

If nature's instructions are carried through the eye of a needle, through the molecular darkness of a minute world below the field of human vision and of time's decay, the same, it might be said, is true of those monumental structures known as civilizations. They are transmitted from one generation to another in invisible puffs of air known as words—words that can also be symbolically incised on clay. As the delicate printing on the mud at the water's edge retraces a visit of autumn birds long since departed, so the little scrabbled tablets in perished cities carry the seeds of human thought across the deserts of millennia. In this instance the teacher is the social brain, but it, too, must be compressed into minute hieroglyphs, and the minds that wrought the miracle efface themselves amidst the jostling torrent of messages, which, like the genetic code, are shuffled and reshuffled as they hurry through eternity. Like a mutation, an idea may be recorded in the wrong time, to lie latent like a recessive gene and spring once more to life in an auspicious era.

Occasionally, in the moments when an archaeologist lifts the slab over a tomb that houses a great secret, a few men gain a unique glimpse through that dark portal out of which all men living have emerged, and through which messages again must pass. Here the Mexican archaeologist Ruz Lhuillier speaks of his first penetration of the great tomb hidden beneath dripping stalactites at the pyramid of Palenque: "Out of the dark shadows, rose a fairy-tale vision, a weird ethereal spectacle from another world. It was like a magician's cave carved out of ice, with walls glittering and sparkling like snow crystals." After shining his torch over hieroglyphs and sculptured figures, the explorer remarked wonderingly: "We were the first people for more than a thousand years to look at it."

Or again, one may read the tale of an unknown pharaoh who had secretly arranged that a beloved woman of his household should be buried in the tomb of the god-king—an act of compassion carrying a personal message across the millennia in defiance of all precedent.

Up to this point we have been talking of the single hidden teacher, the taunting voice out of that old Biblical whirlwind which symbolizes nature. We have seen incredible organic remembrance passed through the needle's eye of a microcosmic world hidden completely beneath the observational powers of creatures preoccupied and ensorcelled by dissolution and decay. We have seen the human mind unconsciously seize upon the principles of that very code to pass its own societal memory forward into time. The individual, the momentary living cell of the society, vanishes, but the institutional structures stand, or if they change, do so in an invisible flux not too dissimilar from that persisting in the stream of genetic continuity.

Upon this world, life is still young, not truly old as stars are measured. Therefore it comes about that we minimize the role of the synapsid reptiles, our remote forerunners, and correspondingly exalt our own intellectual achievements. We refuse to consider that in the old eye of the hurricane we may be, and doubtless are, in aggregate, a slightly more diffuse and dangerous dragon of the primal morning that still enfolds us.

Note that I say "in aggregate." For it is just here, among men, that the role of messages, and, therefore, the role of the individual teacher—or, I should say now, the hidden teachers—begin to be more plainly apparent and their instructions become more diverse. The dead pharaoh, though unintentionally, by a revealing act, had succeeded in conveying an impression of human tenderness that has outlasted the trappings of a vanished religion.

Like most modern educators I have listened to student demands to grade their teachers. I have heard the words repeated until they have become a slogan, that no man over thirty can teach the young of this generation. How would one grade a dead pharaoh, millennia gone, I wonder, one who did not intend to teach, but who, to a few perceptive minds, succeeded by the simple nobility of an act.

Many years ago, a student who was destined to become an internationally known anthropologist sat in a course in linguistics and heard his instructor, a man of no inconsiderable wisdom, describe some linguistic peculiarities of Hebrew words. At the time, the young student, at the urging of his family, was contemplating a career in theology. As the teacher warmed to his subject, the student, in the back row, ventured excitedly, "I believe I can understand that, sir. It is very similar to what exists in Mohegan."

The linguist paused and adjusted his glasses. "Young man," he said, "Mohegan is a dead language. Nothing has been recorded of it since the eighteenth century. Don't bluff."

"But sir," the young student countered hopefully, "It can't be dead so long as an old woman I know still speaks it. She is Pequot-Mohegan. I learned a bit of vocabulary from her and could speak with her myself. She took care of me when I was a child."

"Young man," said the austere, old-fashioned scholar, "be at my house for dinner at six this evening. You and I are going to look into this matter."

A few months later, under careful guidance, the young student published a paper upon Mohegan linguistics, the first of a long series of studies upon the forgotten languages and ethnology of the Indians of the northeastern forests. He had changed his vocation and turned to anthropology because of the attraction of a hidden teacher. But just who was the teacher? The young man himself, his instructor, or that solitary speaker of a dying tongue who had so yearned to hear her people's voice that she had softly babbled it to a child?

Later, this man was to become one of my professors. I absorbed much from him, though I hasten to make the reluctant confession that he was considerably beyond thirty. Most of what I learned was gathered over cups of coffee in a dingy campus restaurant. What we talked about were things some centuries older than either of us. Our common interest lay in snakes, scapulimancy, and other forgotten rites of benighted forest hunters.

I have always regarded this man as an extraordinary individual, in fact, a hidden teacher. But alas, it is all now so old-fashioned. We never protested the impracticality of his quaint subjects. We were all too ready to participate in them. He was an excellent canoeman, but he took me to places where I fully expected to drown before securing my degree. To this day, fragments of his unused wisdom remain stuffed in some back attic of my mind. Much of it I have never found the opportunity to employ, yet it has somehow colored my whole adult existence. I belong to that elderly professor in somewhat the same way that he, in turn, had become the wood child of a hidden forest mother.

There are, however, other teachers. For example, among the hunting peoples there were the animal counselors who appeared in prophetic dreams. Or, among the Greeks, the daemonic supernaturals who stood at the headboard while a man lay stark and listened —sometimes to dreadful things. "You are asleep," the messengers proclaimed over and over again, as though the man lay in a spell to hear his doom pronounced. "You, Achilles, you, son of Atreus. You are asleep, asleep," the hidden ones pronounced and vanished.

We of this modern time know other things of dreams, but we know also that they can be interior teachers and healers as well as the anticipators of disaster. It has been said that great art is the night thought of man. It may emerge without warning from the soundless depths of the unconscious, just as supernovas may blaze up suddenly in the farther reaches of void space. The critics, like astronomers, can afterward triangulate such worlds but not account for them.

A writer friend of mine with bitter memories of his youth, and estranged from his family, who, in the interim, had died, gave me this account of the matter in his middle years. He had been working, with an unusual degree of reluctance, upon a novel that contained certain autobiographical episodes. One night he dreamed; it was a very vivid and stunning dream in its detailed reality.

He found himself hurrying over creaking snow through the blackness of a winter night. He was ascending a familiar path through a long-vanished orchard. The path led to his childhood home. The house, as he drew near, appeared dark and uninhabited, but, impelled by the power of the dream, he stepped upon the porch and tried to peer through a dark window into his own old room.

"Suddenly," he told me, "I was drawn by a strange mixture of repulsion and desire to press my face against the glass. I knew intuitively they were all there waiting for me within, if I could but see them. My mother and my father. Those I had loved and those I hated. But the window was black to my gaze. I hesitated a moment and struck a match. For an instant in that freezing silence I saw my father's face glimmer wan and remote behind the glass. My mother's face was there, with the hard, distorted lines that marked her later years.

"A surge of fury overcame my cowardice. I cupped the match before me and stepped closer, closer toward that dreadful confrontation. As the match guttered down, my face was pressed almost to the glass. In some quick transformation, such as only a dream can effect, I saw that it was my own face into which I stared, just as it was reflected in the black glass. My father's haunted face was but my own. The hard lines upon my mother's aging countenance were slowly reshaping themselves upon my living face. The light burned out. I awoke sweating from the terrible psychological tension of that nightmare. I was in a far port in a distant land. It was dawn. I could hear the waves breaking on the reef."

"And how do you interpret the dream?" I asked, concealing a sympathetic shudder and sinking deeper into my chair.

"It taught me something," he said slowly, and with equal slowness a kind of beautiful transfiguration passed over his features. All the tired lines I had known so well seemed faintly to be subsiding.

"Did you ever dream it again?" I asked out of a comparable experience of my own.

"No, never," he said, and hesitated. "You see, I had learned it was just I, but more, much more, I had learned that I was they. It makes a difference. And at the last, late—much too late—it was all right. I understood. My line was dying, but I understood. I hope they understood, too." His voice trailed into silence.

"It is a thing to learn," I said. "You were seeking something and it came." He nodded, wordless. "Out of a tomb," he added after a silent moment, "my kind of tomb—the mind."

On the dark street, walking homeward, I considered my friend's experience. Man, I concluded, may have come to the end of that wild being who had mastered the fire and the lightning. He can create the web but not hold it together, not save himself except by transcending his own image. For at last, before the ultimate mystery, it is himself he shapes. Perhaps it is for this that the listening web lies open: that by knowledge we may grow beyond our past, our follies, and ever closer to what the Dreamer in the dark intended before the dust arose and walked. In the pages of an old book it has been written that we are in the hands of a Teacher, nor does it yet appear what man shall be.

# The Fifth Planet

"It isn't there any more," he said. He was the only man I ever knew who hunted for bones in the stars, and I remember we were standing out among his sheep in the clear starshine when he said it. "It isn't there any more," he repeated. And innocently enough I asked, "What isn't?"—not really thinking at all but just making conversation and watching the silver light drifting over the gray backs of the sheep.

"The fifth planet," he answered. I thought a minute and counted in my head twice over to make sure, and then I said a little soothingly, as one talks to a confused child, "But the fifth planet is Jupiter. There it is over there. All you have to do is swing the tripod around and you'll pick it up all right. Planets don't disappear that easy, thank God."

"The fifth one did all the same," he said. But he shifted the tripod and took a sight toward Jupiter, and the sheep went on munching. I decided I hadn't heard him correctly. After all there is a good deal of wind in those high valleys, and even the frost made little pinging sounds cracking the stones.

We might have been standing on the moon ourselves, it was so cold. I wanted badly to go in and sit by the fire, but it was like this night after night, and nothing for me to do about it if I wanted companionship. He was a bone hunter like myself, in a kind of way. There aren't many of us, nor enough help to stand by, so I couldn't let him down even though I knew he was crazy as hell. If I was playing a hundred-to-one shot when I looked for bones around his ranch by day, he was playing it a million to one at night. That just doesn't make sense. Your life isn't long enough to fool with odds like that. Just the same, there we were out with those sheep and pointing his little telescope looking for bones in the sky.

I suppose that was the thing that intrigued me the first season we met. I'm not a star hunter, though like most people who work with the earth and its past, I have my normal share of curiosity about the universe. It was a far-off interest, though, and besides I was near-sighted from too much peering at the ground. Radnor was different. He already had a squint when I met him, from straining over that telescope, and he was the sort of chap who generally ends up in a cistern or a cesspool while marching around after the stars.

He wasn't a professional. That kind never is. He was a pure bona fide amateur, and part of the lunatic fringe. He got into this thing by accident, and like most such people, he didn't know when to stop. It began with Williams and a flight of meteors. It ended with—well that's the story. But this is how it began.


## II

Williams came up there on the hunt for a meteor. Not an ordinary one, you understand, but the real stuff. A twenty-tonner heard and seen passing over three states. I knew Williams quite well—we worked at the same institution once—and I knew there wasn't a keener eye for a starfall and where it was going.

He'd plotted it all out from the reports, triangulated, and headed up there into that high tableland. Of course he ran into Radnor. He would have to in order to operate in there at all. It was Radnor's ranch and Radnor that helped him. They were lucky, sure. A ranch hand had seen the hole where it struck. They got it, and it was quite a feather in Williams's cap. In any sane place in the world they would have packed it off posthaste to a museum, with a few drinks for the local boys, and things would have gone back to normalcy fast.

The trouble was that nothing up there was normal. In the first place, digging out that big chunk of iron took time, equipment, and all sorts of supplies. Williams stayed at Radnor's place for weeks, and knowing Williams as I did it was easy to guess what happened:

# THE FIFTH PLANET

Williams simply took the malleable clay of Jim Radnor, sheepman, and made a star hunter out of him. That might have been all right, in a nice amateur sort of way, if they had kept it to the front porch on a Sunday evening, but that wasn't how Williams did things.

He was a born teacher—if he wasn't an astronomer I'd have said preacher and been closer to the truth—and he set out to convert Radnor. He aimed to convince Radnor of the importance of meteorite observation, which might have been all right too—there's no real harm in it if your mind runs that way—but then he added that last devilish touch that only a fanatic like Williams would have used to corrode the soul of a good sheepman.

It was unethical, to my mind, immoral really, because it is the kind of thing which the innocent amateur isn't ready to withstand. He hasn't built up to it with the necessary preparation. You take him, addlepated and open-mouthed, and let him look into space until his brain is reeling. Then you whisper over his shoulder something about life out there in that void, and the only way we can ever learn if it exists. And you speak—oh, I knew old Williams well, you know— of the freezing dark that surrounds us and the loneliness that comes to the astronomer in that room under the slit dome. You speak of the suns going by, and the great fires roaring in the solitude of space. You speak of endless depths, great distances all cold and still and empty of the life of man. And then far off, like an insect singing, you begin to whisper the hope of life on other planets, and whether it is true or untrue, and whether there has ever been or will be things like ourselves out there to share our loneliness. And then you tell again how the secret may be found.

## III

It's not my secret. I won't vouch for it, you understand. It's Williams's field, not mine, but I know what he is capable of and the kind of kinks he can tie in people's heads. I've heard that wistful insect singing too, down another dimension—time—which is why I go on bone hunting. Well, he must have done it to Radnor. When I dropped in, a year later, the man had all the symptoms.

I've never known a nicer fellow than Jim. One of those odd,

big-handed, practical fellows with a streak of romance that had lain dormant till Williams touched it off. Unmarried, too. Probably a wife could have handled him, or driven Williams away before the damage was done, but he had had no protection, so there he was with the little telescope Williams had gotten for him, and nothing on his mind but stars.

He had a bunch of file cards in boxes all over his bedroom. I've never seen anything like it. There was no system, no alphabet, but all observations on meteorites and things pertaining to them filed in a colossal jumble. It made him feel scientific, I guess. He told me about the boxes and said he had "facts" in them.

"Now, Jim," I said, for I knew him well, having been in and out of that country before on a mission concerning a small mouselike animal a million years deceased, "now, Jim, what in the name of God are *you* looking for? One crank in this country is bad enough. I don't like competition."

"Bones," he said.

"What?" I exclaimed.

"Bones," he repeated.

"I don't get you," I said. "You've got a nice little telescope that Williams gave you. You've card files full of stuff on meteorites. You're mumbling to me about the Doppler effect and the red shift. What has all that to do with bones? You're in astronomy."

"I'm hunting for interplanetary bones," he said then. He looked at his shoes, and I guess he thought I wouldn't like it very well, being in bones myself. He needn't have worried. I saw where Williams had led him, and I had no intention of following.

"Oh!" I said. And then I just remarked casually I'd be off for the hills in the morning. I knew what Williams could do to a man. He might have done it to me once, if I hadn't been near-sighted. Williams was a fanatic. It wasn't that there was basically anything wrong with his theory, if he'd been content to leave it at that. You'll find it all there in the books. Where the fanaticism came in was in his utter ruthlessness, and his power over people. He knew his theory was a million-to-one shot—a twice-ten-million-to-one shot. And his idea of shortening the odds was to get twenty thousand jug-headed enthusiasts to waste their lives looking for the proof.

# THE FIFTH PLANET

The proof, of course, was bones, interplanetary fossils. Nobody had ever found them and nobody ever—well, I don't know now. The older you get the less you know. At the last Radnor had his say, but he never showed me anything. That isn't science, you know.

It was meteorites that were the key. The theory runs that they, or some of them, are the products of a smash-up in space, the fragments of a lost planetary body. The chemical composition suggests it. Some are heavy metal such as we expect at our own earth's core; others resemble rocks at the earth's surface. The variation suggests that some of them, at least, originated at different depths in another planet. A planet blown to hell and gone. Just here is where Williams got in his play. Instead of sitting quietly in a good club with his drink and the meteorites, he takes the next impossible step.

The meteorites, he says, keep coming in—big ones and little ones, raining in with the earth's attraction. Okay then, keep looking, keep watching. Some day you'll get an unconsumed mass of sedimentary rock off that vanished planet. Sedimentary rock, mind you; fossil-bearing rock. Get it and you've got the secret of the galaxies. One fossil speeding in from outer space, one bit of fossil life unknown to this planet, one skull from a meteor's heart, and space out there— I remember Williams's gesture at that point of his talk—becomes alive. Man is no longer lonely. Life is no longer a unique and terrible accident. It, too, holds its place with the spinning suns.

My God, when I was younger Williams could make the hair stand up along my neck. Think of it! To know if life was out there, or even had been out there. To know whether there were interplanetary parallelisms, perhaps even men—beings, anyhow. To know and to find it all in a whirling piece of rock coming down from the night sky.

No, Williams never told me the chances; I learned of them from other men. I learned that meteorites of sedimentary rock have never been found. I learned that the surface layers of a planet form such a small proportion of its actual bulk that, dispersed in outer space, the number of such fragments coming in, if they came at all, would be infinitesimal. The fossil-bearing rocks of a planet would be in about the same proportion as dirt on the surface of a suddenly exploded golf ball to the substance of the ball itself. The odds were too great, you see, too great for a short-lived creature like man. The odds, those infernal odds!

But I have said that Williams was a fanatic. He was—a cold madman. He tracked meteors everywhere. He organized societies of meteor enthusiasts. He lectured on meteors. He told his tale. He increased the watchers. I followed his progress for years. I saw him pile up meteors like iron junk in his rooms. All iron, no once-living stone that had felt air and known the sun. The fossils might be out there—yes, they might—but living men don't win on a million-to-one shot. Williams was getting old.

He was getting old when he came the long way up that mesa in pursuit of his last flaming disappointment. He was old when he met Radnor. And he took the last of his fury and his hunger and his eloquence and poured them into that romantic, stubborn, religious-minded man.

"It's a question of time, that's all," Radnor said to me later after I had come down from the hills for supplies. He said it with the assurance of one of those damned one-track amateurs that pull Pluto out of a hat after the professionals have gone home to bed.

I spat into the fire.

"All we need is watchers, more and more watchers. Then . . ."

It was Williams all over again. But there was a difference. I could hear it at the back of his talk. "You will see. It will prove how small we are and how great, also. There will be signs, progress, evidence eventually of how high life can go, evidence from an older planet. Evidence of the Great Plan."

"All right, Jim," I said, seeing him eye the door. I was growing used to his routine. "All right," I said meekly, "we'll go out and watch." It was one of those periods of heavy star fall, but the heavy ones don't come often, not even high up where we were.


IV

I think it was on the third night that I heard him mention that fifth planet, and again the next night. I tried tactfully to correct him once more. Actually I was afraid the stuff was going to his head.

# THE FIFTH PLANET

"Look, Radnor," I said, "what do you mean by the fifth planet? I tell you it's Jupiter."

He looked at me and I could see his stubborn, intense eyes back in their shadowy hollows. "Not by Bode's law," he contradicted, and mumbled some figures at me. I remembered his piles of cards, then, and the way Williams must have hammered him.

"Jupiter is the sixth planet," he went on, more to himself than me. "There's a gap between Mars and Jupiter—something is missing there. There's a gap in the planet distances. The fifth planet isn't there."

"Pure accident," I grumbled, feeling out of my depth.

"No," said Radnor, and we both instinctively stared up at something we couldn't see. "There's something there, all right. You've forgotten the asteroids—Ceres and the rest. They're moving where there should be a planet. It's the fifth one, and they're all that's left of it. Something went wrong there."

A meteor trailed high above us, dissolved, and vanished. "Of course," I said. "Stones, aren't they? Just fragments, I remember. Part of something bigger. No air, nothing but thousands of stones on a planet's pathway."

"The fifth planet," he said again. "It's part of the fifth planet that comes down here in little pieces. Williams was sure of it. He said——"

"It was beyond Mars," I conceded to humor him. "There might have been a chance for life there. Curious, what happened . . ."

I turned away then. It was cold and our breath made little frost rings in the dark. "Come on," I urged, but he just stood there brooding as I went in. I left early the next morning. I won't say with relief, for I liked Radnor. But, after all, this was Radnor in a new phase. Later, in the smoker, as the train started to roll eastward, I thought briefly of Williams and his strange influence upon men of Radnor's type. I thought also of that wide and red-stoned plateau, and the things that came down upon it out of the dark. Then someone started a game of poker, and with the miles clicking off behind us, I forgot, a little deliberately perhaps, the whole episode.

One has to live, you know, and I've always had a feeling that space was not in my line.

V

I don't think, as things turned out, that it was in Radnor's line either. Men of his religious nature get centered on a symbol, finally. With some of them it may be gold tablets buried on a mountain, or a book with cryptic inscriptions. Or it may be just a voice in the woods that they alone can hear. With Radnor I guess it was the fifth planet, and I should have known it when I left him out there in the frost that night.

I never expected to see him again. In a job like mine you go many places, have casual contacts with any number of people, and are apt never to turn up in the same spot twice. As it happens in this case, I wish I never had, but I did.

It was a small matter—a question of the proper zoning of a new fossil—but it brought me back two thousand miles, and two years later. I thought of Radnor, of course. I even went to the trouble of clipping a couple of astronomical articles out of the science section of the *New York Times* for him. I figured he'd like them for those overloaded fact boxes he kept.

Things never change in a country like that. There were the same little desert owls flitting from fence post to fence post as when I went away. The road unwound into the same red distance. It was evening when I got to the ranch, and Radnor received me hospitably enough. I must say he had aged a bit, and his eyes seemed apathetic, but after all, none of us gets any younger.

After supper we talked sheep for a while. It seemed safe, and I was not unskilled at it, but after a time a silence fell between us. It was then I drew out the clippings.

He read the first one without comment and dropped it on the white tablecloth. I handed him the second. I remember it had something to do with a recent discovery about the Martian atmosphere and gave strong support to the theory that there might be life on that planet. Knowing Radnor as I had, I expected this one to be good for an evening's conversation. He looked at the headline with an expression of mingled indifference and dislike. "They shouldn't publish that sort of thing," he said.

"I thought you might like it for those big files of yours," I countered uneasily. He raised his head and looked through me the way that little black telescope of his used to pick up holes in space. "I burned them," he said flatly.

It was awkward, and the whole thing was beginning to get on my nerves. I wanted to get up, and I did. I lit a cigar and studied his face over it. I made one more effort. "How about the scope?" I suggested. "It's a clear night and I reckon you can show me a lot now." Then I started moving for the door.

He pulled himself together with a visible effort and followed me out. For all his peculiarities he was a courteous man, and I had been his friend. On the porch he halted me. There was a high, thin starlight, I remember, and it did odd things to his face.

"I don't look any more," he said, and then repeated it. I dropped into a chair and he sat uneasily facing me on the porch railing. A sort of tension was building up steadily between us.

"I don't look any more because I know," he said. "I know about it already. 'Seek and you shall find,' the Book says. It doesn't say what you will find, it just says you will find. Up here there are ways. Williams knew them."

I looked past him into the night. There was nowhere else to look except out on that great windswept plateau. A long streamer of green light shot across the horizon. The stones are still coming in, I thought wearily, but with the other part of my mind I said to Radnor, putting my words carefully together, "I don't follow you. Do you mean you found something?"

He ignored the interruption. "I believed in the Plan," he said, "what some people call the Divine Plan. I believed in life. I believed it was advancing, rising, becoming more intelligent. I believed it might have been further along out there"—he gestured mutely. "I believed it would give us hope to know."

I heard him, but I put the question bluntly. After all, it might be a matter for science and scientist is what I called myself. "What did you find," I asked, "specifically?"

"The Plan is not what you think," he said. His eyes in that strange light were alien and as cryptic as before. "The Plan is not what you think it is. I know about it now. And life—" He made another gesture, wide, indifferent, and final. There was a greater emptiness than space within him. I could feel it grow as we sat there.

I did not ask that question again. You can call me a fool, but you did not sit there as I did in that valley out of time, while star falls whispered overhead, and a fanatic talked icy insanity at your elbow. I tell you the man frightened me—or maybe it was space itself. I got the feeling somehow that he wanted me to ask again what he had found. And by then I didn't want to hear. Why? Well, that kind of experience is painful, and you try to forget afterward, but I think he must have hit some weak spot in my psychology, probed unaware some unexpressed deep horror of my own. Anyhow I had a feeling that I might believe his answer, and I knew in the same clairvoyant instant of revulsion that I could not bear to hear him give it. "Have you got a match?" I said.

He sighed and came a long way back from somewhere. I thought I saw how it was with him then. Williams had finished him as he had finished others. Well, space is not my job. I checked my data in the hills next morning and talked a lot about sheep, and left— maybe a little sooner than I normally would.

I had a card once from Radnor afterward. It was five years later, and I remember it well, because it came a week after Hiroshima. There was nothing on the card but one line, as though it had been hanging in the air all that time and had just caught up to me. "The Plan is not what you think it is," it read. "Do you see now?"

For a time I puzzled over it, unsure that I did. But after Nagasaki the thing began to be a tune in my head like the little songs the wind makes under telegraph wires. It just went on sighing, "You see? You see?" Of course I knew he was crazy, but just the same he was right about one thing. The fifth planet is gone. And maybe I see.

# The Last Neanderthal

For thou shalt be in league with the stones of the field: and the
beasts of the field shall be at peace with thee.

—Job 5:23

## I

It has long been the thought of science, particularly in evolutionary
biology, that nature does not make extended leaps, that her creatures
slip in slow disguise from one shape to another. A simple observation
will reveal, however, that there are rocks in deserts that glow with
heat for a time after sundown. Similar emanations may come from
the writer or the scientist. The creative individual is someone upon
whom mysterious rays have converged and are again reflected, not
necessarily immediately, but in the course of years. That all of this
wispy geometry of dreams and memories should be the product of
a kind of slow-burning oxidation carried on in an equally diffuse and
mediating web of nerve and sense cells is surprising enough, but that
the emanations from the same particulate organ, the brain, should
be so strikingly different as to disobey the old truism of an unleaping
nature is quite surprising, once one comes to contemplate the reality.

The same incident may stand as a simple fact to some, an intangi-
ble hint of the nature of the universe to others, a useful myth to a
savage, or any number of other things. The receptive mind makes
all the difference, shadowing or lighting the original object. I was an
observer, intent upon my own solitary hieroglyphics.

It happened a long time ago at Curaçao, in the Netherlands
Antilles, on a shore marked by the exposed ribs of a wrecked
freighter. The place was one where only a student of desolation

would find cause to linger. Pelicans perched awkwardly on what remained of a rusted prow. On the edge of the littered beach beyond the port I had come upon a dead dog wrapped in burlap, obviously buried at sea and drifted in by the waves. The dog was little more than a skeleton but still articulated, one delicate bony paw laid gracefully—as though its owner merely slept, and would presently awaken—across a stone at the water's edge. Around his throat was a waterlogged black strap that showed he had once belonged to someone. This dog was a mongrel whose life had been spent among the island fishermen. He had known only the small sea-beaten boats that come across the strait from Venezuela. He had romped briefly on shores like this to which he had been returned by the indifferent sea.

I stepped back a little hesitantly from the smell of death, but still I paused reluctantly. Why, in this cove littered with tin cans, bottles, and cast-off garments, did I find it difficult, if not a sacrilege, to turn away? Because, the thought finally came to me, this particular tattered garment had once lived. Scenes on the living sea that would never in all eternity recur again had streamed through the sockets of those vanished eyes. The dog was young, the teeth in its jaws still perfect. It was of that type of loving creature who had gamboled happily about the legs of men and striven to partake of their endeavors.

Someone had seen crudely to his sea burial, but not well enough to prevent his lying now where came everything abandoned. Nevertheless, vast natural forces had intervened to clothe him with a pathetic dignity. The tide had brought him quietly at night and placed what remained of him asleep upon the stones. Here at sunrise I had stood above him in a light he would never any longer see. Even if I had had a shovel the stones would have prevented his burial. He would wait for a second tide to spirit him away or lay him higher to bleach starkly upon coral and conch shells, mingling the little lime of his bones with all else that had once stood upright on these shores.

As I turned upward into the hills beyond the beach I was faintly aware of a tracery of lizard tails amidst the sand and the semi-desert shrubbery. The lizards were so numerous on the desert floor that their swift movement in the bright sun left a dizzying impression, like spots dancing before one's eyes. The creatures had a tangential way of darting off to the side like inconsequential thoughts that never paused long enough to be fully apprehended. One's eyesight was oppressed by subtly moving points where all should have been quiet. Similar darting specks seemed to be invading my mind. Offshore I could hear the sea wheezing and suspiring in long gasps among the caverns of the coral. The equatorial sun blazed on my unprotected head and hummingbirds flashed like little green flames in the underbrush. I sought quick shelter under a manzanillo tree, whose poisoned apples had tempted the sailors of Columbus.

I suppose the apples really made the connection. Or perhaps merely the interior rustling of the lizards as I passed some cardboard boxes beside a fence brought the thing to mind. Or again, it may have been the tropic sun, lending its flames to life with a kind of dreadful indifference as to the result. At any rate, as I shielded my head under the leaves of the poison tree, the darting lizard points began to run together into a pattern.

Before me passed a broken old horse plodding before a cart laden with bags of cast-off clothing, discarded furniture, and abandoned metal. The horse's harness was a makeshift combination of straps mended with rope. The bearded man perched high in the driver's seat looked as though he had been compounded from the assorted junk heap in the wagon bed. What finally occupied the center of my attention, however, was a street sign and a year—a year that scurried into shape with the flickering alacrity of the lizards. "R Street," they spelled, and the year was 1923.

By now the man on the wagon is dead, his cargo dispersed, never to be reassembled. The plodding beast has been overtaken by whatever fate comes upon a junkman's horse. Their significance upon that particular day in 1923 had been resolved to this, just this: The wagon had been passing the intersection between R and Fourteenth streets when I had leaned from a high-school window a block away, absorbed as only a sixteen-year-old may sometimes be with the sudden discovery of time. It is all going, I thought with the bitter desperation of the young confronting history. No one can hold us. Each and all, we are riding into the dark. Even living, we cannot remember half the events of our own days.

# NATURE AND AUTOBIOGRAPHY

At that moment my eye had fallen upon the junk dealer passing his fateful corner. Now, I had thought instantly, now, save him, immortalize the unseizable moment. The junkman is the symbol of all that is going or is gone. He is passing the intersection into nothingness. Say to the mind, "Hold him, do not forget."

The darting lizard points beyond the manzanillo tree converged and tightened. The phantom horse and the heaped, chaotic wagon were still jouncing across the intersection upon R Street. They had never crossed it; they would not. Forty-five years had fled away. I was not wrong about the powers latent in the brain. The scene was still in process.

I estimated the lowering of the sun with one eye while at the back of my mind the lizard rustling continued. The blistering apples of the manzanillo reminded me of an inconsequential wild-plum fall far away in Nebraska. They were not edible but they contained the same, if a simpler, version of the mystery hidden in our heads. They were hoarding and dispersing energy while the inanimate universe was running down around us.

"We must regard the organism as a configuration contrived to evade the tendency of the universal laws of nature," John Joly the geologist had once remarked. Unlike the fire in a thicket, life burned cunningly and hoarded its resources. Energy provisions in the seed provided against individual death. Of all the unexpected qualities of an unexpected universe, the sheer organizing power of animal and plant metabolism is one of the most remarkable, but, as in the case of most everyday marvels, we take it for granted. Where it reaches its highest development, in the human mind, we forget it completely. Yet out of it history is made—the junkman on R Street is prevented from departing. Growing increasingly archaic, that phantom would be held at the R Street intersection while all around him new houses arose and the years passed unremembered. He would not be released until my own mind began to crumble.

The power to free him is not mine. He is held enchanted because long ago I willed a miniature of history, confined to a single brain. That brain is devouring oxygen at a rate out of all proportion to the rest of the body. It is involved in burning, evoking, and transposing visions, whether of lizard tails, alphabets from the sea, or the realms beyond the galaxy. So important does nature regard this unseen combustion, this smoke of the planet's autumn, that a starving man's brain will be protected to the last while his body is steadily consumed. It is a part of unexpected nature.

In the rational universe of the physical laboratory this sullen and obstinate burning might not, save for our habit of taking the existent for granted, have been expected. Nonetheless, it is here, and man is its most tremendous manifestation. One might ask, Would it be possible to understand humanity a little better if one could follow along just a step of the evolutionary pathway in person? Suppose that there still lived . . . but let me tell the tale, make of it what you will.

## II

Years after the experience I am about to describe, I came upon a recent but Neanderthaloid skull in the dissecting room—a rare-enough occurrence, one that the far-out flitting of forgotten genes struggles occasionally to produce, as if life sometimes hesitated and were inclined to turn back upon its pathway. For a time, remembering an episode of my youth, I kept the indices of cranial measurement by me.

Today, thinking of that experience, I have searched vainly for my old notebook. It is gone. The years have a way of caring for things that do not seek the safety of print. The earlier event remains, however, because it was not a matter of measurements or anthropological indices but of a living person whom I once knew. Now, in my autumn, the face of that girl and the strange season I spent in her neighborhood return in a kind of hazy lesson that I was too young to understand.

It happened in the West, somewhere in that wide drought-ridden land of empty coulees that carry in sudden spates of flood the boulders of the Rockies toward the sea. I suppose that, with the outward flight of population, the region is as wild now as it was then, some forty years ago. It would be useless to search for the place upon a map, though I have tried. Too many years and too many uncertain miles lie behind all bone hunters. There was no town to fix upon a road map. There was only a sod house tucked behind a butte, out of the prevailing wind. And there was a little spring-fed pond in a grassy meadow—that I remember.

Bone hunting is not really a very romantic occupation. One walks day after day along miles of frequently unrewarding outcrop. One grows browner, leaner, and tougher, it is true, but one is far from the bright lights, and the prospect, barring a big strike, like a mammoth, is always to abandon camp and go on. It was really a gypsy profession, then, for those who did the field collecting.

In this case, we did not go on. There was an eroding hill in the vicinity, and on top of that hill, just below sod cover, were the foot bones, hundreds of them, of some lost Tertiary species of American rhinoceros. It is useless to ask why we found only foot bones or why we gathered the mineralized things in such fantastic quantities that they must still lie stacked in some museum storeroom. Maybe the creatures had been immured standing up in a waterhole and in the millions of succeeding years the rest of the carcasses had eroded away from the hilltop stratum. But there were the foot bones, and the orders had come down, so we dug carpals and metacarpals till we cursed like an army platoon that headquarters has forgotten.

There was just one diversion: the spring, and the pond in the meadow. There, under the bank, we cooled our milk and butter purchased from the soddy inhabitants. There we swam and splashed after work. The country people were reserved and kept mostly to themselves. They were uninterested in the dull bones on the hilltop unenlivened by skulls or treasure. After all, there was reason for their reserve. We must have appeared, by their rural standards, harmless but undoubtedly touched in the head. The barrier of reserve was never broken. The surly farmer kept to his parched acres and estimated to his profit our damage to his uncultivated hilltop. The slatternly wife tended a few scrawny chickens. In that ever-blowing landscape their windmill largely ran itself.

Only a stocky barefoot girl of twenty sometimes came hesitantly down the path to our camp to deliver eggs. Some sixty days had drifted by upon that hillside. I began to remember the remark of an old fossil hunter who in his time had known the Gold Coast and the African veldt. "When calico begins to look like silk," he had once warned over a fire in the Sierras, "it is time to go home."

But enough of that. We were not bad young people. The girl shyly brought us the eggs, the butter, and the bacon and then withdrew. Only after some little time did her appearance begin to strike me as odd. Men are accustomed to men in their various color variations around the world. When the past intrudes into a modern setting, however, it is less apt to be visible, because to see it demands knowledge of the past, and the past is always camouflaged when it wears the clothes of the present.

The girl came slowly down the trail one evening, and it struck me suddenly how alone she looked and how, well, *alien,* she also appeared. Our cook was stoking up the evening fire, and as the shadows leaped and flickered I, leaning invisibly against a rock, was suddenly transported one hundred thousand years into the past. The shadows and their dancing highlights were the cause of it. They had swept the present out of sight. That girl coming reluctantly down the pathway to the fire was removed from us in time, and subconsciously she knew it as I did. By modern standards she was not pretty, and the gingham dress she wore, if anything, defined the difference.

Short, thickset, and massive, her body was still not the body of a typical peasant woman. Her head, thrust a little forward against the light, was massive-boned. Along the eye orbits at the edge of the frontal bone I could see outlined in the flames an armored protuberance that, particularly in women, had vanished before the close of the Würmian ice. She swung her head almost like a great muzzle beneath its curls, and I was struck by the low bun-shaped breadth at the back. Along her exposed arms one could see a flash of golden hair.

No, we are out of time, I thought quickly. We are each and every one displaced. She is the last Neanderthal, and she does not know what to do. We are those who eliminated her long ago. It is like an old scene endlessly re-enacted. Only the chipped stones and the dead game are lacking.

I came out of the shadow then and spoke gently to her, taking the packages. It was the most one could do across that waste of infinite years. She spoke almost inaudibly, drawing an unconscious circle in the dust with a splayed bare foot. I saw, through the thin dress, the powerful thighs, the yearning fertility going unmated in this lonesome spot. She looked up, and a trick of the fire accentuated the cavernous eye sockets so that I saw only darkness within. I accompanied her a short distance along the trail. "What is it you are digging for?" she managed to ask.

"It has to do with time," I said slowly. "Something that happened a long time ago."

She listened incuriously, as one at the morning of creation might do.

"Do you like this?" she persisted. "Do you always just go from one place to another digging these things? And who pays for it, and what comes of it in the end? Do you have a home?" The soddy and her burly father were looming in the dusk. I paused, but questions flung across the centuries are hard to answer.

"I am a student," I said, but with no confidence. How could I say that suddenly she herself and her ulnar-bowed and golden-haired forearms were a part of a long reach backward into time?

"Of what has been, and what will come of it we are trying to find out. I am afraid it will not help one to find a home," I said, more to myself than her. "Quite the reverse, in fact. You see—"

The dark sockets under the tumbled hair seemed somehow sadly vacant. "Thank you for bringing the things," I said, knowing the customs of that land. "Your father is waiting. I will go back to camp now." With this I strode off toward our fire but went, on impulse, beyond it into the full-starred night.

This was the way of things along the Wild Cat escarpment. There was sand blowing and the past mingling with the present in more ways than professional science chose to see. There were eroded farms no longer running cattle and a diminishing population waiting, as this girl was waiting, for something they would never possess. They were, without realizing it, huntsmen without game, women without warriors. Obsolescence was upon their way of life.

But about the girl lingered a curious gentleness that we know now had long ago touched the vanished Neanderthals she so resembled. It would be her fate to marry eventually one of the illiterate hard-eyed uplanders of my own kind. Whatever the subtle genes had resurrected in her body would be buried once more and hidden in the creature called *sapiens*. Perhaps in the end his last woman would stand unwanted before some fiercer, brighter version of himself. It would be no more than justice. I was farther out in the deep spaces than I knew, and the fire was embers when I returned.

The season was waning. There came, inevitably, a time when the trees began to talk of winter in the crags above the camp. I have repeated all that can be said about so fragile an episode. I had exchanged in the course of weeks a few wistful, scarcely understood remarks. I had waved to her a time or so from the quarry hilltop. As the time of our departure neared I had once glimpsed her shyly surveying from a rise beyond the pond our youthful plungings and naked wallowings in the spring-fed water. Then suddenly the leaves were down or turning yellow. It was time to go. The fossil quarry and its interminable foot bones were at last exhausted.

But something never intended had arisen for me there by the darkening water—some agonizing, lifelong nostalgia, both personal and, in another sense, transcending the personal. It was—how shall I say it?—the endurance in a single mind of two stages of man's climb up the energy ladder that may be both his triumph and his doom.

Our battered equipment was assembled in the Model T's, which, in that time, were the only penetrators of deep-rutted upland roads. Morose good-byes were expressed; money was passed over the broken sod cover on the hilltop. Hundreds of once galloping rhinoceros foot bones were stowed safely away. And that was it. I stood by the running board and slowly, very slowly, let my eyes wander toward that massive, archaic, and yet tragically noble head—of a creature so far back in time it did not know it represented tragedy. I made, I think, some kind of little personal gesture of farewell. Her head raised in recognition and then dropped. The motors started. *Homo sapiens,* the energy devourer, was on his way once more.

What was it she had said, I thought desperately as I swung aboard. Home, she had questioned, "Do you have a home?" Perhaps I once did, I was to think many times in the years that followed, but I, too, was a mental atavism. I, like that lost creature, would never find the place called home. It lay somewhere in the past down that hundred-thousand-year road on which travel was impossible. Only ghosts with uncertain eyes and abashed gestures would meet there. Upon a surging tide of power first conceived in the hearth fires of dead caverns mankind was plunging into an uncontrolled future beyond anything the people of the Ice had known.

The cell that had somehow mastered the secret of controlled energy, of surreptitious burning to a purpose, had finally produced the mind, judiciously, in its turn, controlling the inconstant fire at the cave mouth. Beyond anything that lost girl could imagine, words in the mouth or immured in libraries would cause substance to vanish and the earth itself to tremble. The little increments of individual energy dissolving at death had been coded and passed through the centuries by human ingenuity. A climbing juggernaut of power was leaping from triumph to triumph. It threatened to be more than man and all his words could master. It was more and less than man.

I remembered those cavernous eye sockets whose depths were forever hidden from me in the firelight. Did they contain a premonition of the end we had invited, or was it only that I was young and hungry for all that was untouchable? I have searched once more for the old notebooks but, again, in vain. They would tell me, at best, only how living phantoms can be anatomically compared with those of the past. They would tell nothing of that season of the falling leaves or how I learned under the night sky of the utter homelessness of man.

## III

I have seen a tree root burst a rock face on a mountain or slowly wrench aside the gateway of a forgotten city. This is a very cunning feat, which men take too readily for granted. Life, unlike the inanimate, will take the long way round to circumvent barrenness. A kind of desperate will resides even in a root. It will perform the evasive tactics of an army, slowly inching its way through crevices and hoarding energy until someday it swells and a living tree upheaves the heaviest mausoleum. This covert struggle is part of the lifelong battle waged against the Second Law of Thermodynamics, the heat death that has been frequently assumed to rule the universe. At the hands of man that hoarded energy takes strange forms, both in the methods of its accumulation and in the diverse ways of its expenditure.

For hundreds of thousands of years, a time longer than all we know of recorded history, the kin of that phantom girl had lived without cities along the Italian Mediterranean or below the northern tentacles of the groping ice. The low archaic skull vault had been as capacious as ours. Neanderthal man had, we now know after long digging, his own small dreams and kindnesses. He had buried his dead with offerings—there were even evidences that they had been laid, in some instances, upon beds of wild flowers. Beyond the chipped flints and the fires in the cavern darkness his mind had not involved itself with what was to come upon him with our kind—the first bowmen, the great artists, the terrible creatures of his blood who were never still.

It was a time of autumn driftage that might have lasted and been well forever. Whether it was his own heavy brow that changed in the chill nights or that somewhere his line had mingled with a changeling cuckoo brood who multiplied at his expense we do not know with certainty. We know only that he vanished, though sometimes, as in the case of my upland girl, a chance assemblage of archaic genes struggles to re-emerge from the loins of *sapiens*.

But the plucked flint had flown; the heavy sad girls had borne the children of the conquerors. Rain and leaves washed over the cave shelters of the past. Bronze replaced flint, iron replaced bronze, while the killing never ceased. The Neanderthals were forgotten; their grottoes housed the oracles of later religions. Marble cities gleamed along the Mediterranean. The ice and the cave bear had vanished. White-robed philosophers discoursed in Athens. Armed galleys moved upon the waters. Agriculture had brought wealth and diversification of labor. It had also brought professional soldiery. The armored ones were growing and, with them, slavery, torture, and death upon all the seas of the world.

The energy that had once sufficed only to take man from one camping place to another, the harsh but innocent world glimpsed by Cook in the eighteenth century on the shores of Australia, century by century was driving toward a climax. The warriors with the tall foreheads given increasingly to fanatic religions and monumental

149

art had finally grown to doubt the creations of their own minds.

The remnants of what had once been talked about in Athens and been consumed in the flames of Alexandria hesitantly crept forth once more. Early in the seventeenth century Sir Francis Bacon asserted that "by the agency of man a new aspect of things, a new universe, comes into view." In those words he was laying the basis of what he came to call "the second world," that world which could be drawn out of the natural by the sheer power of the human mind. Man had, of course, unwittingly been doing something of the sort since he came to speak. Bacon, however, was dreaming of the new world of invention, of toleration, of escape from irrational custom. He was the herald of the scientific method itself. Yet that method demands history also—the history I as an eager student had long ago beheld symbolically upon a corner in the shape of a junkman's cart. Without knowledge of the past, the way into the thickets of the future is desperate and unclear.

Bacon's second world is now so much with us that it rocks our conception of what the natural order was, or is, or in what sense it can be restored. A mathematical formula traveling weakly along the fibers of the neopallium may serve to wreck the planet. It is a kind of metabolic energy never envisaged by the lichen attacking a rock face or dreamed of in the flickering shadows of a cave fire. Yet from these ancient sources man's hunger has been drawn. Its potential is to be found in the life of the world we call natural, just as its terrifying intricacy is the product of the second visionary world evoked in the brain of man.

The two exist on the planet in an increasingly uneven balance. Into one or the other or into a terrifying nothing one of these two worlds must finally subside. Man, whose strange metabolism has passed beyond the search for food to the naked ingestion of power, is scarcely aware that the energy whose limited planetary store lies at the root of the struggle for existence has passed by way of his mind into another dimension. There the giant shadows of the past continue to contend. They do so because life is a furnace of concealed flame.

Some pages back I spoke of a wild-plum thicket. I did so because I had a youthful memory of visiting it in autumn. All the hoarded juices of summer had fallen with that lush untasted fruit upon the grass. The tiny engines of the plant had painstakingly gathered throughout the summer rich stores of sugar and syrup from the ground. Seed had been produced; birds had flown away with fruit that would give rise to plum trees miles away. The energy dispersion was so beneficent on that autumn afternoon that earth itself seemed anxious to promote the process against the downward guttering of the stars. Even I, tasting the fruit, was in my animal way scooping up some of it into thoughts and dreams.

Long after the Antillean adventure I chanced on an autumn walk to revisit the plum thicket. I was older, much older, and I had come largely because I wondered if the thicket was still there and because this strange hoarding and burning at the heart of life still puzzled me. I have spoken figuratively of fire as an animal, as being perhaps the very *essence* of animal. Oxidation, I mean, as it enters into life and consciousness.

Fire, as we have learned to our cost, has an insatiable hunger to be fed. It is a nonliving force that can even locomote itself. What if now—and I half closed my eyes against the blue plums and the smoke drifting along the draw—what if now it is only concealed and grown slyly conscious of its own burning in this little house of sticks and clay that I inhabit? What if I am, in some way, only a sophisticated fire that has acquired an ability to regulate its rate of combustion and to hoard its fuel in order to see and walk?

The plums, like some gift given from no one to no one visible, continued to fall about me. I was old now, I thought suddenly, glancing at a vein on my hand. I would have to hoard what remained of the embers. I thought of the junkman's horse and tried to release him so that he might be gone.

Perhaps I had finally succeeded. I do not know. I remembered that star-filled night years ago on the escarpment and the heavy-headed dreaming girl drawing a circle in the dust. Perhaps it was time itself she drew, for my own head was growing heavy and the smoke from the autumn fields seemed to be penetrating my mind. I wanted to drop them at last, these carefully hoarded memories. I wanted to strew them like the blue plums in some gesture of love toward the universe all outward on a mat of leaves. Rich, rich and not to be hoarded, only to be laid down for someone, anyone, no longer to be carried and remembered in pain like the delicate paw lying forever on the beach at Curaçao.

I leaned farther back, relaxing in the leaves. It was a feeling I had never had before, and it was strangely soothing. Perhaps I was no longer *Homo sapiens,* and perhaps that girl, the last Neanderthal, had known as much from the first. Perhaps all I was, really, was a pile of autumn leaves seeing smoke wraiths through the haze of my own burning. Things get odder on this planet, not less so. I dropped my head finally and gazed straight up through the branches at the sun. It was all going, I felt, memories dropping away in that high indifferent blaze that tolerated no other light. I let it be so for a little, but then I felt in my pocket the flint blade that I had carried all those years from the gravels on the escarpment. It reminded me of a journey I would not complete and the circle in the dust around which I had magically traveled for so long.

I arose then and, biting a plum that tasted bitter, I limped off down the ravine. One hundred thousand years had made little difference—at least, to me. The secret was to travel always in the first world, not the second; or, at least, to know at each crossroad which world was which. I went on, clutching for stability the flint knife in my pocket. A blue smoke like some final conflagration swept out of the draw and preceded me. I could feel its heat. I coughed, and my eyes watered. I tried as best I could to keep pace with it as it swirled on. There was a crackling behind me as though I myself were burning, but the smoke was what I followed. I held the sharp flint like a dowser's twig, cold and steady in my hand.

# II
# Early Poems

# The Spider

His science has progressed past stone,
His strange and dark geometries,
Impossible to flesh and bone,
Revive upon the passing breeze
The house the blundering foot destroys.
Indifferent to what is lost
He trusts the wind and yet employs
The jeweled stability of frost.
Foundations buried underfoot
Are forfeit to the mole and worm
But spiders know it and will put
Their trust in airy dreams more firm
Than any rock and raise from dew
Frail stairs the careless wind blows through.

# Tasting the Mountain Spring

The spring comes to us through a mile of wood,
Beginning in the high cold acres where
Snow water starts, but seeping downward there
Feeds roots—things at the abysmal sources of
All life. Sticks and wet stones and thirsts
Of worm and toadstool, unseen starry bursts
Of damp wood-pollen fill it—taste enough
To let you know it has come down the brink
Of more than thunder. . . . In this foaming ditch
Water with earth's iron tainted and defiled
Mingles with stars, but, for myself, I drink
Like fawn or antelope, untasting which,
So long as all that water's quick and wild.

# Things Will Go

When it is all done
Who will know? Who will care?
The snake will still be gliding by the stone,
The frog stare
From his place on the lily pad.
Things will go
Like water, like wind,
As they always have gone since the first
Ooze sprouted and finned.
This does not matter. What's done
Has always been so.
I shall tell myself this, not believe
Like the others I know.

# Leaving September

If I have once forgotten on this field
The long light of the dusk, or far away
The sheep on tawny grass, how stones will yield
Small bitter puffballs, or a cricket stay
To wring wry tunes from emptiness and dearth,
Let me remember; let me hold them now
Close to the heart—while I upon the earth
Am the stone field and pain the heavy plow.
Not in wide measures is the harvest culled;
Not by disaster nor by cutting hail
Is the loss seen, the grief in somewise dulled—
Being done at last. Ours is a different scale—
Leaving September stars and a little smoke
And memory tight as a lichen to an oak.

# Nocturne in Silver

Here where the barbed wire straggles in the marsh
And alkali crusts all the weeds like frost,
I have come home, I have come home to hear
The new young frogs that cry along the lost

Wild ditches where at midnight only cows
And fools with eery marsh fire in their brains
Blunder toward midnight. Silvery and clear
Cry the new frogs; the blood runs in my veins

Coldly and clearly. I am mottled, too,
And feel a silver bubble in my throat.
Lock doors, turn keys, or follow in your fear.
My eyes are green, and warily afloat

In the June darkness. I am done with fire.
Water quicksilver-like that slips through stone
Has quenched my madness—if you find me here
My lineage squat and warty will be known.

# Winter Sign

A spider web pulled tight between two stones
With nothing left but autumn leaves to catch
Is maybe a winter sign, or the thin blue bones
Of a hare picked clean by ants. A man can attach

Meanings enough to the wind when his luck is out,
But, having stumbled into this season of grief,
I mean to reflect on the life that is here and about
In the fall of the leaves—not on the dying leaf.

Something more tough, reliable, and stark
Carries the blood of life toward a farther spring—
Something that lies concealed in the soundless dark
Of burr and pod, in the seeds that hook and sting.

I have learned from these that love which endures the night
May smolder in outward death while the colors blaze,
But trust my love—it is small, burr-coated, and tight.
It will stick to the bone. It will last through the autumn days.

# October Has
# the Heart

Left to his ruin with the autumn leaf,
The spider, black and yellow, treading air
By means of gossamer, goes like a thief
Up, up, and up—till from that trembling stair
He launches out for some far other vine
Where pumpkins lie like moons among the corn.
As through some old, some bitter-clear thin wine
The world lies still—no green leaf hides the thorn.
October has the heart; no more dark things
Cry in the blood; the quick impatient storms
Are all gone past, and with them all high wings.
Clear in this autumn quiet something forms:
Something to last—what Keats once bent to learn
Painted forever on a certain urn.

# Dusk Interval

Here is the waste, the stone, the streaming sunset,
Where no clouds pass.
Here, where the hawk's dark wing goes lonely over
Sheep-bitten grass,

Green ice once crawled and plowed the meadow.
The boulders lie
As they were dropped in that tremendous plowing.
The crows cry

Clamorous above it in the twilit evening . . .
They do not stoop.
The rich grain and the harvest are not found here.
Night hawks loop

Erratic spirals in the windy starlight.
The fallow ground
Is sleeping, and I know with what ghost sleeping,
Deep under sound.

Oh, not for long the grass, the bells of grasses:
The mice who love
Their hidden runways will soon pass. The boulders
Will lift and move.

This land is sleeping in a dream of mammoth.
Their heavy tread
Will sound again. Sometime their feet will shudder
The last man from his bed.

# Let the
# Red Fox Run

Red-bellied let the red fox run
Under the raining leaf, and weather
And summer go beyond recall
My heart will strain no more at its tether.

I will not be out in the sharp hill frost,
I will not be there when the fox goes over
A wall where the broken boulders spill
The shape of a farm back into the clover.

I will not be running with all that runs
(Its torn breath streaking down the furrow).
I will take my ease while the hunt pounds by,
Safe at last in earth's darkest burrow.

But somewhere still in the brain's gray vault,
Where the light grows dim and the owls are crying,
I shall run with the fox through the leaf-strewn wood.
I shall not be present at my own dying.

# The Fishers

The trout stream is fished out and still;
The fishers with their flies have gone.
Nor upstream now, nor down the hill
Move any men with waders on.
The water keeps on coming down;
Still water running green and deep
Harbors a stealthy life where brown
Old leaves go sailing into sleep.
The fishers say the stream is bad.
No rainbow flash against the sun
Will make the souls of fishers glad,
But say for fishers I am one
And here, at least, can still be caught
The slippery minnows of a thought.

# III
# Science and
# Humanism

# The Star Thrower

Who is the man walking in the Way? An eye glaring in the skull.

—Seccho

## I

It has ever been my lot, though formally myself a teacher, to be taught surely by none. There are times when I have thought to read lessons in the sky, or in books, or from the behavior of my fellows, but in the end my perceptions have frequently been inadequate or betrayed. Nevertheless, I venture to say that of what man may be I have caught a fugitive glimpse, not among multitudes of men, but along an endless wave-beaten coast at dawn. As always, there is this apparent break, this rift in nature, before the insight comes. The terrible question has to translate itself into an even more terrifying freedom.

If there is any meaning to this book [*The Unexpected Universe*], it began on the beaches of Costabel with just such a leap across an unknown abyss. It began, if I may borrow the expression from a Buddhist sage, with the skull and the eye. I was the skull. I was the inhumanly stripped skeleton without voice, without hope, wandering alone upon the shores of the world. I was devoid of pity, because pity implies hope. There was, in this desiccated skull, only an eye like a pharos light, a beacon, a search beam revolving endlessly in sunless noonday or black night. Ideas like swarms of insects rose to the beam, but the light consumed them. Upon that shore meaning had ceased. There were only the dead skull and the revolving eye. With such an eye, some have said, science looks upon the world. I

169

do not know. I know only that I was the skull of emptiness and the endlessly revolving light without pity.

Once, in a dingy restaurant in the town, I had heard a woman say: "My father reads a goose bone for the weather." A modern primitive, I had thought, a diviner, using a method older than Stonehenge, as old as the arctic forests.

"And where does he do that?" the woman's companion had asked amusedly.

"In Costabel," she answered complacently, "in Costabel." The voice came back and buzzed faintly for a moment in the dark under the revolving eye. It did not make sense, but nothing in Costabel made sense. Perhaps that was why I had finally found myself in Costabel. Perhaps all men are destined at some time to arrive there as I did.

I had come by quite ordinary means, but I was still the skull with the eye. I concealed myself beneath a fisherman's cap and sunglasses, so that I looked like everyone else on the beach. This is the way things are managed in Costabel. It is on the shore that the revolving eye begins its beam and the whispers rise in the empty darkness of the skull.

The beaches of Costabel are littered with the debris of life. Shells are cast up in windrows; a hermit crab, fumbling for a new home in the depths, is tossed naked ashore, where the waiting gulls cut him to pieces. Along the strip of wet sand that marks the ebbing and flowing of the tide, death walks hugely and in many forms. Even the torn fragments of green sponge yield bits of scrambling life striving to return to the great mother that has nourished and protected them.

In the end the sea rejects its offspring. They cannot fight their way home through the surf which casts them repeatedly back upon the shore. The tiny breathing pores of starfish are stuffed with sand. The rising sun shrivels the mucilaginous bodies of the unprotected. The seabeach and its endless war are soundless. Nothing screams but the gulls.

In the night, particularly in the tourist season, or during great storms, one can observe another vulturine activity. One can see, in the hour before dawn on the ebb tide, electric torches bobbing like fireflies along the beach. This is the sign of the professional shellers seeking to outrun and anticipate their less aggressive neighbors. A kind of greedy madness sweeps over the competing collectors. After a storm one can see them hurrying along with bundles of gathered starfish, or, toppling and overburdened, clutching bags of living shells whose hidden occupants will be slowly cooked and dissolved in the outdoor kettles provided by the resort hotels for the cleaning of specimens. Following one such episode I met the star thrower.

As soon as the ebb was flowing, as soon as I could make out in my sleeplessness the flashlights on the beach, I arose and dressed in the dark. As I came down the steps to the shore I could hear the deeper rumble of the surf. A gaping hole filled with churning sand had cut sharply into the breakwater. Flying sand as light as powder coated every exposed object like snow. I made my way around the altered edges of the cove and proceeded on my morning walk up the shore. Now and then a stooping figure moved in the gloom or a rain squall swept past me with light pattering steps. There was a faint sense of coming light somewhere behind me in the east.

Soon I began to make out objects, up-ended timbers, conch shells, sea wrack wrenched from the far-out kelp forests. A pink-clawed crab encased in a green cup of sponge lay sprawling where the waves had tossed him. Long-limbed starfish were strewn everywhere, as though the night sky had showered down. I paused once briefly. A small octopus, its beautiful dark-lensed eyes bleared with sand, gazed up at me from a ragged bundle of tentacles. I hesitated, and touched it briefly with my foot. It was dead. I paced on once more before the spreading whitecaps of the surf.

The shore grew steeper, the sound of the sea heavier and more menacing, as I rounded a bluff into the full blast of the offshore wind. I was away from the shellers now and strode more rapidly over the wet sand that effaced my footprints. Around the next point there might be a refuge from the wind. The sun behind me was pressing upward at the horizon's rim—an ominous red glare amidst the tumbling blackness of the clouds. Ahead of me, over the projecting point, a gigantic rainbow of incredible perfection had sprung shim-mering into existence. Somewhere toward its foot I discerned a human figure standing, as it seemed to me, within the rainbow, though unconscious of his position. He was gazing fixedly at something in the sand.

Eventually he stooped and flung the object beyond the breaking surf. I labored toward him over a half-mile of uncertain footing. By the time I reached him the rainbow had receded ahead of us, but something of its color still ran hastily in many changing lights across his features. He was starting to kneel again.

In a pool of sand and silt a starfish had thrust its arms up stiffly and was holding its body away from the stifling mud.

"It's still alive," I ventured.

"Yes," he said, and with a quick yet gentle movement he picked up the star and spun it over my head and far out into the sea. It sank in a burst of spume, and the waters roared once more.

"It may live," he said, "if the offshore pull is strong enough." He spoke gently, and across his bronzed worn face the light still came and went in subtly altering colors.

"There are not many come this far," I said, groping in a sudden embarrassment for words. "Do you collect?"

"Only like this," he said softly, gesturing amidst the wreckage of the shore. "And only for the living." He stooped again, oblivious of my curiosity, and skipped another star neatly across the water.

"The stars," he said, "throw well. One can help them."

He looked full at me with a faint question kindling in his eyes, which seemed to take on the far depths of the sea.

"I do not collect," I said uncomfortably, the wind beating at my garments. "Neither the living nor the dead. I gave it up a long time ago. Death is the only successful collector." I could feel the full night blackness in my skull and the terrible eye resuming its indifferent journey. I nodded and walked away, leaving him there upon the dune with that great rainbow ranging up the sky behind him.

I turned as I neared a bend in the coast and saw him toss another star, skimming it skillfully far out over the ravening and tumultuous water. For a moment, in the changing light, the sower appeared magnified, as though casting larger stars upon some greater sea. He had, at any rate, the posture of a god.

But again the eye, the cold world-shriveling eye, began its inevitable circling in my skull. He is a man, I considered sharply, bringing my thought to rest. The star thrower is a man, and death is running more fleet than he along every seabeach in the world.

I adjusted the dark lens of my glasses and, thus disguised, I paced slowly back by the starfish gatherers, past the shell collectors, with their vulgar little spades and the stick-length shelling pincers that eased their elderly backs while they snatched at treasures in the sand. I chose to look full at the steaming kettles in which beautiful voiceless things were being boiled alive. Behind my sunglasses a kind of litany began and refused to die down. *"As I came through the desert thus it was, as I came through the desert."*

In the darkness of my room I lay quiet with the sunglasses removed, but the eye turned and turned. In the desert, an old monk had once advised a traveler, the voices of God and the Devil are scarcely distinguishable. Costabel was a desert. I lay quiet, but my restless hand at the bedside fingered the edge of an invisible abyss. "Certain coasts"—the remark of a perceptive writer came back to me—"are set apart for shipwreck." With unerring persistence I had made my way thither.

## II

There is a difference in our human outlook, depending on whether we have been born on level plains, where one step reasonably leads to another, or whether, by contrast, we have spent our lives amidst glacial crevasses and precipitous descents. In the case of the mountaineer, one step does not always lead rationally to another save by a desperate leap over a chasm, or by an even more hesitant tiptoeing across precarious snow bridges.

Something about these opposed landscapes has its analogue in the mind of man. Our prehistoric life, one might say, began amidst enforested gloom with the abandonment of the protected instinctive life of nature. We sought, instead, an adventurous existence amidst the crater lands and ice fields of self-generated ideas. Clambering onward, we have slowly made our way out of a maze of isolated peaks into the level plains of science. Here, one step seems definitely to succeed another, the universe appears to take on an imposed order, and the illusions through which mankind has painfully made its way for many centuries have given place to the enormous vistas of past and future time. The encrusted eye in the stone speaks to us of undeviating sunlight; the calculated elliptic of Halley's comet no longer forecasts world disaster. The planet plunges on through a chill void of star years, and there is little or nothing that remains unmeasured.

Nothing, that is, but the mind of man. Since boyhood I had been traveling across the endless coordinated realms of science, just as, in the body, I was a plains dweller, accustomed to plodding through distances unbroken by precipices. Now that I come to look back, there was one contingent aspect of that landscape I inhabited whose significance, at the time, escaped me. "Twisters," we called them locally. They were a species of cyclonic, bouncing air funnel that could suddenly loom out of nowhere, crumpling windmills or slashing with devastating fury through country towns. Sometimes, by modest contrast, more harmless varieties known as dust devils might pursue one in a gentle spinning dance for miles. One could see them hesitantly stalking across the alkali flats on a hot day, debating, perhaps, in their tall, rotating columns, whether to ascend and assume more formidable shapes. They were the trickster part of an otherwise pedestrian landscape.

Infrequent though the visitations of these malign creations of the air might be, all prudent homesteaders in those parts had provided themselves with cyclone cellars. In the careless neighborhood in which I grew up, however, we contented ourselves with the queer yarns of cyclonic folklore and the vagaries of weather prophecy. As a boy, aroused by these tales and cherishing a subterranean fondness for caves, I once attempted to dig a storm cellar. Like most such projects this one was never completed. The trickster element in nature, I realize now, had so buffeted my parents that they stoically rejected planning. Unconsciously, they had arrived at the philosophy that foresight merely invited the attention of some baleful intelligence that despised and persecuted the calculating planner. It was not until many years later that I came to realize that a kind of maleficent primordial power persists in the mind as well as in the wandering dust storms of the exterior world.

A hidden dualism that has haunted man since antiquity runs

across his religious conceptions as the conflict between good and evil. It persists in the modern world of science under other guises. It becomes chaos versus form or antichaos. Form, since the rise of the evolutionary philosophy, has itself taken on an illusory quality. Our apparent shapes no longer have the stability of a single divine fiat. Instead, they waver and dissolve into the unexpected. We gaze backward into a contracting cone of life until words leave us and all we know is dissolved into the simple circuits of a reptilian brain. Finally, sentience subsides into an animalcule.

Or we revolt and refuse to look deeper, but the void remains. We are rag dolls made out of many ages and skins, changelings who have slept in wood nests or hissed in the uncouth guise of waddling amphibians. We have played such roles for infinitely longer ages than we have been men. Our identity is a dream. We are process, not reality, for reality is an illusion of the daylight—the light of our particular day. In a fortnight, as aeons are measured, we may lie silent in a bed of stone, or, as has happened in the past, be figured in another guise. Two forces struggle perpetually in our bodies: Yam, the old sea dragon of the original Biblical darkness, and, arrayed against him, some wisp of dancing light that would have us linger, wistful, in our human form. "Tarry thou, till I come again"—an old legend survives among us of the admonition given by Jesus to the Wandering Jew. The words are applicable to all of us. Deep-hidden in the human psyche there is a similar injunction, no longer having to do with the longevity of the body but, rather, a plea to wait upon some transcendent lesson preparing in the mind itself.

Yet the facts we face seem terrifyingly arrayed against us. It is as if at our backs, masked and demonic, moved the trickster as I have seen his role performed among the remnant of a savage people long ago. It was that of the jokester present at the most devout of ceremonies. This creature never laughed; he never made a sound. Painted in black, he followed silently behind the officiating priest, mimicking, with the added flourish of a little whip, the gestures of the devout one. His timed and stylized posturings conveyed a derision infinitely more formidable than actual laughter.

In modern terms, the dance of contingency, of the indeterminable, outwits us all. The approaching fateful whirlwind on the plain had mercifully passed me by in youth. In the moment when I witnessed that fireside performance I knew with surety that primitive man had lived with a dark message. He had acquiesced in the admission into his village of a cosmic messenger. Perhaps the primitives were wiser in the ways of the trickster universe than ourselves; perhaps they knew, as we do not, how to ground or make endurable the lightning.

At all events, I had learned, as I watched that half-understood drama by the leaping fire, why man, even modern man, reads goose bones for the weather of his soul. Afterward I had gone out, a troubled unbeliever, into the night. There was a shadow I could not henceforth shake off, which I knew was posturing and would always posture behind me. That mocking shadow looms over me as I write. It scrawls with a derisive pen and an exaggerated flourish. I know instinctively it will be present to caricature the solemnities of my deathbed. In a quarter of a century it has never spoken.

Black magic, the magic of the primeval chaos, blots out or transmogrifies the true form of things. At the stroke of twelve the princess must flee the banquet or risk discovery in the rags of a kitchen wench; coach reverts to pumpkin. Instability lies at the heart of the world. With uncanny foresight folklore has long toyed symbolically with what the nineteenth century was to proclaim a reality—namely, that form is an illusion of the time dimension, that the magic flight of the pursued hero or heroine through frogskin and wolf coat has been, and will continue to be, the flight of all men.

Goethe's genius sensed, well before the publication of the *Origin of Species*, the thesis and antithesis that epitomize the eternal struggle of the immediate species against its dissolution into something other: in modern terms, fish into reptile, ape into man. The power to change is both creative and destructive—a sinister gift, which, unrestricted, leads onward toward the formless and inchoate void of the possible. This force can only be counterbalanced by an equal impulse toward specificity. Form, once arisen, clings to its identity. Each species and each individual holds tenaciously to its present nature. Each strives to contain the creative and abolishing maelstrom that pours unseen through the generations. The past vanishes;

the present momentarily persists; the future is potential only. In this specious present of the real, life struggles to maintain every manifestation, every individuality, that exists. In the end, life always fails, but the amorphous hurrying stream is held and diverted into new organic vessels in which form persists, though the form may not be that of yesterday.

The evolutionists, piercing beneath the show of momentary stability, discovered, hidden in rudimentary organs, the discarded rubbish of the past. They detected the reptile under the lifted feathers of the bird, the lost terrestrial limbs dwindling beneath the blubber of the giant cetaceans. They saw life rushing outward from an unknown center, just as today the astronomer senses the galaxies fleeing into the infinity of darkness. As the spinning galactic clouds hurl stars and worlds across the night, so life, equally impelled by the centrifugal powers lurking in the germ cell, scatters the splintered radiance of consciousness and sends it prowling and contending through the thickets of the world.

All this devious, tattered way was exposed to the ceaselessly turning eye within the skull that lay hidden upon the bed in Costabel. Slowly that eye grew conscious of another eye that searched it with equal penetration from the shadows of the room. It may have been a projection from the mind within the skull, but the eye was, nevertheless, exteriorized and haunting. It began as something glaucous and blind beneath a web of clinging algae. It altered suddenly and became the sand-smeared eye of the dead cephalopod I had encountered upon the beach. The transformations became more rapid with the concentration of my attention, and they became more formidable. There was the beaten, bloodshot eye of an animal from somewhere within my childhood experience. Finally, there was an eye that seemed torn from a photograph, but that looked through me as though it had already raced in vision up to the steep edge of nothingness and absorbed whatever terror lay in that abyss. I sank back again upon my cot and buried my head in the pillow. I knew the eye and the circumstance and the question. It was my mother. She was long dead, and the way backward was lost.

## III

Now it may be asked, upon the coasts that invite shipwreck, why the ships should come, just as we may ask the man who pursues knowledge why he should be left with a revolving search beam in the head whose light falls only upon disaster or the flotsam of the shore. There is an answer, but its way is not across the level plains of science, for the science of remote abysses no longer shelters man. Instead, it reveals him in vaporous metamorphic succession as the homeless and unspecified one, the creature of the magic flight.

Long ago, when the future was just a simple tomorrow, men had cast intricately carved game counters to determine its course, or they had traced with a grimy finger the cracks on the burnt shoulder blade of a hare. It was a prophecy of tomorrow's hunt, just as was the old farmer's anachronistic reading of the weather from the signs on the breastbone of a goose. Such quaint almanacs of nature's intent had sufficed mankind since antiquity. They would do so no longer, nor would formal apologies to the souls of the game men hunted. The hunters had come, at last, beyond the satisfying supernatural world that had always surrounded the little village, into a place of homeless frontiers and precipitous edges, the indescribable world of the natural. Here tools increasingly revenged themselves upon their creators and tomorrow became unmanageable. Man had come in his journeying to a region of terrible freedoms.

It was a place of no traditional shelter, save those erected with the aid of tools, which had also begun to achieve a revolutionary independence from their masters. Their ways had grown secretive and incalculable. Science, more powerful than the magical questions that might be addressed by a shaman to a burnt shoulder blade, could create these tools but had not succeeded in controlling their ambivalent nature. Moreover, they responded all too readily to that urge for tampering and dissolution which is part of our primate heritage.

We had been safe in the enchanted forest only because of our weakness. When the powers of that gloomy region were given to us, immediately, as in a witch's house, things began to fly about unbidden. The tools, if not science itself, were linked intangibly to the subconscious poltergeist aspect of man's nature. The closer man and the natural world drew together, the more erratic became the behavior of each. Huge shadows leaped triumphantly after every blinding illumination. It was a magnified but clearly recognizable version of the black trickster's antics behind the solemn backs of the priesthood. Here, there was one difference. The shadows had passed out of all human semblance; no societal ritual safely contained their posturings, as in the warning dance of the trickster. Instead, unseen by many because it was so gigantically real, the multiplied darkness threatened to submerge the carriers of the light.

Darwin, Einstein, and Freud might be said to have released the shadows. Yet man had already entered the perilous domain that henceforth would contain his destiny. Four hundred years ago Francis Bacon had already anticipated its dual nature. The individuals do not matter. If they had not made their discoveries, others would have surely done so. They were good men, and they came as enlighteners of mankind. The tragedy was only that at their backs the ritual figure with the whip was invisible. There was no longer anything to subdue the pride of man. The world had been laid under the heavy spell of the natural; henceforth, it would be ordered by man.

Humanity was suddenly entranced by light and fancied it reflected light. Progress was its watchword, and for a time the shadows seemed to recede. Only a few guessed that the retreat of darkness presaged the emergence of an entirely new and less tangible terror. Things, in the words of G. K. Chesterton, were to grow incalculable by being calculated. Man's powers were finite; the forces he had released in nature recognized no such limitations. They were the irrevocable monsters conjured up by a completely amateur sorcerer.

But what, we may ask, was the nature of the first discoveries that now threaten to induce disaster? Pre-eminent among them was, of course, the perception to which we have already referred: the discovery of the interlinked and evolving web of life. The great Victorian biologists saw, and yet refused to see, the war between form and formlessness, chaos and antichaos, which the poet Goethe had sensed contesting beneath the smiling surface of nature. "The dangerous gift from above," he had termed it, with uneasy foresight.

By contrast, Darwin, the prime student of the struggle for existence, sought to visualize in a tangled bank of leaves the silent and

179

insatiable war of nature. Still, he could imply with a veiled compla-
cency that man might "with some confidence" look forward to a
secure future "of inappreciable length." This he could do upon the
same page in the *Origin of Species* where he observes that "of the
species now living very few will transmit progeny to a far distant
futurity." The contradiction escaped him; he did not wish to see it.
Darwin, in addition, saw life as a purely selfish struggle, in which
nothing is modified for the good of another species without being
directly advantageous to its associated form.

If, he contended, one part of any single species had been formed
for the exclusive good of another, "it would annihilate my theory."
Powerfully documented and enhanced though the statement has
become, famine, war, and death are not the sole instruments biolo-
gists today would accept as the means toward that perfection of
which Darwin spoke. The subject is subtle and intricate; let it suffice
to say here that the sign of the dark cave and the club became so
firmly fixed in human thinking that in our time it has been invoked
as signifying man's true image in books selling in the hundreds of
thousands.

From the thesis and antithesis contained in Darwinism we come
to Freud. The public knows that, like Darwin, the master of the
inner world took the secure, stable, and sunlit province of the mind
and revealed it as a place of contending furies. Ghostly transforma-
tions, flitting night shadows, misshapen changelings existed there, as
real as anything that haunted the natural universe of Darwin. For
this reason, appropriately, I had come as the skull and the eye to
Costabel—the coast demanding shipwreck. Why else had I remem-
bered the phrase, except for a dark impulse toward destruction
lurking somewhere in the subconscious? I lay on the bed while the
agonized eye in the remembered photograph persisted at the back
of my closed lids.

It had begun when, after years of separation, I had gone dutifully
home to a house from which the final occupant had departed. In a
musty attic—among old trunks, a broken aquarium, and a dusty
heap of fossil shells collected in childhood—I found a satchel. The
satchel was already a shabby antique, in whose depths I turned up
a jackknife and a "rat" of hair such as women wore at the beginning

of the century. Beneath these lay a pile of old photographs and a note—two notes, rather, evidently dropped into the bag at different times. Each, in a thin, ornate hand, reiterated a single message that the writer had believed important. "This satchel belongs to my son, Loren Eiseley." It was the last message. I recognized the trivia. The jackknife I had carried in childhood. The rat of hair had belonged to my mother, and there were also two incredibly pointed slippers that looked as though they had been intended for a formal ball, to which I knew well my mother would never in her life have been invited. I undid the rotted string around the studio portraits.

Mostly they consisted of stiff, upright bearded men and heavily clothed women equally bound to the formalities and ritual that attended upon the photography of an earlier generation. No names identified the pictures, although here and there a reminiscent family trait seemed faintly evident. Finally I came upon a less formal photograph, taken in the eighties of the last century. Again no names identified the people, but a commercial stamp upon the back identified the place: Dyersville, Iowa. I had never been in that country town, but I knew at once it was my mother's birthplace.

Dyersville, the thought flashed through my mind, making the connection now for the first time: the dire place. I recognized at once the two sisters at the edge of the photograph, the younger clinging reluctantly to the older. Six years old, I thought, turning momentarily away from the younger child's face. Here it began, her pain and mine. The eyes in the photograph were already remote and shadowed by some inner turmoil. The poise of the body was already that of one miserably departing the peripheries of the human estate. The gaze was mutely clairvoyant and lonely. It was the gaze of a child who knew unbearable difference and impending isolation.

I dropped the notes and pictures once more into the bag. The last message had come from Dyersville: "my son." The child in the photograph had survived to be an ill-taught prairie artist. She had been deaf. All her life she had walked the precipice of mental breakdown. Here on this faded porch it had begun—the long crucifixion of life. I slipped downstairs and out of the house. I walked for miles through the streets.

Now at Costabel I put on the sunglasses once more, but the face from the torn photograph persisted behind them. It was as though I, as man, was being asked to confront, in all its overbearing weight, the universe itself. "Love not the world," the Biblical injunction runs, "neither the things that are in the world." The revolving beam in my mind had stopped, and the insect whisperings of the intellect. There was, at last, an utter stillness, a waiting as though for a cosmic judgment. The eye, the torn eye, considered me.

"But I *do* love the world," I whispered to a waiting presence in the empty room. "I love its small ones, the things beaten in the strangling surf, the bird, singing, which flies and falls and is not seen again." I choked and said, with the torn eye still upon me, "I love the lost ones, the failures of the world." It was like the renunciation of my scientific heritage. The torn eye surveyed me sadly and was gone. I had come full upon one of the last great rifts in nature, and the merciless beam no longer was in traverse around my skull.

But no, it was not a rift but a joining: the expression of love projected beyond the species boundary by a creature born of Darwinian struggle, in the silent war under the tangled bank. "There is no boon in nature," one of the new philosophers had written harshly in the first years of the industrial cities. Nevertheless, through war and famine and death, a sparse mercy had persisted, like a mutation whose time had not yet come. I had seen the star thrower cross that rift and, in so doing, he had reasserted the human right to define his own frontier. He had moved to the utmost edge of natural being, if not across its boundaries. It was as though at some point the supernatural had touched hesitantly, for an instant, upon the natural.

Out of the depths of a seemingly empty universe had grown an eye, like the eye in my room, but an eye on a vastly larger scale. It looked out upon what I can only call itself. It searched the skies and it searched the depths of being. In the shape of man it had ascended like a vaporous emanation from the depths of night. The nothing had miraculously gazed upon the nothing and was not content. It was an intrusion into, or a projection out of, nature for which no precedent existed. The act was, in short, an assertion of value arisen from the domain of absolute zero. A little whirlwind of commingling molecules had succeeded in confronting its own universe.

# THE STAR THROWER

Here, at last, was the rift that lay beyond Darwin's tangled bank. For a creature, arisen from that bank and born of its contentions, had stretched out its hand in pity. Some ancient, inexhaustible, and patient intelligence, lying dispersed in the planetary fields of force or amidst the inconceivable cold of interstellar space, had chosen to endow its desolation with an apparition as mysterious as itself. The fate of man is to be the ever-recurrent, reproachful Eye floating upon night and solitude. The world cannot be said to exist save by the interposition of that inward eye—an eye various and not under the restraints to be apprehended from what is vulgarly called the natural.

I had been unbelieving. I had walked away from the star thrower in the hardened indifference of maturity. But thought mediated by the eye is one of nature's infinite disguises. Belatedly, I arose with a solitary mission. I set forth in an effort to find the star thrower.

## IV

Man is himself, like the universe he inhabits, like the demoniacal stirrings of the ooze from which he sprang, a tale of desolations. He walks in his mind from birth to death the long resounding shores of endless disillusionment. Finally, the commitment to life departs or turns to bitterness. But out of such desolation emerges the awesome freedom to choose—to choose beyond the narrowly circumscribed circle that delimits the animal being. In that widening ring of human choice, chaos and order renew their symbolic struggle in the role of titans. They contend for the destiny of a world.

Somewhere far up the coast wandered the star thrower beneath his rainbow. Our exchange had been brief because upon that coast I had learned that men who ventured out at dawn resented others in the greediness of their compulsive collecting. I had also been abrupt because I had, in the terms of my profession and experience, nothing to say. The star thrower was mad, and his particular acts were a folly with which I had not chosen to associate myself. I was an observer and a scientist. Nevertheless, I had seen the rainbow attempting to attach itself to earth.

On a point of land, as though projecting into a domain beyond us, I found the star thrower. In the sweet rain-swept morning, that great many-hued rainbow still lurked and wavered tentatively beyond him. Silently I sought and picked up a still-living star, spinning it far out into the waves. I spoke once briefly. "I understand," I said. "Call me another thrower." Only then I allowed myself to think, He is not alone any longer. After us there will be others.

We were part of the rainbow—an unexplained projection into the natural. As I went down the beach I could feel the drawing of a circle in men's minds, like that lowering, shifting realm of color in which the thrower labored. It was a visible model of something toward which man's mind had striven, the circle of perfection.

I picked and flung another star. Perhaps far outward on the rim of space a genuine star was similarly seized and flung. I could feel the movement in my body. It was like a sowing—the sowing of life on an infinitely gigantic scale. I looked back across my shoulder. Small and dark against the receding rainbow, the star thrower stooped and flung once more. I never looked again. The task we had assumed was too immense for gazing. I flung and flung again while all about us roared the insatiable waters of death.

But we, pale and alone and small in that immensity, hurled back the living stars. Somewhere far off, across bottomless abysses, I felt as though another world was flung more joyfully. I could have thrown in a frenzy of joy, but I set my shoulders and cast, as the thrower in the rainbow cast, slowly, deliberately, and well. The task was not to be assumed lightly, for it was men as well as starfish that we sought to save. For a moment, we cast on an infinite beach together beside an unknown hurler of suns. It was, unsought, the destiny of my kind since the rituals of the Ice Age hunters, when life in the Northern Hemisphere had come close to vanishing. We had lost our way, I thought, but we had kept, some of us, the memory of the perfect circle of compassion from life to death and back again to life—the completion of the rainbow of existence. Even the hunters in the snow, making obeisance to the souls of the hunted, had known the cycle. The legend had come down and lingered that he who gained the gratitude of animals gained help in need from the dark wood.

I cast again with an increasingly remembered sowing motion and went my lone way up the beaches. Somewhere, I felt, in a great atavistic surge of feeling, somewhere the Thrower knew. Perhaps he smiled and cast once more into the boundless pit of darkness. Perhaps he, too, was lonely, and the end toward which he labored remained hidden—even as with ourselves.

I picked up a star whose tube feet ventured timidly among my fingers while, like a true star, it cried soundlessly for life. I saw it with an unaccustomed clarity and cast far out. With it, I flung myself as forfeit, for the first time, into some unknown dimension of existence. From Darwin's tangled bank of unceasing struggle, selfishness, and death, had arisen, incomprehensibly, the thrower who loved not man, but life. It was the subtle cleft in nature before which biological thinking had faltered. We had reached the last shore of an invisible island—yet, strangely, also a shore that the primitives had always known. They had sensed intuitively that man cannot exist spiritually without life, his brother, even if he slays. Somewhere, my thought persisted, there is a hurler of stars, and he walks, because he chooses, always in desolation, but not in defeat.

In the night the gas flames under the shelling kettles would continue to glow. I set my clock accordingly. Tomorrow I would walk in the storm. I would walk against the shell collectors and the flames. I would walk remembering Bacon's forgotten words "for the uses of life." I would walk with the knowledge of the discontinuities of the unexpected universe. I would walk knowing of the rift revealed by the thrower, a hint that there looms, inexplicably, in nature something above the role men give her. I knew it from the man at the foot of the rainbow, the starfish thrower on the beaches of Costabel.

# Science and the
# Sense of the Holy

I

When I was a young man engaged in fossil hunting in the Nebraska badlands I was frequently reminded that the ravines, washes, and gullies over which we wandered resembled the fissures in a giant exposed brain. The human brain contains the fossil memories of its past—buried but not extinguished moments—just as this more formidable replica contained deep in its inner stratigraphic convolutions earth's past in the shape of horned titanotheres and stalking, dirk-toothed cats. Man's memory erodes away in the short space of a lifetime. Jutting from the coils of the earth brain over which I clambered were the buried remnants, the changing history, of the entire age of mammals—millions of years of vanished daylight with their accompanying traces of volcanic outbursts and upheavals. It may well be asked why this analogy of earth's memory should so preoccupy the mind of a scientist as to have affected his entire outlook upon nature and upon his kinship with—even his concern for—the plant and animal world about him.

Perhaps the problem can best be formulated by pointing out that there are two extreme approaches to the interpretation of the living world. One was expressed by Charles Darwin at the age of twenty-eight; one by Sigmund Freud in his mature years. Other men of science have been arrayed on opposite sides of the question, but the eminence of these two scholars will serve to point up a controversy that has been going on since science arose, sometimes quietly, sometimes marked by vitriolic behavior, as when a certain specialist wed-

186

ded to his own view of the universe hurled his opponent's book into his wastebasket only to have it retrieved and cherished by a graduate student who became a lifelong advocate of the opinions reviled by his mentor. Thus it is evident that, in the supposed objective world of science, emotion and temperament may play a role in our selection of the mental tools with which we choose to investigate nature.

Charles Darwin, at a time when the majority of learned men looked upon animals as either automatons or creatures created merely for human exploitation, jotted thoughtfully into one of his early journals upon evolution the following observation:

"If we choose to let conjecture run wild, then animals, our fellow brethren in pain, disease, suffering and famine—our slaves in the most laborious works, our companions in our amusements—they may partake of our origin in one common ancestor—we may be all netted together."

What, we may now inquire, is the world view here implied, one way in which a great scientist looked upon the subject matter that was to preoccupy his entire working life? In spite of the fact that Darwin was, in his later years, an agnostic, in spite of confessing he was "in thick mud" so far as metaphysics was concerned, the remark I have quoted gives every sign of that feeling of awe, of dread of the holy playing upon nature, which characterizes the work of a number of naturalists and physicists down even to the present day. Darwin's remark reveals an intuitive sensitivity to the life of other creatures about him, an attitude quite distinct from that of the laboratory experimentalist who is hardened to the infliction of pain. In addition, Darwin's final comment that we may be all netted together in one gigantic mode of experience, that we are in a mystic sense one single diffuse animal, subject to joy and suffering beyond what we endure as individuals, reveals a youth drawn to the world of nature by far more than just the curiosity to be readily satisfied by the knife or the scalpel.

If we turn to Sigmund Freud by way of contrast we find an oddly inhibited reaction. Freud, though obviously influenced by the elegant medical experimenters of his college days, groped his way alone, and by methods not subject to quantification or absolute verification, into the dark realms of the subconscious. His reaction to the natural world, or at least his feelings and intuitions about it, are basically cold, clinical, and reserved. He of all men recognized what one poet has termed "the terrible archaeology of the brain." Freud states that "nothing once constructed has perished, and all the earlier stages of development have survived alongside the latest." But for Freud, convinced that childhood made the man, adult reactions were apt to fall under the suspicion of being childhood ghosts raised up in a disguised fashion. Thus, insightful though he could be, the very nature of his study of man tended to generate distrust of that outgoing empathy we observed in the young Darwin. "I find it very difficult to work with these intangible qualities," confessed Freud. He was suspicious of their representing some lingering monster of childhood, even if reduced in size. Since Freud regarded any type of religious feeling—even the illuminative quality of the universe—as an illusion, feelings of awe before natural phenomena such as that manifested by Darwin were to him basically remnants of childhood and to be dismissed accordingly.

In *Civilization and Its Discontents* Freud speaks with slight condescension of a friend who claimed a sensation of eternity, something limitless, unbounded—"oceanic," to use the friend's expression. The feeling had no sectarian origin, no assurance of immortality, but implied just such a sense of awe as might lie at the root of the religious impulse. "I cannot," maintained Freud, "discover this 'oceanic' impulse in myself." Instead he promptly psychoanalyzes the feeling of oneness with the universe into the child's pleasure ego which holds to itself all that is comforting; in short, the original ego, the infant's ego, included everything. Later, by experience, contended Freud, our adult ego becomes only a shrunken vestige of that far more extensive feeling which "expressed an inseparable connection . . . with the external world."

In essence, then, Freud is explaining away one of the great feelings characteristic of the best in man by relegating it to a childhood atavistic survival in adult life. The most highly developed animals, he observes, have arisen from the lowest. Although the great saurians are gone, the dwarfed crocodile remains. Presumably if Freud had completed the analogy he would have been forced to say that crocodilian adults without awe and with egos shrunken safely into their petty concerns represented a higher, more practical evolutionary level than the aberrant adult who persists in feelings of wonder before which Freud recoiled with a nineteenth-century mechanist's distaste, although not without acknowledging that this lurking childlike corruption might be widespread. He chose to regard it, however, as just another manifestation of the irrational aspect of man's divided psyche.

Over six decades before the present, a German theologian, Rudolf Otto, had chosen for his examination what he termed *The Idea of the Holy (Das Heilige)*. Appearing in 1917 in a time of bitterness and disillusionment, his book was and is still widely read. It cut across denominational divisions and spoke to all those concerned with that *mysterium tremendum*, that very awe before the universe which Freud had sighed over and dismissed as irrational. I think it safe to affirm that Freud left adult man somewhat shrunken and misjudged—misjudged because some of the world's scientists and artists have been deeply affected by the great mystery, less so the child at one's knee who frequently has to be disciplined to what in India has been called the "opening of the heavenly eye."

Ever since man first painted animals in the dark of caves he has been responding to the holy, to the numinous, to the mystery of being and becoming, to what Goethe very aptly called "the weird portentous." Something inexpressible was felt to lie behind nature. The bear cult, circumpolar in distribution and known archaeologically to extend into Neanderthal times, is a further and most ancient example. The widespread beliefs in descent from a totemic animal, guardian helpers in the shapes of animals, the concept of the game lords who released or held back game to man are all part of a variety of a sanctified, reverent experience that extends from the beautiful rock paintings of South Africa to the men of the Labradorean forests or the Plains Indian seeking by starvation and isolation to bring the sacred spirits to his assistance. All this is part of the human inheritance, the wonder of the world, and nowhere does that wonder press closer to us than in the guise of animals which, whether supernaturally as in the caves of our origins or, as in Darwin's sudden illumination, perceived to be, at heart, one form, one awe-inspiring mystery, seemingly diverse and apart but derived from the same genetic source. Thus the *mysterium* arose not by primitive campfires alone.

Skins may still prickle in a modern classroom.

In the end, science as we know it has two basic types of practitioners. One is the educated man who still has a controlled sense of wonder before the universal mystery, whether it hides in a snail's eye or within the light that impinges on that delicate organ. The second kind of observer is the extreme reductionist who is so busy stripping things apart that the tremendous mystery has been reduced to a trifle, to intangibles not worth troubling one's head about. The world of the secondary qualities—color, sound, thought—is reduced to illusion. The *only* true reality becomes the chill void of ever-streaming particles.

If one is a biologist this approach can result in behavior so remarkably cruel that it ceases to be objective but rather suggests a deep grain of sadism that is not science. To list but one example, a recent newspaper article reported that a great urban museum of national reputation had spent over a half-million dollars on mutilating experiments with cats. The experiments are too revolting to chronicle here and the museum has not seen fit to enlighten the public on the knowledge gained at so frightful a cost in pain. The cost, it would appear, lies not alone in animal suffering but in the dehumanization of those willing to engage in such blind, random cruelty. The practice was defended by museum officials, who in a muted show of scientific defense maintained the right to study what they chose "without regard to its demonstrable practical value."

This is a scientific precept hard to override since the days of Galileo, as the official well knew. Nevertheless, behind its seamless façade of probity many terrible things are and will be done. Blaise Pascal, as far back as the seventeenth century, foresaw our two opposed methods. Of them he said: "There are two equally dangerous extremes, to shut reason out, and to let nothing else in." It is the reductionist who, too frequently, would claim that the end justifies the means, who would assert reason as his defense and let that *mysterium* which guards man's moral nature fall away in indifference, a phantom without reality.

"The whole of existence frightens me," protested the philosopher Søren Kierkegaard; "from the smallest fly to the mystery of the Incarnation, everything is unintelligible to me, most of all myself."

# SCIENCE AND THE SENSE OF THE HOLY

By contrast, the evolutionary reductionist Ernst Haeckel, writing in 1877, commented that "the cell consists of matter . . . composed chiefly of carbon with an admixture of hydrogen, nitrogen and sulphur. These component parts, properly united, produce the soul and body of the animated world, and suitably nourished become man. With this single argument the mystery of the universe is explained, the Deity annulled and a new era of infinite knowledge ushered in." Since these remarks of Haeckel's, uttered a hundred years ago, the genetic alphabet has scarcely substantiated in its essential intricacy Haeckel's carefree dismissal of the complexity of life. If anything, it has given weight to Kierkegaard's wary statement or at least heightened the compassionate wonder with which we are led to look upon our kind.

"A conviction akin to religious feeling of the rationality or intelligibility of the world lies behind all scientific work of a high order," says Albert Einstein. Here once more the eternal dichotomy manifests itself. Thoreau, the man of literature, writes compassionately, "Shall I not have intelligence with the earth? Am I not partly leaves and vegetable mould myself?" Or Walt Whitman, the poet, protests in his *Song of Myself:* "whoever walks a furlong without sympathy walks to his own funeral drest in a shroud."

"Magnifying and applying come I"—he thunders—
"Outbidding at the start the old cautious hucksters . . .
Not objecting to special revelations, considering a curl of smoke
     or a hair
on the back of my hand just as curious as any revelation."

Strange, is it not, that so many of these voices are not those of children, but those of great men—Newton playing on the vast shores of the universe, or Whitman touched with pity or Darwin infused with wonder over the clambering tree of life. Strange, that all these many voices should be dismissed as the atavistic yearnings of an unreduced childlike ego seeking in "oceanic" fashion to absorb its entire surroundings, as though in revolt against the counting house, the laboratory, and the computer.

## II

Not long ago in a Manhattan art gallery there were exhibited paint-
ings by Irwin Fleminger, a modernist whose vast lawless Martianlike
landscapes contain cryptic human artifacts. One of these paintings
attracted my eye by its title: "Laws of Nature." Here in a jumbled
desert waste without visible life two thin laths had been erected a
little distance apart. Strung across the top of the laths was an insub-
stantial string with even more insubstantial filaments depending
from the connecting cord. The effect was terrifying. In the huge
inhuman universe that constituted the background, man, who was
even more diminished by his absence, had attempted to delineate
and bring under natural law an area too big for his comprehension.
His effort, his "law," whatever it was, denoted a tiny measure in the
midst of an ominous landscape looming away to the horizon. The
frail slats and dangling string would not have sufficed to fence a
chicken run.

The message grew as one looked. With all the great powers of
the human intellect we were safe, we understood, in degree, a
space between some slats and string, a little gate into the world of
infinitude. The effect was crushing and it brought before one that
sense of the "other" of which Rudolf Otto spoke, the sense be-
yond our senses, unspoken awe, or, as the reductionist would have
it, nothing but waste. There the slats stood and the string drooped
hopelessly. It was the natural law imposed by man, but outside its
compass, again to use the words of Thoreau, was something ter-
rific, not bound to be kind to man. Not man's at all really—a star's
substance totally indifferent to life or what laws life might concoct.
No man would greatly extend that trifling toy. The line sagged
hopelessly. Man's attempt had failed, leaving but an artifact in the
wilderness. Perhaps, I thought, this is man's own measure. Perhaps
he has already gone. The crepitation at my spine increased. I felt
the mood of the paleolithic artists, lost in the mysteries of birth
and coming, as they carved pregnant beasts in the dark of caves
and tried by crayons to secure the food necessarily wrung from
similar vast landscapes. Their art had the same holy quality that
shows in the ivory figurines, the worship before the sacred mother

who brought man mysteriously into the limited world of the cave mouth.

The numinous then is touched with superstition, the reductionist would say, but all the rituals suggest even toward hunted animals a respect and sympathy leading to ceremonial treatment of hunted souls; whereas by contrast in the modern world the degradation of animals in experiments of little, or vile, meaning, were easily turned to the experimental human torture practiced at Dachau and Buchenwald by men dignified with medical degrees. So the extremes of temperament stand today: the man with reverence and compassion in his heart whose eye ranges farther than the two slats in the wilderness, and the modern vandal totally lacking in empathy for life beyond his own, his sense of wonder reduced to a crushing series of gears and quantitative formula, the educated vandal without mercy or tolerance, the collecting man that I once tried to prevent from killing an endangered falcon, who raised his rifle, fired, and laughed as the bird tumbled at my feet. I suppose Freud might have argued that this was a man of normal ego, but I, extending my childlike mind into the composite life of the world, bled accordingly.

Perhaps Freud was right, but let us look once more at this brain that in many distinguished minds has agonized over life and the mysterious road by which it has come. Certainly, as Darwin recognized, it was not the tough-minded, logical inductionists of the early nineteenth century who in a deliberate distortion of Baconian philosophy solved the problem of evolution. Rather, it was what Darwin chose to call "speculative" men, men, in other words, with just a touch of the numinous in their eye, a sense of marvel, a glimpse of what was happening behind the visible, who saw the whole of the living world as though turning in a child's kaleidoscope.

Among the purely human marvels of the world is the way the human brain after birth, when its cranial capacity is scarcely larger than that of a gorilla or other big anthropoid, spurts onward to treble its size during the first year of life. The human infant's skull will soar to a cranial capacity of 950 cubic centimeters while the gorilla has reached only 380 cubic centimeters. In other words, the human brain grows at an exponential rate, a spurt which carries it almost to adult capacity at the age of fourteen.

This clever and specifically human adaptation enables the human offspring successfully to pass the birth canal like a reasonably small-headed animal, but in a more larval and helpless condition than its giant relatives. The brain burgeons after birth, not before, and it is this fact which enables the child, with proper care, to assimilate all that larger world which will be forever denied to its relative the gorilla. The big anthropoids enjoy no such expansion. Their brains grow without exponential quickening into maturity. Somewhere in the far past of man something strange happened in his evolutionary development. His skull has enhanced its youthful globularity; he has lost most of his body hair and what remains grows strangely. He demands, because of his immature emergence into the world, a lengthened and protected childhood. Without prolonged familial attendance he would not survive, yet in him reposes the capacity for great art, inventiveness, and his first mental tool, speech, which creates his humanity. He is without doubt the oddest and most unusual evolutionary product that this planet has yet seen.

The term applied to this condition is neoteny, or pedomorphism. Basically the evolutionary forces, and here "forces" stands for complete ignorance, seem to have taken a roughhewn ordinary primate and softened and eliminated the adult state in order to allow for a fantastic leap in brain growth. In fact, there is a growing suspicion that some, at least, of the African fossils found and ascribed to the direct line of human ascent in eastern Africa may never, except for bipedalism and some incipient tool-using capacities, have taken the human road at all.

Some with brains that seem to have remained at the same level through long ages have what amounts quantitatively to no more than an anthropoid brain. Allowing for upright posture and free use of the hand, there is no assurance that they spoke or in any effective way were more than well-adapted bipedal apes. Collateral relatives, in short, but scarcely to be termed men. All this is the more remarkable because their history can now be traced over roughly five if not six million years—a singularly unprogressive period for a creature destined later to break upon the world with such remarkable results after so long a period of gestation.

Has something about our calculations gone wrong? Are we study-
ing, however necessarily, some bipedal cousins but not ancestral
men? The human phylogeny which we seemed well on the way to
arranging satisfactorily is now confused by a multiplicity of material
contended over by an almost equal number of scholars. Just as a
superfluity of flying particles is embarrassing the physicist, so man's
evolution, once thought to be so clearly delineated, is showing signs
of similar strain. A skull from Lake Rudolf with an estimated capac-
ity of 775 cubic centimeters or even 800 and an antiquity ranging
into the three-million-year range is at the human Rubicon, yet much
younger fossils are nowhere out of the anthropoid range.

Are these all parts of a single variable subhumanity from which
we arose, or are some parts of this assemblage neotenous of brain and
others not? The scientific exchanges are as stiff with politeness as
exchanges between enemies on the floor of the Senate. "Professor
so-and-so forgets the difficult task of restoring to its proper position
a frontal bone trampled by cattle." A million years may be covertly
jumped because there is nothing to be found in it. We must never
lose sight of one fact, however: it is by neotenous brain growth that
we came to be men, and certain of the South African hominids to
which we have given such careful attention seem to have been
remarkably slow in revealing such development. Some of them, in
fact, during more years than present mankind has been alive seem
to have flourished quite well as simple grassland apes.

Why indeed should they all have become men? Because they
occupied the same ecological niche, contend those who would lump
this variable assemblage. But surely paleontology does not always so
bind its deliberations. We are here dealing with a gleam, a whisper,
a thing of awe in the mind itself, that oceanic feeling which even
the hardheaded Freud did not deny existed though he tried to assign
it to childhood.

With animals whose precise environment through time may over-
lap, extinction may result among contending forms; it can and did
happen among men. But with the first stirrings of the neotenous
brain and its superinduced transformation of the family system a
new type of ecological niche had incipiently appeared—a speaking

niche, a wondering niche which need not have been first manifested in tools but in family organization, in wonder over what lay over the next hill or what became of the dead. Whether man preferred seeds or flesh, how he regarded his silent collateral relatives, may not at first have induced great competition. Only those gifted with the pedomorphic brain would in some degree have fallen out of competition with the real. It would have been their danger and at the same time their beginning triumph. They were starting to occupy, not a niche in nature, but an invisible niche carved into thought which in time would bring them suffering, superstition, and great power.

It cannot, in the beginning, be recognized clearly because it is not a matter of molar teeth and seeds, or killer instincts and ill-interpreted pebbles. Rather it was something happening in the brain, some blinding, irradiating thing. Until the quantity of that gray matter reached the threshold of human proportions no one could be sure whether the creature saw with a human eye or looked upon life with even the faint stirrings of some kind of religious compassion.

The new niche in its beginnings is invisible; it has to be inferred. It does not lie waiting to be discovered in a pebble or a massive molar. These things are important in the human dawn but so is the mystery that ordained that mind should pass the channel of birth and then grow like a fungus in the night—grow and convolute and overlap its older buried strata, while a 600-pound gorilla retains by contrast the cranial content of a very small child. When man cast off his fur and placed his trust in that remarkable brain linked by neural pathways to his tongue he had potentially abandoned niches for dreams. Henceforth the world was man's niche. All else would live by his toleration—even the earth from which he sprang. Perhaps this is the hardest, most expensive lesson the layers of the fungus brain have yet to learn: that man is not as other creatures and that without the sense of the holy, without compassion, his brain can become a gray stalking horror—the deviser of Belsen.

Its beginning is not the only curious thing about that brain. There are some finds in South Africa dating into immediately post-glacial times that reveal a face and calvaria more "modern" in appearance, more pedomorphic, than that of the average European. The skull is marked by cranial capacities in excess of 1700 cubic centimeters—

big brained by any standards. The mastoids are childlike, the teeth reduced, the cranial base foreshortened. These people, variously termed Boskopoid or Strandlooper, have, in the words of one anthropologist, "the amazing cranium to face ratio of almost five to one. In Europeans it is about three to one. Face size has been modernized and subordinated to brain growth." In a culture still relying on coarse fare and primitive implements, the face and brain had been subtly altered in the direction science fiction writers like to imagine as the direction in which mankind is progressing. Yet here the curious foetalization of the human body seems to have outrun man's cultural status, though in the process giving warning that man's brain could still pass the straitened threshold of its birth.

How did these people look upon the primitive world into which they found themselves precipitated? History gives back no answer save that here there flourished striking three-dimensional art—the art of the brother animal seen in beauty. Childlike, Freud might have muttered, with childlike dreams, rushed into conflict with the strong, the adult and shrunken ego, the ego that gets what it wants. Yet how strangely we linger over this lost episode of the human story, its pathos, its possible meaning. From whence did these people come? We are not sure. We are not even sure that they derive from one of the groups among the ruck of bipedal wandering apes long ago in Kenya that reveal some relationship to ourselves. Their development was slow, if indeed some of them took that road, the strange road to the foetalized brain that was to carry man outside of the little niche that fed him his tuberous, sandy diet.

We thought we were on the verge of solving the human story, but now we hold in our hands gross jaws and delicate, and are unsure of our direction save that the trail is longer than we had imagined twenty years ago. Yet still the question haunts us, the numinous, the holy in man's mind. Early man laid gifts beside the dead, but then in the modern unbelieving world, Ernst Haeckel's world, a renowned philosopher says, "The whole of existence frightens me," or another humbler thinker says, "In the world there is nothing to explain the world" but remembers the gold eyes of the falcon thrown brutally at his feet. He shivers while Freud says, "As for me I have never had such feelings." They are a part of childhood, Freud argues, though there are some who counter that in childhood—yes, even Freud might grant it—the man is made, the awe persists or is turned off by blows or the dullness of unthinking parents. One can only assert that in science, as in religion, when one has destroyed human wonder and compassion, one has killed man, even if the man in question continues to go about his laboratory tasks.

## III

Perhaps there is one great book out of all American literature which best expresses the clash between the man who has genuine perception and the one who pursues nature as ruthlessly as a hunted animal. I refer to *Moby Dick*, whose narrator, Ishmael, is the namesake of a Biblical wanderer. Every literate person knows the story of Moby Dick and his pursuit by the crazed Captain Ahab who had yielded a leg to the great albino whale. It is the whale and Ahab who dominate the story. What does the whale represent? A symbol of evil, as some critics have contended? Fate, destiny, the universe personified, as other scholars have protested?

Moby Dick is "all a magnet," remarks Ahab cryptically at one moment. "And be he agent or be he principal I will wreak my hate upon him." Here, reduced to the deck of a whaler out of Nantucket, the old immortal questions resound, the questions labeled science in our era. Nothing is to go unchallenged. Thrice, by different vessels, Ahab is warned away from his contemplated conquest. The whale does not pursue Ahab, Ahab pursues the whale. If there is evil represented in the white whale it cannot be personalized. The evils of self-murder, of megalomania, are at work in a single soul calling up its foreordained destruction. Ahab heartlessly brushes aside the supplications of a brother captain to aid in the search for his son, lost somewhere in a boat in the trail of the white whale's passing. Such a search would only impede the headlong fury of the pursuit.

In Ahab's anxiety to "strike through the mask," to confront "the principal," whether god or destiny, he is denuding himself of all humanity. He has forgotten his owners, his responsibility to his crew. His single obsession, the hidden obsession that lies at the root of much Faustian overdrive in science, totally possesses him. Like Faust he must know, if the knowing kills him, if naught lies beyond. "All my means are sane," he writes, like Haeckel and many another since. "My motive and my object mad."

So it must have been in the laboratories of the atom breakers in their first heady days of success. Yet again on the third day Starbuck, the doomed mate, cries out to Ahab, "Desist. See. Moby Dick seeks thee not. It is thou, thou, that madly seekest him." This then is not the pursuit of evil. It is man in his pride that the almighty gods will challenge soon enough. Not for nothing is Moby Dick a white snow hill rushing through Pacific nights. He carries upon his brow the inscrutability of fate. Agent or principal, Moby Dick presents to Ahab the mystery he may confront but never conquer. There is no harpoon tempered that will strike successfully the heart of the great enigma.

So much for the seeking peg-legged man without heart. We know he launched his boats and struck his blows and in the fury of return-ing vengeance lost his ship, his comrades, and his own life. If, indeed, he pierced momentarily the mask of the "agent," it was not long enough to tell the tale. But what of the sometimes silent narrator, the man who begins the book with the nonchalant an-nouncement, "Call me Ishmael," the man whose Biblical namesake had every man's hand lifted against him? What did he tell? After all, Moby Dick is his book.

Ishmael, in contrast to Ahab, is the wondering man, the acceptor of all races and their gods. In contrast to the obsessed Ahab he paints a magnificent picture of the peace that reigned in the giant whale schools of the 1840s, the snuffling and grunting about the boats like dogs, loving and being loved, huge mothers gazing in bliss upon their offspring. After hours of staring in those peaceful depths, "Deep down," says Ishmael, "there I still bathe in eternal mildness of joy." The weird, the holy, hangs undisturbed over the whales' huge cradle. Ishmael knows it, others do not.

At the end, when Ahab has done his worst and the *Pequod* with the wounded whale is dragged into the depths amidst shrieking seafowl, it is Ishmael, buoyed up on the calked coffin of his cannibal friend Queequeg, who survives to tell the tale. Like Whitman, like

W. H. Hudson, like Thoreau, Ishmael, the wanderer, has noted more of nature and his fellow men than has the headstrong pursuer of the white whale, whether "agent" or "principal," within the universe. The tale is not of science, but it symbolizes on a gigantic canvas the struggle between two ways of looking at the universe: the magnification by the poet's mind attempting to see all, while disturbing as little as possible, as opposed to the plunging fury of Ahab with his cry, "Strike, strike through the mask, whatever it may cost in lives and suffering." Within our generation we have seen the one view plead for endangered species and reject the despoliation of the earth; the other has left us lingering in the shadow of atomic disaster. Actually, the division is not so abrupt as this would imply, but we are conscious as never before in history that there is an invisible line of demarcation, an ethic that science must sooner or later devise for itself if mankind is to survive. Herman Melville glimpsed in his huge mythology of the white beast that was nature's agent something that only the twentieth century can fully grasp.

It may be that those childlike big-brained skulls from Africa are not of the past but of the future, man, not, in Freud's words, retaining an atavistic child's ego, but pushing onward in an evolutionary attempt to become truly at peace with the universe, to know and enjoy the sperm-whale nursery as did Ishmael, to paint in three dimensions the beauty of the world while not to harm it.

Yesterday, wandering along a railroad spur line, I glimpsed a surprising sight. All summer long, nourished by a few clods of earth on a boxcar roof, a sunflower had been growing. At last, the car had been remembered. A train was being made up. The box car with its swaying rooftop inhabitant was coupled in. The engine tooted and slowly, with nodding dignity, my plant began to travel.

Throughout the summer I had watched it grow but never troubled it. Now it lingered and bowed a trifle toward me as the winds began to touch it. A light not quite the sunlight of this earth was touching the flower, or perhaps it was the watering of my aging eye—who knows? The plant would not long survive its journey but the flower seeds were autumn-brown. At every jolt for miles they would drop along the embankment. They were travelers—travelers like Ishmael and myself, outlasting all fierce pursuits and destined to re-emerge into future autumns. Like Ishmael, I thought, they will speak with the voice of the one true agent: "I only am escaped to tell thee."

# The Winter
# of Man

"We fear," remarked an Eskimo shaman responding to a religious question from the explorer Knud Rasmussen some fifty years ago. "We fear the cold and the things we do not understand. But most of all we fear the doings of the heedless ones among ourselves."

Students of the earth's climate have observed that man, in spite of the disappearance of the great continental ice fields, still lives on the steep edge of winter or early spring. The pulsations of these great ice deserts, thousands of feet thick and capable of overflowing mountains and valleys, have characterized the nature of the world since man, in his thinking and speaking phase, arose. The ice which has left the marks of its passing upon the landscape of the Northern Hemisphere has also accounted, in its long, slow advances and retreats, for movements, migrations and extinctions throughout the plant and animal kingdoms.

Though man is originally tropical in his origins, the ice has played a great role in his unwritten history. At times it has constricted his movements, affecting the genetic selection that has created him. Again, ice has established conditions in which man has had to exert all his ingenuity in order to survive. By contrast, there have been other times when the ice has withdrawn farther than today and then, like a kind of sleepy dragon, has crept forth to harry man once more. For something like a million years this strange and alternating contest has continued between man and the ice.

When the dragon withdrew again some fifteen or twenty thousand years ago, man was on the verge of literacy. He already possessed great art, as the paintings in the Lascaux cavern reveal. It was an art devoted to the unseen, to the powers that control the movement of game and the magic that drives the hunter's shaft to its target. Without such magic man felt weak and helpless against the vagaries of nature. It was his first attempt at technology, at control of nature by dominating the luck element, the principle of uncertainty in the universe.

A few millennia further on in time man had forgotten the doorway of snow through which he had emerged. He would only rediscover the traces of the ice age in the nineteenth century by means of the new science of geology. At first he would not believe his own history or the reality of the hidden ice dragon, even though Greenland and the polar world today lie shrouded beneath that same ice. He would not see that what the Eskimo said to Rasmussen was a belated modern enactment of an age-old drama in which we, too, had once participated. "We fear," the Eskimo sage had said in essence, "we fear the ice and cold. We fear nature which we do not understand and which provides us with food or brings famine."

Man, achieving literacy on the far Mediterranean shores in an instant of golden sunlight would take the world as it was, to be forever. He would explore the intricacies of thought and wisdom in Athens. He would dream the first dreams of science and record them upon scrolls of parchment. Twenty-five centuries later those dreams would culminate in vast agricultural projects, green revolutions, power pouring through great pipelines, or electric energy surging across continents. Voices would speak into the distances of space. Huge jet transports would hurtle through the skies. Radio telescopes would listen to cosmic whispers from beyond our galaxy. Enormous concentrations of people would gather and be fed in towering metropolises. Few would remember the Greek word *hubris*, the term for overweening pride, that pride which eventually causes some unseen balance to swing in the opposite direction.

Today the ice at the poles lies quiet. There have been times in the past when it has maintained that passivity scores of thousands of years—times longer, in fact, than the endurance of the whole of urban civilization since its first incipient beginnings no more than seven thousand years ago. The temperature gradient from the poles to the equator is still steeper than throughout much of the unglaciated periods of the past. The doorway through which man has come is just tentatively closing behind him.

So complex is the problem of the glacial rhythms that no living scientist can say with surety the ice will not return. If it does the swarming millions who now populate the planet may mostly perish in misery and darkness, inexorably pushed from their own lands to be rejected in desperation by their neighbors. Like the devouring locust swarms that gather in favorable summers, man may have some of that same light-winged ephemeral quality about him. One senses it occasionally in those places where the dropped, transported boulders of the ice fields still hint of formidable powers lurking somewhere behind the face of present nature.

These fractured mementoes of devastating cold need to be contemplated for another reason than themselves. They constitute exteriorly what may be contemplated interiorly. They contain a veiled warning, perhaps the greatest symbolic warning man has ever received from nature. The giant fragments whisper, in the words of Einstein, that "nature does not always play the same game." Nature is devious in spite of what we have learned of her. The greatest scholars have always sensed this. "She will tell you a direct lie if she can," Charles Darwin once warned a sympathetic listener. Even Darwin, however, alert as he was to vestigial traces of former evolutionary structures in our bodies, was not in a position to foresee the kind of strange mental archaeology by which Sigmund Freud would probe the depths of the human mind. Today we are aware of the latent and shadowy powers contained in the subconscious: the alternating winter and sunlight of the human soul.

Has the earth's glacial winter, for all our mastery of science, surely subsided? No, the geologist would answer. We merely stand in a transitory spot of sunshine that takes on the illusion of permanence only because the human generations are short.

Has the wintry bleakness in the troubled heart of humanity at least equally retreated?—that aspect of man referred to when the Eskimo, adorned with amulets to ward off evil, reiterated: "Most of all we fear the secret misdoings of the heedless ones among our-selves."

No, the social scientist would have to answer, the winter of man has not departed. The Eskimo standing in the snow, when ques-tioned about his beliefs, said: "We do not believe. We only fear. We fear those things which are about us and of which we have no sure knowledge. . . ."

But surely we can counter that this old man was an ignorant remnant of the Ice Age, fearful of a nature he did not understand. Today we have science; we do not fear the Eskimo's malevolent ghosts. We do not wear amulets to ward off evil spirits. We have pierced to the far rim of the universe. We roam mentally through light-years of time.

Yes, this could be admitted, but we also fear. We fear more deeply than the old man in the snow. It comes to us, if we are honest, that perhaps nothing has changed the grip of winter in our hearts, that winter before which we cringed amidst the ice long ages ago.

For what is it that we do? We fear. We do not fear ghosts but we fear the ghost of ourselves. We have come now, in this time, to fear the water we drink, the air we breathe, the insecticides that are dusted over our giant fruits. Because of the substances we have poured into our contaminated rivers, we fear the food that comes to us from the sea. There are also those who tell us that by our own heedless acts the sea is dying.

We fear the awesome powers we have lifted out of nature and cannot return to her. We fear the weapons we have made, the hatreds we have engendered. We fear the crush of fanatic people to whom we readily sell these weapons. We fear for the value of the money in our pockets that stands symbolically for food and shelter. We fear the growing power of the state to take all these things from us. We fear to walk in our streets at evening. We have come to fear even our scientists and their gifts.

We fear, in short, as that self-sufficient Eskimo of the long night had never feared. Our minds, if not our clothes, are hung with invisible amulets: nostrums changed each year for our bodies whether it be chlorophyl toothpaste, the signs of astrology, or cold cures that do not cure: witchcraft nostrums for our society as it fractures into contending multitudes all crying for liberation without responsibility.

We fear, and never in this century will we cease to fear. We fear the end of man as that old shaman in the snow had never had cause to fear it. There is a winter still about us—the winter of man that has followed him relentlessly from the caverns and the ice. The old Eskimo spoke well. It is the winter of the heedless ones. We are in the winter. We have never left its breath.

# Man Against
# the Universe

I

Man against the universe. But who is man and how is the universe to be defined? Sigmund Freud, in the modern era, remarked that man's mind has suffered from the impact of three significant events. The first took place when Nicolaus Copernicus, over four centuries ago, succeeded in demonstrating that the earth revolved around the sun, thus removing man from his privileged position at the center of the cosmos. The second blow which man's religious sensitivity sustained might well be dated to Darwin's demonstration in 1859 that man was only one part of nature's living web and was akin to, indeed was descended from, the animal life of the past. Finally, Freud himself, the great conquistador of psychology, created the third trauma by revealing the subterranean irrational qualities of the human mind.

The five-hundredth anniversary of Copernicus's birth was only recently celebrated. In the 1970s science has lengthened out the period in which man was a mere wandering proto-homonid on the African savanna. Thanks to the researches of Harlow Shapley, for fifty years we have known we are not even located at the heart of our own galaxy but like a sand grain are drifting on a remote arm of a spiral nebula which contains uncounted members. In truth, we can find no center. As far as the eye can reach, the objects of our attention are fleeing outward through billions of light-years.

Yet to say that man's self-examination began with the dawn of Copernican science would be to ignore that tremendous confrontation between Job and the voice from the whirlwind, in which the humbled Job is asked where he was when the foundations of the earth were laid. Furthermore, the ancient Orient had always viewed the world as illusory and envisioned the good life as primarily a way of hastening one's escape from the suffering wheel of existence. Thus man's sense of alienation, his feelings of inadequacy and trepidation before the natural world about him, long preceded the psychical disturbances that Freud regarded as induced by modern science. As Robin Collingwood pointed out some years ago, Anicius Boethius's *Consolation of Philosophy*, written in the sixth century A.D., had the distinction of being one of the most widely read books of the Middle Ages. For a thousand years every literate individual sought solace and comfort in the *Consolation*. It was never a proscribed book. Nevertheless it touches upon the infinitesimal space occupied by man in the scheme of things. Copernicus, on the other hand, had actually opened the possibility that human power extended into the celestial realms. In no mean sense he was a necessary forerunner of the space voyagers.

Yet any great scholar or artist is likely to find his conceptions denigrated in some quarters. To say that the entirety of mankind has been overwhelmed and psychologically traumatized beyond recall is to overestimate the achievements of any single intellectual. Today there exist millions of people who are totally encapsulated in another era and to whom Darwin and Darwin's ideas mean nothing. The accretion of ideas through the centuries does change the intellectual climate. Rarely, however, is the contemporary mass conscious of the innovator in its midst. This was particularly true before the rise of the news-disseminating media, but even today the content of much of science and philosophy is confined to learned circles and only rarely reaches a wider audience. As our probes into nature become more sophisticated, the greater becomes our reliance upon the specialist, while he, in turn, appeals to a minute audience of his peers.

The truth is that no man expounds upon great ideas to a single audience. He speaks, instead, to audiences, and these in turn will be receiving his message, like the far-traveling light from a star, sometimes centuries after he has delivered it. Man is not one public; he is many and the messages he receives are likely to become garbled in transmission. Again, the ideas of the most honest and well-intentioned scholar may be distorted, reoriented, or trimmed to fit the public needs of a given epoch. In addition, it could be argued that no great act of scientific synthesis is really fixed in the public mind until that public has been prepared to receive it through anticipatory glimpses.

Darwin, for example, had the way partly prepared for his ideas by the geological and paleontological efforts of the generation before him. The fact that geological time had been vastly extended had been recognized. Animal breeders were beginning to discern a lurking dynamism, a potential for change concealed in their domestic creations. In the 1840s Robert Chambers, an enterprising journalist and amateur geologist, had written a widely circulated popular book espousing, albeit anonymously, the evolutionary cause. Even the concept of natural selection, Darwin's major claim to originality, had been anticipated, in admittedly firefly glimpses, by several previous writers. Without detracting in the least from Darwin's massive and major achievement, one may observe that the literate public was in some measure ready to receive his views. In spite of some contemporary furor, the educated world accepted him within his lifetime.

By contrast, Gregor Mendel, as significant in his own way as Darwin, never received serious recognition in scientific circles and had been dead for thirty-five years before his discoveries in genetics were appreciated. He was ahead of his century and was what today might be called a laboratory geneticist carrying out seemingly unspectacular experiments upon pea plants in a kitchen garden. He was a monk burdened with the religious duties of his monastery. He had no romantic aura of wealth, no spectacular world voyage, no eminent scientific colleagues and defenders to heighten his prestige. Mendel's discoveries, though essential to the full understanding of the evolutionary mechanism, were of a sufficiently mathematical cast to belong to the biological studies of the twentieth century, not the nineteenth.

Though his work could be regarded as leading on to a far more sophisticated understanding of the miracle of life and its interrelatedness, Mendel went unnoticed by the public. No philosopher has tried to describe what Mendel's discoveries might have done to our world view, in the way either of shock or of renewed uplift. Such horizons of thought are implicit in his work and need not be equated with a more simplistic nineteenth-century Darwinism. The simple point is, however, that Mendel never had the kind of philosophical attention that would have attracted Freud. His thought lay outside the stream of public attention and he never would have gained Freud's interest as the purveyor of psychological shock.

Freud gauged his own impact upon society, but I wonder, with all due respect to his discoveries in the basement depths of the intellect, whether his claim to having destroyed man's faith in the godlike attributes of reason is justified, or whether he has expressed merely the happy ardor of the triumphant psychiatrist. For out of the depths of unreason, the murkiness of the subconscious, have come also some of the most poignant works of great art and literature. Even scientists have, on occasion, acknowledged indebtedness to that subterranean river. Freud did not in actuality destroy man's faith in mind. He merely added to its mystery by the realization that it could create besides flawed half-idiot phantasms, a more incredible beauty than could be conjured up in daylight. Before Freud was born, Ralph Waldo Emerson, a man of no inconsiderable literary gifts, had written: "I conceive a man as always spoken to from behind, and unable to turn his head and see the speaker." From those words emerges the voice of nineteenth-century romanticism. With Emerson and Darwin as opposed yet converging forces in nineteenth-century thought I shall now concern myself.

## II

George Boas, one of our most eminent intellectual historians, remarked, some thirty years ago, that there are always at least two philosophies in a country: one based upon the way people live, and the other upon the results of meditation upon the universe. In the end, one is apt to contend against the other. A perfect example of this may be observed in the rise of those doctrines labeled by critics as romanticism. They reached a peculiar intensity in the early nineteenth century, chiefly as a revolt against the formalism and social restraint of the eighteenth century.

One can venture that one of the first principles to emerge from the romantic revolt was the assertion of the self against the universe —the self, "dirty and amused" or titillated with midnight terrors but for all that having escaped forever out of the constraining formal gardens of custom into a wilder nature of crags and leaping torrents. Reason gave way for the moment to the long-restrained but impassioned reality of the heart. People wept over the new poetry, and the new poetry—that of Byron, Shelley, Keats, Coleridge—was full of picturesque revolutionaries and moon-haunted landscapes that would have seemed absurd to Lord Chesterfield and his contemporaries—men who believed that gentlemen neither laughed nor wept, at least in public. So much was the nostalgic time-sense deepened that people of means began to replace their formal gardens with artificially constructed ruins in which to brood. The experience of nature became tinged with a belief in a higher awareness, as though in the observation of nature itself one saw into the mind of the Divinity. Something subjective, lingering behind one's casual impressions, was thus sensed in nature. An intensified empathy, a willingness to transcend the ordinary modes of thinking, became a part of the suddenly emancipated and magnified self.

This feeling for nature as a thought to be encompassed, a human ego sustained by a creative power greater than itself yet capable of assimilation by the individual, crossed the Atlantic and took on a peculiarly American tinge among Emerson and his followers, who became known as transcendentalists. The mystical aspect of this experience is described by Emerson early in his career. "Standing on bare ground," he says, "my head bathed by the blithe air and uplifted into infinite space, all mean egotism vanishes. I become a transparent eyeball; I am nothing, I see all; the currents of the Universal Being circulate through me; I am part or parcel of God."

If such remarks now seem a trifle grandiose it is because this first careless rapture, what we might call the utter intoxication with wild nature which descended upon the first romantics, has largely departed. These first innovators were dreamers, sleepwalkers upon mountain heights, who groped their way out of formal gardens to be hurried along through obscure lanes and falling leaves. One's destination mattered less than the sudden freedom from restraint.

In New England with its Puritan heritage it is not surprising that, instead of being engaged with the tale of the Ancient Mariner or the defiant acts of Byronic heroes, verse should remain spare and clipped, but that the granite hillsides should take on an unearthly light in the prose that flowered by Walden Pond. Emerson was the basic sustainer, teacher, and father of the American movement. He had traveled abroad, talked with Coleridge, visited Stonehenge with Carlyle. There he had remarked in a flash of insight that the huge broken slabs reminded him of some ancient egg out of which all the ecclesiastical structures and history of the British isles had proceeded. Unconsciously the great essayist's gift for words had forecast something of his own role in American thought. His utterance was destined to inspire the democratic embrace of Whitman, as well as the austerities of Thoreau.

Of all the Concord circle Emerson was perhaps the most widely read in science. He was familiar with Sir Charles Lyell's work in geology and was well aware that Christian chronology had become a mere "kitchen clock" compared with the vast time depths the earth sciences were beginning to reveal. "What terrible questions we are learning to ask," brooded the man sometimes accused of walking with his head in the clouds. He saw us as already divesting ourselves of the theism of our fathers.

No, it cannot be asserted that this romantic of the winds and stars did not comprehend true nature. Louis Agassiz, the exponent of the Ice Age, was his friend. Emerson could speak without reluctance of early man's chewed marrow bones, of pain and disillusion, of the exploration of dreams and their midnight revelations. Yet he remained deceptively aloof, and it is perhaps this quality which has led to much castigation and to assumptions that his puritanism could never tolerate a full evolutionary philosophy.

"I found," he once humorously remarked, "when I had finished my new lecture that it was a very good house, only the architect had unfortunately omitted the stairs." And so indeed Emerson had. For all that, however, the stairs, or the somewhat wispy and transparent ghost of them, exist. It is what he called the infinitude of the private man. But if the private man is to understand his infinitude he must be led to explore it, to clamber up any available ladder. This was Emerson's primary occupation and to it he brought not alone a truly prophetic glimpse of nature before Darwin, but also a remarkably clear perception of the fauna contained in man's own psyche.

To explain the intellectual relationship between such opposites as Darwin and Emerson is not easy. At first glance, though contemporaries in time, they appear poles apart in thought, even though both have derived much from the scientific discoveries of their elders. Darwin would never have compared himself to a transparent eyeball, neither would Emerson have ever used Darwin's words "on the clumsy . . . blundering and horribly cruel works of Nature." Darwin was also willing to confess that nature was capable of telling "a direct lie," but in spite of his occasional protestations, weariness, and doubt I cannot quite visualize him confiding, as did Emerson, that his journals were full of disjointed dreams and all manner of rambling reveries and "audacities." "I delight in telling what I think," Emerson affirms in a letter, "but if you ask how I dare say so, or why it is so, I am the most helpless of mortal men." Here Emerson is the honest romantic admitting that the voice of the speaker he was never destined to see pre-empted his thoughts. Yet he knew his own gifts well, and the powers he had "by the help of some fine words" to make "every old wagon and woodpile oscillate a little and threaten to dance."

Darwin was capable of perceiving, from the presence of vestigial organs in living creatures, the fact that they were engaged on an invisible journey. Animals slipped through the interstices between one medium and another, dragging with them evolutionary traces of the past in the shape of functionless claws or rudimentary teeth. Nevertheless, no professional biologist should be unaware of Emerson's pronouncement that "there is a crack in everything God has made." Emerson is perfectly aware that the oak glades about Concord present, at best, peripheral vistas into a nature whose "interiors are terrific, full of hydras and crocodiles." In his journals there is a hidden melancholy not always to be found in his published essays.

The Romantic Movement has been studied in many aspects—its effects on the social order, its effects upon philosophy, literature, music, and the graphic arts. I know of no adequate treatment of its impact upon the science of the nineteenth century and I shall not attempt one here. It should be recognized, however, that nature in the eyes of the early romantics was revelatory. History, the ruins of the past, partook of that revelation. So did the geological catastrophism of the early century. Men began to look behind self-evident nature, the fixed nature of the existing world, toward some *mysterium* not evident to the directly observant eye. The fixed scale of nature that satisfied the scholars of the seventeenth and eighteenth centuries showed signs of disintegration. Progress and innovation came to be regarded as ushering in a better world. The existent began to be replaced by process. As Emerson put it, "We wake and find ourselves on a stair; there are stairs below us which we seem to have ascended, there are stairs above us . . . which go out of sight."

Though Darwin, in public moments, claimed his thinking to be inductive and purely Baconian, he was already as a youth being swept along in the romantic current which included enthusiasm for Odyssean voyages, evidences of past time, and the looming shadow, not just of tomorrow, but of a different tomorrow in some manner derived from today. When in 1831 he set sail in the *Beagle* all these matters were swirling in the heads of his contemporaries, however much the first discoverers would politely deny themselves in order to avert the wrath of the orthodox. In 1818, when Darwin was a boy of nine, Keats wrote about the struggle for existence, of which men were to hear so much after the publication of the *Origin of Species:*

> I was at home
> And should have been most happy—but I saw
> Too far into the sea, where every maw
> The greater on the less feeds evermore.
> But I saw too distinct into the core
> Of an eternal fierce destruction,
> And so from happiness I was far gone.

Keats, the prescient romantic, saw what Darwin was later to see and what Emerson also glimpsed and recorded as "the virulence that still remains uncured in the universe."

As Darwin centered upon that "fierce destruction" whose creative role he sought to unravel, he appealed less to the tame logicians of his era and more and more to "speculative men," men with imagination, men who loved extremes of argument—in short, romantic men. In a burst of enthusiasm Darwin himself once cried, shedding his Baconian mask for a moment, "I am but a gambler and love a wild experiment." In those words Darwin had revealed the soul of a romantic, a man willing to follow a dancing boglight through the obscurity of forgotten ages.

Nevertheless, when he came to write the conclusion of the *Origin of Species,* a certain orthodox benignity is allowed once more to conceal the ferocity of the world whose cruelty and waste he had once exclaimed over. "As natural selection works solely by and for the good of each being," the author philosophizes, "all corporeal and mental endowments will tend to progress toward perfection." "Thus," concludes Darwin, "from the war of nature, from famine and death, the most exalted object which we are capable of conceiving, namely, the production of the higher animals, directly follows. There is grandeur in this view of life, with its several powers, having been originally breathed by the Creator into a few forms or into one; and that, whilst this planet has gone cycling on according to the fixed law of gravity, from so simple a beginning endless forms most beautiful and most wonderful have been and are being evolved." Of this type of conclusion the mystical Emerson had remarked soberly on an earlier but similar occasion, "What is so ungodly as these polite bows to God in English books?"

The man whom reality eluded, or so it was said, produced in 1841 a statement that anticipates the full flowering of process philosophy in the twentieth century but would equally and more eloquently have graced Darwin's final paragraphs in the *Origin of Species.* "The method of nature," Emerson muses, "who could ever analyze it? That rushing stream will not stop to be observed. We can never surprise nature in a corner, never find the end of a thread, never tell where to set the first stone. The bird hastens to lay her egg. The egg hastens to be a bird. [Nature's] smoothness is the smoothness of the pitch of a cataract. Its permanence is a perpetual inchoation."

Unlike Darwin's somewhat sly intimations of perfection and progress it was the idealist, not the concealed materialist, who wrote: "That no single end may be selected and nature judged thereby, appears from this, that if man himself be considered as the end, and it be assumed that the final cause of the world is to make holy or wise or beautiful men, we see that it has not succeeded."

As a result of his contemplations, even though he did not possess the Darwinian key of natural selection, Emerson is aware of nature's infinite prodigality and wastefulness of suns and systems. He recognizes that nature can only be conceived as existing to a universal end, and not to a particular one, such as man. "To a universe of ends," Emerson adds as an afterthought, "a work of ecstasy." Nature, he maintained, is unspecific. "[It] knows neither palm nor oak, but only vegetable life, which sprouts into forests and festoons the globe." Nowhere is anything final. Nature has no private will; it will answer no private question. "The world," Emerson meditates, looking on with that far-reaching sun-struck eyeball which earned him critical derision, "leaves no track in space, and the greatest action of man no mark in the vast idea."

And yet Emerson cared—more, perhaps, than has been allowed. Crouched midway on that desperate stair whose steps pass from dark to dark, he spoke as Darwin chose not to speak in his final peroration. Emerson saw, with a terrible clairvoyance, the downward pull of the past. "The transmigration of souls is no fable," he wrote. "I would it were; but men and women are only half human. Every animal in the barnyard, the field and the forest, of the earth and of the waters . . . has contrived to get a footing and to leave the print of its features and form in someone or other of these upright heaven-facing speakers." He could sense, not Darwin's automatic trend toward perfection, but the weary slipping, the sensed entropy, the ebbing away of the human spirit into fox and weasel as it struggled upward while all its past tugged upon it from below. This is the Gethsemane of the man whom Walt Whitman called, and rightly, "transcendental of limits, a pure American for daring."

## III

When I was young, in a time of boyhood marked by a world as fresh and green and utterly marvelous as on the day of its creation, I found myself attracted by a huge tropical shell which lay upon my aunt's dressing table. The twentieth century was scarcely a decade old, and people did not travel or collect as they do now. My uncle and aunt lived far inland in the central states and what wandering relative had given them the beautiful iridescent shell I do not know. It was held up to my youthful ear and I was told to listen carefully and I would hear the sea. Out of the great shell, even in that silent bedroom, I, who had never seen the ocean, heard the whispered sibilance, the sigh of waves upon the beach, the little murmurs of moving water, the confused mewing of gulls in the sun-bright air. It was my first miracle, indeed perhaps my first awareness of the otherness of nature, of myself outside, in a sense, and listening, as though beyond light-years, to a remote event. Perhaps, in that Victorian bedroom with its knickknacks and curios, I had suddenly fallen out of the nature I inhabited and turned, for the first time, to survey her with surprise.

The sounds stayed with me through the years or I would not be able to recall them now. Neither does it matter that in my college days I learned that it was not the sea to which I had listened, but the vastly magnified whispers of my blood and the house around me. Either was marvel enough—that a shell, a shell shaped in the seas' depths, should, without intent, so concentrate the essence of the world as to bring its absent images before me.

The taxonomists, the classifiers, have tried with Latin appellations to define man to their satisfaction. They have called him wise and raised up justifiable doubt, as did Freud. They have called him the tool user, the fabricator. They have, by turns, characterized him as the only being who laughs or who weeps. They have spoken of him as a time binder who transmits thought through the generations and thus reorients and changes the world. There are also those who have categorized him as the sole religious animal or, finally, as *Homo duplex*, the creature composed of flesh and spirit.

The appeal of this last definition gives me pause, even though I am a professional anthropologist who must employ the diction of his trade. For is it not true, as Emerson indicated before the rise of scientific anthropology, that man, in becoming aware of nature, has entered upon a confused and endless exploration, a transcendental search for order? Both the theologian and the scientist, each in his way, pursue that quest.

In one of the most profound and succinct analogies ever penned by a philosopher, George Santayana once ventured: "The universe is the true Adam, the creation the true fall." He saw, immured in his study, that in the instant when the universe was brought out of the void of non-being its particles, achieving such powers as are present in man, would yearn for understanding of their destiny. Alienated and alone, listening to the murmur in the shell, the individual would search his mind in vain. Primitively he would seek to placate the unseen spirits in running water, or the ghost that rules in the fir tree. Divorced from the whole, he would always be intimidated by those mocking questions from the whirlwind, "Where wast thou, where wast thou? Declare if thou knowest it all."

No clearer evidence is needed to refute Freud's argument that the great traumas from which man has suffered are the products of modern science. The fall out of nature into knowledge was sustained long ago in the caverns of mankind's birth. Between the telescope and the microscope the Adamic universe has widened, that is all. If we still suffer from renewed shocks of a scientific nature, we have, at the same time, been released from the bonds of barbarous superstition. If the particle cannot rejoin the mass, it has at least achieved, in twentieth-century quantum mechanics, a creative liberty not granted under the Newtonian Mechanic God.

When I first read Emerson's *Method of Nature* I was amazed at how much of a forerunner of process philosophy he was, and how, some twenty years before the *Origin of Species,* as I have noted, he had expressed so skillfully nature's lack of any single observable objective. Not for man, not for mouse. Total nature, as he put it, was coincident with no private will, yet it was "growing like a field of maize in July."

At the time I encountered those passages I was a young man steeped in the scientific tradition, and I was struck with Emerson's articulate insight. Why then, one might ponder, if Emerson glimpsed only a universe of ends, and if every natural object is only an emanation from another, and if—I can put it in no other way—each emanation explodes into another future, did Emerson, after beclouding human hope, direct so much of his attention toward the species he had so eloquently dismissed? For, along with fox and woodchuck, we would appear as but momentary and superficial tenants of the globe.

It was not until many years later, when I had abandoned certain of the logical disciplines of my youth, that I began to sense why Emerson, with seeming inconsistency, had rounded home in that same essay to extol the nature of man. I think it was upon encountering a phrase in Whitman, and knowing there was an intellectual affinity between the two men, that I paused. The lines read:

There was a child went forth every day
And the first object he looked upon, that object he became . . .

It is not alone that the species is an emanation, I considered; our very thoughts transform us from minute to minute, hour to hour. How powerfully this quotation reflects Emerson's earlier statement: "The termination of the world in a man appears to be the last victory of intelligence. The universal does not attract us until housed in an individual. Who heeds the waste abyss of possibility?

Who indeed, until the possibility is embodied, "not to be diffused," in Whitman's words, but to be realized. I had listened long ago to the impingement of secret and rumorous whispers from the air upon the coiled interior of a shell. Man it was who held and interpreted the shell, first in the romantic sea vision of youth, last as a symbol of all that the human ear might encompass from the resounding shores of the universe, as well as his own interior.

"We must admire in man," continued Emerson, who, in *The Method of Nature*, was careful not to admire him overmuch, "the form of the formless, the concentration of the vast, the house of reason, the cave of memory." The cave of memory! It is this, this echoing upheld shell, that enabled Emerson to interpose insignificant transitory man as the counterweight to stars and wasteful galaxies, to say, in fact, that man can carry the chemistry and the distance of a star inside his head. "What is a man," he jotted in his journals, "but nature's finer success in self-explication?" The explication is not eternal, any more than today is for always. The world, Emerson made clear, is in process, is departing, as men and ideas are similarly departing. The self-explication of today is approximate and will demand rearrangement as long as a critical and enlightened eye remains to examine nature. Nor does Emerson have illusions about the number of minds that can genuinely perceive nature. Furthermore, he is aware that what he terms nature's "suburbs and extremities" may contain truths that turn the world from a lumber room to an ordered creation. This observation was written in the same year that Darwin, home from probing such natural extremities as the Galápagos, conceived of the principle of natural selection.

Emerson had had, like Darwin, an illness and a voyage—that strange road taken by so many of the nineteenth-century romantics —romantics who were finally to displace the sedate white doorstone into nature by something wild and moon-haunted, whether in science or art. He may have had, as he himself once ventured, "an excess of faith"—faith in man that may cause us to stir uneasily now, but which he expressed at a time when London was truly a city of dreadful night. Above all, he seemed to sense intuitively what Alfred Russel Wallace had believed—that man possesses latent mental powers beyond what he might culturally express in a given epoch. In Ice Age caverns he had painted with an artist's eye; modern primitives can master music, writing, and machines they have never previously experienced. In the words of the eminent French biologist Jean Rostand, "Already at the origin of the species man was equal to what he was destined to become." A careful reading of the American transcendentalist would demonstrate that he had an intuitive grasp of this principle—so firm that neither the size of the universe nor the imperfections of our common humanity distressed him overmuch. He knew, with a surety our age is in danger of losing, that if there was ever a good man there will be more. Nature strives at better than her actual creatures. We are, Emerson maintains, "a conditional population." If atavistic reptiles still swim in the depths of man's psyche, they are not the only inhabitants of that hidden region.

Tomorrow lurks in us, the latency to be all that was not achieved before. This is what led proto-man, five million years ago, to start upon a journey, at a time when night and day were strange and miraculous, as was the trumpeting of mammoths or the march of reindeer. It was for this that man adorned his caverns in the morning

of time. It was for this that he worshiped the bear. For man had
fallen out of the secure world of instinct into a place of wonder. That
wonder is still expanding, changing as man's mind keeps pace with
it. He stands and listens with a shell pressed to his ear. He is still
a child before the infinite spaces but he is in no way frightened. It
was thus that his journey began—perhaps with a message drawn
from an echoing shell. Now he listens with his own giant fabricated
ear to messages from beyond infinity. In the old house of nature
there are monsters in every cupboard. That is why, as nature's
children, we are inveterate romantics and go visiting. This is why the
great American essayist anticipated the whole of the unborn science
of anthropology when he said, "The entrance of [nature] into his
mind seems to be the birth of man." If it brought him fear it opened
to his aroused curiosity every nook and cranny of the world. It left
him, in fact, the inheritor of an echoing and ghost-ridden mansion.
The shifting unseen potential that we call nature has left to man but
one observable dictum, to grow. Only our unforeseeable tomorrow
can determine whether we will grow in the wisdom Emerson an-
ticipated.

# Thoreau's Vision
# of the Natural World

## I

Somewhere in the coverts about Concord, a lynx was killed well over a century ago and examined by Henry David Thoreau; measured, in fact, and meditated upon from nose to tail. Others called it a Canadian lynx, far strayed from the northern wilds. No, insisted Thoreau positively, it is indigenous, indigenous but rare. It is a night haunter; it is a Concord lynx. On this he was adamant. Not long ago, over in Vermont, an intelligent college girl told me that, walking in the woods, her Labrador retriever had startled and been attacked by a Canadian lynx which she had been fully competent to recognize. I was too shy, however, to raise the question of whether the creature might have been, as Thoreau defiantly asserted, a genuine New England lynx, persisting but rare since colonial times.

Thoreau himself was a genuine Concord lynx. Of that there can be no doubt. We know the place of his birth, his rarity, something of his habits, his night travels, that he had, on occasion, a snarl transferred to paper, and that he frequented swamps, abandoned cellar holes, and woodlots. His temperament has been a subject of much uncertainty, as much, in truth, as the actual shape of those human figures which he was wont to examine looming in fogs or midsummer hazes. Thoreau sometimes had difficulty in seeing men or, by contrast, sometimes saw them too well. Others had difficulty in adjusting their vision to the Concord lynx himself, with the result that a varied and contentious literature has come down to us. Even the manner of his death is uncertain, for though the cause is known, some have maintained that he benefited a weak constitution by a rugged outdoor life. Others contend that he almost deliberately stoked the fires of consumption by prolonged exposure in inclement weather.

As is the case with most wild animals at the periphery of the human vision, Thoreau's precise temperament is equally a matter of conjecture even though he left several books and a seemingly ingenuous journal which one eminent critic, at least, regards as a cunningly contrived mythology. He has been termed a stoic, a contentious moralizer, a parasite, an arsonist, a misanthrope, a supreme egotist, a father-hater who projected his animus on the state, a banal writer who somehow managed to produce a classic work of literature. He has also been described as a philosophical anarchist and small-town failure, as well as an intellectual aristocrat. Some would classify him simply as a nature writer, others as a failed scientist who did not comprehend scientific method. Others speak of his worldwide influence upon the social movements of the twentieth century, of his exquisite insight and style, of his relentless searching for something never found—a mystic in the best sense of the term. He has also been labeled a prig by a notable man of English letters. There remains from those young people who knew him the utterly distinct view that he was a friendly, congenial, and kindly man. At the time of his funeral, and long before fame attended his memory, the schools of Concord were dismissed in his honor.

In short, the Concord lynx did not go unwept to his grave. Much of the later controversy that has created a Browningesque *Ring and the Book* atmosphere about his intentions and character is the product of a sophisticated literary world he abhorred in life. Something malevolent frequently creeps into this atmosphere even though it is an inevitable accompaniment of the transmission of great books through the ages. Basically the sensitive writer should stay away from his own kind. Jealousies, tensions, feuds, unnecessary discourtesies that are hard to bear in print are frequently augmented by close contact, even if friendships begin well. The writer's life is a lonely one and doubtless should remain so, but a prurient curiosity allows no great artist to rest easy in his grave. Critical essays upon Thoreau now number hundreds of items, very little of which, I suspect, would move the Concord lynx to do more than retire farther into whatever thickets might remain to him. Neither science nor literature was his total concern. He was a fox at the wood's edge, regarding human preoccupations with doubt. Indeed he had rejected an early invitation to join the American Association for the Advancement of Science. The man had never entertained illusions about the course of technological progress and the only message that he, like an Indian, had gotten from the telegraph was the song of the wind through its wires.

As a naturalist he possessed the kind of memory which fixes certain scenes in the mind forever—a feeling for the vastness and mystery contained in nature, a powerful aesthetic response when, in his own words, "a thousand bare twigs gleam like cobwebs in the sun." He had been imprinted, as it were, by his home landscape at an early age. Similarly, whatever I may venture upon the meaning of Thoreau must come basically from memory alone, with perhaps some examination of the tone of his first journal as contrasted with his last. My present thoughts convey only the residue of what, in the course of time, I have come to feel about his intellectual achievement—the solitary memory that Thoreau himself might claim of a journey across austere uplands.

In addition, my observations come mostly from the realm of science, whereas the preponderance of what had been written about Thoreau has come from the region he appeared to inhabit: namely, literature. His scientific interests have frequently been denigrated, and he himself is known more than once to have deplored the "inhumanity of science." Surely then, one cannot, as a representative of this alien discipline, be accused of either undue tolerance or weak sympathy for a transcendental idealism that has largely fallen out of fashion. Yet it is an aspect of this philosophy, more particularly as it is found modified in Thoreau, that I wish to consider. For Thoreau, like Emerson, is an anticipator, a forerunner of the process philosophers who have so largely dominated the twentieth century. He stands at the border between existent and potential nature.

# THOREAU'S VISION OF THE NATURAL WORLD

## II

Behind all religions lurks the concept of nature. It persists equally in the burial cults of Neanderthal man, in Cro-Magnon hunting art, in the questions of Job and in the answering voice from the whirlwind. In the end it is the name of man's attempt to define and delimit his world, whether seen or unseen. He knows intuitively that nature is a reality which existed before him and will survive his individual death. He may include in his definition that which is, or that which may be. Nature remains an otherness which incorporates man, but which man instinctively feels contains secrets denied to him.

A professional atheist must still account for the fleeting particles that appear and vanish in the perfected cyclotrons of modern physics. We may see behind nature a divinity which rules it, or we may regard nature itself as a somewhat nebulous and ill-defined deity. Man knows that he springs from nature and not nature from him. This is very old and primitive knowledge. Man, as the "thinking reed," the memory beast, and the anticipator of things to come, has devised hundreds of cosmogonies and interpretations of nature. More lately, with the dawn of the scientific method, he has sought to probe nature's secrets by experiment rather than unbounded speculation.

Still, of all words coming easily to the tongue, none is more mysterious, none more elusive. Behind nature is hidden the chaos as well as the regularities of the world. And behind all that is evident to our senses is veiled the insubstantial deity that only man, of all earth's creatures, has had the power either to perceive or to project into nature.

As scientific agnostics we may draw an imaginary line beyond which we deny ourselves the right to pass. We may adhere to the tangible, but we will still be forced to speak of the "unknowable" or of "final causes" even if we proclaim such phrases barren and of no concern to science. In our minds we will acknowledge a line we have drawn, a definition to which we have arbitrarily restricted ourselves, a human limit that may or may not coincide with reality. It will still be nature that concerns us as it concerned the Neanderthal. We cannot exorcise the word, refine it semantically though we may. Nature is the receptacle which contains man and into which he finally sinks to rest. It implies all, absolutely all, that man knows or can know. The word ramifies and runs through the centuries, assuming different connotations.

Sometimes it appears as ghostly as the unnamed shadow behind it; sometimes it appears harsh, prescriptive, and solid. Again matter becomes interchangeable with energy; fact becomes shadow, law becomes probability. Nature is a word that must have arisen with man. It is part of his otherness, his humanity. Other beasts live within nature. Only man has ceaselessly turned the abstraction around and around upon his tongue and found fault with every definition, found himself looking ceaselessly outside of nature toward something invisible to any eye but his own and indeed not surely to be glimpsed by him.

To propound that Henry David Thoreau is a process philosopher, it is necessary first to understand something of the concepts entertained by early nineteenth-century science and philosophy, and also to consider something of the way in which these intellectual currents were changing. New England's ties to English thought preponderated, although, as is well known, some of the ideas had their roots on the continent. An exhaustive analysis is unnecessary to the present purpose. Thoreau was a child of his time but he also reached beyond it.

In early-nineteenth-century British science there was a marked obsession with Baconian induction. The more conservative-minded, who dreaded the revelations of the new geology, sought, in their emphatic demand for facts, to drive wide-ranging and useful hypotheses out of currency. The thought of Bacon, actually one of the innovators of scientific method, was being perverted into a convenient barrier against the advance of irreligious science. Robert Chambers, an early evolutionist, had felt the weight of this criticism, and Darwin, later on, experienced it beyond the midcentury. In inexperienced hands it led to much aimless fact-gathering under the guise of proper inductive procedures for true scientists. Some, though not all, of Thoreau's compendiums and detailed observations suggest this view of science, just as do his occasional scornful remarks about museum taxonomy.

In a typical Thoreauvian paradox he could neither leave his bundles of accumulated fact alone, nor resist muttering "it is ebb tide with the scientific reports." Only toward the close of his journals does he seem to be inclining toward a more perceptive scientific use of his materials under the influence of later reading. It is necessary to remember that most of Thoreau's intellectual contacts were with literary men, though Emerson was a wide and eclectic reader who saw clearly that the new uniformitarian geology had transformed our conceptions of the world's antiquity.

The one striking exception to Thoreau's lack of direct contact with the scientific world was his meeting with Louis Agassiz after the European glaciologist, taxonomist, and teacher had joined the staff at Harvard in the 1840s. Brilliant and distinguished naturalist though he was, Louis Agassiz was probably not the best influence upon Thoreau. He traced the structural relations of living things, he introduced America to comparative taxonomy, he taught Thoreau to observe such oddities as frozen and revived caterpillars. His eye, if briefly, was added to Thoreau's eye, not always to the latter's detriment. Typically, Agassiz warned against hasty generalizations while pursuing relentlessly his own interpretation of nature.

The European poet of the Ice Age was, in a very crucial sense, at the same time an anachronism. He did not believe in evolution; he did not grasp the significance of natural selection. "Geology," he wrote in 1857, "only shows that at different periods there have existed different species; but no transition from those of a preceding into those of a following epoch has ever been noticed anywhere." He saw a beneficent intelligence behind nature; he was a Platonist at heart, dealing with the classification of the eternal forms, seeing in the vestigial organs noted by the evolutionist only the direct evidence of divine plan carried through for symmetry's sake even when the organ was functionless.

It is this preternatural intelligence which Thoreau is led to see in the protective arrangement of moth cocoons in winter. "What kind of understanding," he writes, "was there between the mind . . . and that of the worm that fastened a few of these leaves to its cocoon in order to disguise it?" Plainly he is following in the footsteps of the great biologist, who, like many other scholars, recognized a spiritual succession of forms in the strata, but not the genuine organic transformations that had produced the living world. It may be noted in passing that this Platonic compromise with reality was one easily acceptable to most transcendentalists. They were part of a far-removed romantic movement which was to find the mechanistic aspects of nineteenth-century science increasingly intolerable. One need not align oneself totally with every aspect of the Darwinian universe, however, to see that Agassiz's particular teleological interpretation of nature could not be long sustained. Whatever might lie behind the incredible profusion of living forms would not so easily yield its secrets to man.

The mystery in nature Thoreau began to sense early. A granitic realism forced from him the recognition that the natural world is indifferent to human morality, just as the young Darwin had similarly brooded over the biological imperfections and savagery of the organic realm. "How can [man]" protested Thoreau, "perform that long journey who has not conceived whither he is bound, . . . who has no passport to the end?" This is a far cry from the expressions of some of the contemporary transcendentalists who frequently confused nature with a hypostatized divine reason which man could activate within himself. By contrast, Thoreau remarks wearily, "Is not disease the rule of existence?" He had seen the riddled leaf and the worm-infested bud.

If one meditates upon the picture of nature presented by both the transcendental thinkers such as Emerson and the evolutionary doctrine drawn from Darwin, one is struck by the contrast between what appears to be a real and an ideal nature. The transcendentalist lived in two worlds at once, in one of which he was free to transform himself; he could escape the ugly determinism of the real. In Emerson's words, "two states of thought diverge every moment in wild contrast."

The same idea is echoed in the first volume of his journals when the young Thoreau ventures, "On one side of man is the actual and on the other the ideal." These peculiar worlds are simultaneously existent. Life is bifurcated between the observational world and another more ideal but realizable set of "instructions" implanted in our minds, again a kind of Platonic blueprint. We must be taught through the proper understanding of the powers within us. The transcendentalist possessed the strong optimism of the early Republic, the belief in an earthly Eden to be created.

If we examine the Darwinian world of change we recognize that the nature of the evolutionary process is such as to deny any relationships except those that can be established on purely phyletic grounds of uninterrupted descent. The Platonic abstract blueprint of successive types has been dismissed as a hopeful fiction. Vestigial organs are really what their name implies—remnants lingering from a former state of existence. The tapeworm, the sleeping-sickness trypanosome, are as much a product of natural selection as man himself. All currently existing animals and plants have ancestral roots extending back into Archeozoic time. Every species is in some degree imperfect and scheduled to vanish by reason of the very processes which brought it into being. Even in this world of endless struggle, however, Darwin is forced to introduce a forlorn note of optimism which appears in the final pages of the *Origin of Species*. It is his own version of the ideal. Out of the war of nature, of strife unending, he declares, all things will progress toward perfection.

The remark rings somewhat hollowly upon the ear. Darwin's posited ideal world, such as it is, offers no immediate hope that man can embrace. Indeed, it is proffered on the same page where Darwin indicates that of the species now living very few will survive into the remote future. Teleological direction has been read out of the universe. It would re-emerge in the twentieth century in more sophisticated guises that would have entranced Thoreau, but for the moment the "Great Companion" was dead. The Darwinian circle had introduced process into nature but had never paused to examine nature itself. In the words of Alfred North Whitehead, "Science is concerned not with the causes but the coherence of nature." Something, in other words, held the thing called nature together, gave it duration in the midst of change and a queer kind of inhuman rationality.

It may be true enough that Thoreau in his last years never resolved his philosophical difficulties. (Indeed, what man has?) It may also be assumed that the confident and brilliant perceptions of the young writer began to give way in his middle years to a more patient search for truth. The scientist in him was taking the place of the artist. To some of the literary persuasion this may seem a great loss. Considering, however, the toils from which he freed himself, the hope that he renewed, his solitary achievement is remarkable.

One may observe that there are two reigning models involving human behavior today: a conservative and a progressive version. The first may be stated as regarding man in the mass as closely reflecting his primate origins. He is the "ape and tiger" of Huxley's writing. His origins are sufficiently bestial that they place limits upon his ethical possibilities. Latent aggression makes him an uncertain and dangerous creature.

Unconsciously, perhaps, the first evolutionists sought to link man more closely to the animal world from which he had arisen. Paradoxically this conception would literally freeze man upon his evolutionary pathway as thoroughly as though a similar argument had been projected upon him when he was a Cretaceous tree shrew. Certainly one may grant our imperfect nature. Man is in process, as is the whole of life. He may survive or he may not, but so long as he survives he will be part of the changing, onrushing future. He, too, will be subject to alteration. In fact, he may now be approaching the point of consciously inducing his own modification.

How did Thoreau, who matured under the influence of the transcendentalists and the design arguments of Louis Agassiz, react to this shifting, oncoming world of contingency and change? It is evident he was familiar with Charles Lyell's writings, that he knew about the development (that is, evolution) theories of Robert Chambers. The final volume of his journals even suggests that he may have meditated upon Darwin's views before his death in 1862.

Now, in the final years, he seems to gather himself for one last effort. "The development theory implies a greater vital force in nature," he writes, "because it is more flexible and accommodating and equivalent to a sort of constant new creation."

He recognizes the enormous waste in nature but tries carefully to understand its significance just as he grasps the struggle for existence. His eyes are open still to his tenderly cherished facts of snow and leaves and seasons. He counts tree rings and tries to understand forest succession. The world is perhaps vaster than he imagined, but, even from the first, nature was seen as lawless on occasion and capable of cherishing unimaginable potentials. That was where he chose to stand, at the very edge of the future, "to anticipate," as he says in *Walden*, "nature herself."

This is not the conservative paradigm of the neo-Darwinian circle. Instead it clearly forecasts the thought of twentieth-century Alfred North Whitehead. Thoreau strove with an unequaled intensity to observe nature in all its forms, whether in the raw shapes of mountains or the travelings of seeds and deer mice. His consciousness expanded like a sunflower. The more objects he beheld, the more immortal he became. "My senses," he wrote, "get no rest." It was as though he had foreseen Whitehead's dictum that "passage is a quality not only of nature, which is the thing known, but also of sense awareness, which is the procedure of knowing." Thoreau had constituted himself the Knower. "All change," he wrote, "is a miracle to contemplate, but it is a miracle that is taking place every instant." He saw man thrust up through the crust of nature "like a wedge and not till the wound heals . . . do we begin to discover where we are." He viewed us all as mere potential; shadowy, formless perhaps, but as though about to be formed. He had listened alone to the "unspeakable rain"; he had sought in his own way to lead others to a supernatural life in nature. He had succeeded. He had provided for others the passport that at first he thought did not exist; a passport, he finally noted, "earned from the elements."

## III

To follow the involved saunterings of the journals is to observe a man sorting, selecting, questioning less nature than his own way into nature, to find, as Thoreau expressed it, "a patent for himself." Thoreau is never wholly a man of the transcendental camp. He is, in a sense, a double agent. He is drawn both to the spiritual life and to that of the savage. "Are we not all wreckers," he asks, "and do we not contract the habits of wreckers?" The term *"wreckers,"* of course, he uses in the old evil sense of the shore scavengers who with false lights beckoned ships to their doom. And again he queries, "Is our life innocent enough?" It would appear he thinks otherwise, for he writes, "I have a murderer's experience . . ." and he adds, a trifle scornfully, "there is no record of a great success in history."

Thoreau once said disconsolately that he awaited a Visitor who never came, one whom he referred to as the "Great Looker." Some have thought that pique or disappointment shows in these words and affects his subsequent work. I do not choose to follow this line of reasoning, since, on another page of *Walden,* he actually recollects receiving his guest as the "old settler and original proprietor who is reported to have dug Walden pond . . . and fringed it with pine woods." As a somewhat heretical priest once observed, "God asks nothing of the highest soul but attention."

Supplementing that remark Thoreau had asserted, "There has been nothing but the sun and the eye since the beginning." That eye, in the instance of Thoreau, had missed nothing. Even in the depths of winter when nature's inscriptions lay all about him in the snow, he had not faltered to recognize among them the cruel marks of a farmer's whip, steadily, even monotonously, lashing his oxen down the drift-covered road. The sight wounded him. Nature, he knew, was not bound to be kind to man. In fact, there was a kind of doubleness in nature as in the writer. The inner eye was removed; its qualities were more than man, as natural man, could long sustain. The Visitor had come in human guise and looked out upon the world a few brief summers. It is remembered that when at last an acquaintance came to ask of Thoreau on his deathbed if he had made his peace with God, the Visitor in him responded simply, "We have never quarreled."

Thoreau had appropriated the snow as "the great revealer." On it were inscribed all the hieroglyphs that the softer seasons concealed. Last winter, trudging in the woods, I came to a spot where freezing, melting, and refreezing had lifted old footprints into little pinnacles of trapped oak leaves as though a shrub oak had walked upon some errand. Thoreau had recorded the phenomenon over a century ago. There was something uncanny about it, I thought, standing attentively in the snow. A visitor, perhaps the Visitor, had once more passed.

In the very first volume of his journals Thoreau had written, "There is always the possibility, the possibility, I say, of being all, or remaining a particle in the universe." He had, in the end, learned that nature was not an enlarged version of the human ego, that it was not, to use Emerson's phrase, "the immense shadow of man." Toward the close of his life he had turned from literature to the growing, formidable world of the new science—the science that in the twentieth century was destined to reduce everything to infinitesimal particles and finally these to a universal vortex of wild energies.

But the eye persisted, the unexplainable eye that gave even Darwin a cold shudder. All it experienced were the secondary qualities, the illusions that physics had rejected, but the eye remained, just as Thoreau had asserted—the sun and the eye from the beginning. Thoreau was gone, but the eye was multitudinous, ineradicable.

I advanced upon the fallen oak leaves. We were all the eye of the Visitor—the eye whose reason no physics could explain. Generation after generation the eye was among us. We were particles but we were also the recording eye that saw the sunlight—that which physics had reduced to cold waves in a cold void. Thoreau's life had been dedicated to the unexplainable eye.

I had been trained since youth against the illusions, the deceptions of that eye, against sunset as reality, against my own features as anything but a momentary midge swarm of particles. Even this momentary phantasm I saw by the mind's eye alone. I no longer resisted as I walked. I went slowly, making sure that the eye momentarily residing in me saw and recorded what was intended when Thoreau spoke of the quality of the eye as belonging more to God than man.

But there was a message Thoreau intended to transmit. "I suspect," he had informed his readers, "that if you should go to the end of the world, you would find somebody there going further." It is plain that he wanted a message carried that distance, but what was it? We are never entirely certain. He delighted in gnomic utterances such as that in which he pursued the summer on snowshoes.

"I do not think much of the actual," he had added. Is this then the only message of the great Walden traveler in the winter days when the years "came fast as snowflakes"? Perhaps it is so intended, but the words remain cryptic. Thoreau, as is evidenced by his final journals, had labored to lay the foundations of a then unnamed science—ecology. In many ways he had outlived his century. He was always concerned with the actual, but it was the unrolling reality of the process philosopher, "the universe," as he says, "that will not wait to be explained."

For this reason he tended to see men at a distance. For the same reason he saw himself as a first settler in nature, his house the oldest in the settlement. Thoreau reflected in his mind the dreamers of the westward crossing; in this he is totally American.

Yet Thoreau preferred to the end his own white winter spaces. He lingers, curvetting gracefully, like the fox he saw on the river or the falcon in the morning air. He identifies, he enters them, he widens the circumference of life to its utmost bounds. "One world at a time," he jokes playfully on his deathbed, but it is not, in actuality, the world that any of us know or could reasonably endure. It is simply Thoreau's world, "a prairie for outlaws." Each one of us must seek his own way there. This is his final message, for each man is forever the eye and the eye is the Visitor. Whatever remedy exists for life is never to be found at Walden. It exists, if at all, where the real Walden exists, somewhere in the incredible dimensions of the universal Eye.

# Walden: Thoreau's Unfinished Business

The life of Henry David Thoreau has been thoroughly explored for almost a century by critics and biographers, yet the mystery of this untraveled man who read travel literature has nowhere been better expressed than by his own old walking companion Ellery Channing, who once wrote: "I have never been able to understand what he meant by his life. Why was he so disappointed with everybody else? Why was he so interested in the river and the woods . . . ? Something peculiar here I judge."

If Channing, his personal friend, was mystified, it is only to be expected that as Thoreau's literary stature has grown, the ever-present enigma of his life and thought has grown with it. Wright Morris, the distinguished novelist and critic, has asked, almost savagely, the same question in another form. Putting Channing's question in a less personal but more formidable and timeless literary context he ventures, quoting from Thoreau who spent two years upon the Walden experiment and then abandoned it, "If we are alive let us go about our business." "But," counters Morris brutally, "what business?" Thoreau fails to inform us. In the words of Morris, Walden was the opening chapter of a life, one that enthralls us, but with the remaining chapters missing.

For more than a decade after *Walden* was composed, Thoreau continued his intensive exploration of Concord, its inhabitants and its fields, but upon the "business" for which he left Walden he is oddly cryptic. Once, it is true, he muses in his journal that "the utmost possible novelty would be the difference between me and myself a year ago." He must then have been about some business, even though the perceptive critic Morris felt he had already performed it and was at loose ends and groping. The truth is that the critic, in a timeless sense, can be right and in another way wrong, for looking is in itself the business of art.

In a studied paragraph Carl Jung, with no reference to Thoreau, perhaps pierced closest to Thoreau's purpose without ever revealing it. He says in his alchemical studies, "Medieval alchemy prepared the greatest attack on the divine order of the universe which mankind has ever dared. Alchemy is the dawn of the age of natural sciences which, through the *daemonium* of the scientific spirit, drove nature and her forces into the service of mankind to a hitherto unheard of degree. . . . Technics and science have indeed conquered the world, but whether the soul has gained thereby is another matter."

Thoreau was indeed a spiritual wanderer through the deserts of the modern world. Almost by instinct he rejected that beginning wave of industrialism which was later to so entrance his century. He also rejected the peace he had found on the shores of Walden Pond, the alternate glazing and reflection of that great natural eye which impartially received the seasons. It was, in the end, too great for his endurance, too timeless. He was a restless pacer of fields, a reader who, in spite of occasional invective directed against those who presumed to neglect their homes for far places, nevertheless was apt with allusions drawn from travel literature, and quick to discern in man uncharted spaces.

"Few adults," once remarked Emerson, Thoreau's one-time mentor and friend, "can see nature." Thoreau was one of those who could. Moreover he saw nature as another civilization, a thing of vaster laws and vagaries than that encompassed by the human mind. When he visited the Maine woods he felt its wind upon him like the closing of a dank door from some forgotten cellar of the past.

Was it some curious midnight impulse to investigate such matters that led Thoreau to abandon the sunny hut at Walden for "other business"? Even at Walden he had heard, at midnight, the insistent fox, the "rudimental man," barking beyond his lighted window in the forest. The universe was in motion, nothing was fixed. Nature was "a prairie for outlaws," violent, unpredictable. Alone in the environs of Walden Thoreau wandered in the midst of that greater civilization he had discovered as surely as some monstrous edifice come suddenly upon in the Mayan jungles. He never exclaimed about the Indian trails seen just at dusk in a winter snowfall—neither where they went, nor upon what prairie they vanished or in what direction. He never ventured to tell us, but he was one of those great artist-scientists who could pursue the future through its past. This is why he lives today in the heart of young and old alike, "a man of surfaces," one critic has said, but such surfaces—the arrowhead, the acorn, the oak leaf, the indestructible thought-print headed toward eternity—plowed and replowed in the same field. Truly another civilization beyond man, nature herself, a vast lawless mindprint shattering traditional conceptions.

Thoreau, in his final journals, had said that the ancients with their gorgons and sphinxes could imagine more than existed. Modern men, by contrast, could not imagine so much as exists. For more than one hundred years that statement has stood to taunt us. Every succeeding year has proved Thoreau right. The one great hieroglyph, nature, is as unreadable as it ever was and so is her equally wild and unpredictable offspring, man. Like Thoreau, the examiner of lost and fragile surfaces of flint, we are only by indirection students of man. We are, in actuality, students of that greater order known as nature. It is into nature that man vanishes. "Wildness is a civilization other than our own," Thoreau had ventured. Out of it man's trail had wandered. He had come with the great ice, drifting before its violence, scavenging the flints it had dropped. Whatever he was now, the ice had made him, the breath from the dank door, great cold, and implacable winters.

Thoreau in the final pages of *Walden* creates a myth about a despised worm who surmounts death and bursts from his hidden chamber in a wooden table. Was the writer dreaming of man, man freed at last from the manacles of the ice? No word of his intention remains, save of his diligent experiments with frozen caterpillars in his study—a man preoccupied with the persistent flame of life trapped in the murderous cold. Is not the real business of the artist to seek for man's salvation, and by understanding his ingredients to make him less of an outlaw to himself, civilize him, in fact, back into that titanic otherness, that star's substance from which he had arisen? Perhaps encamped sufficiently in the great living web we might emerge again, not into the blind snow-covered eye of Walden's winter, but into the eternal spring man dreams of everywhere and nowhere finds.

Man, himself, is Walden's eye of ice and eye of summer. What now makes man an outlaw, with the fox urgent at his heels, is the fact that one of his eyes is gray and wintry and blind, while with the other is glimpsed another world just tantalizingly visible and dismissed as an illusion. What we know with certainty is that a creature with such disparate vision cannot long survive. It was that knowledge which led Thoreau to strain his eyesight till it ached and to record all he saw. A flower might open a man's mind, a box tortoise endow him with mercy, a mist enable him to see his own shifting and uncertain configuration. But the alchemist's touchstone in Thoreau was to give him sight, not power. Only man's own mind, the artist's mind, can change the winter in man.

## II

There are persons who, because of youthful associations, prefer harsh-etched things before their eyes at morning. The foot of an iron bedstead perhaps, or a weathered beam on the ceiling, an abandoned mine tipple, or even a tombstone. On July 14 of the year 1973, I awoke at dawn and saw above my head the chisel marks on an eighteenth-century beam in the Concord Inn. As I strolled up the street toward the cemetery I saw a few drifters, black and white, stirring from their illegal night's sleep among the gravestones. Later I came to the Thoreau family plot and saw the little yellow stone marked "Henry" that no one is any longer sure indicates the precise place where he lies. Perhaps there is justice in this obscurity because the critics are also unsure of the contradictions and intentions of his journal, even of the classic *Walden.* A ghost then, of shifting features, peers out from between the gravestones, unreal, perhaps uninterpreted still.

I turned away from the early morning damp for a glimpse of the famous pond which in the country of my youth would have been called a lake. I walked its whole blue circumference with an erudite citizen of Concord. It was still an unearthly reflection of the sky, even if here and there beer bottles were bobbing in the shallows. I walked along the tracks of the old railroad where Thoreau used to listen to the telegraph wires. He had an eye for the sharp-edged artifact, I thought. The bobbing bottles, the keys to beer cans, he would have transmitted into cosmic symbols just as he had sensed all past time in the odors of a swamp. "All the ages are represented still," he had said, with nostrils flaring above the vegetation-choked water, "and you can smell them out."

It was the same, he found, with the ashes of Indian campfires, with old bricks and cellarholes. As for arrowheads, he says in a memorable passage, "I landed on two spots this afternoon and picked up a dozen. You would say it had rained arrowheads for they lie all over the surface of America. They lie in the meeting house cellar, and they lie in the distant cowpasture. They are sown like grain . . . over the earth. Each one," Thoreau writes, "yields me a thought. . . . It is humanity inscribed on the face of the earth. It is a footprint—rather a mindprint—left everywhere. . . . They are not fossil bones, but, as it were, fossil thoughts forever reminding me of the mind that shaped them. I am on the trail of mind."

Some time ago in a graduate seminar met in honor of the visit of an eminent prehistorian I watched the scholar and his listeners try to grapple with the significance of an anciently shaped stone. Not one of those present, involved as they were with semantic involutions, could render up so simple an expression as "mindprint." The lonely follower of the plow at Concord had provided both art and anthropology with an expression of horizon-reaching application which it has inexplicably chosen to ignore.

Mindprints are what the first men left, mindprints will be what the last man leaves, even if it is only a beer can dropped rolling from the last living hand, or a sagging picture in a ruined house. Cans, too, have their edges, a certain harshness; they too represent a structure of the mind, perhaps even an attitude. Thoreau might have seen that, too. Indeed he had written long ago: "If the outside of a man is so variegated and extensive, what must the inside be? You are high up the Platte river," he admonished, "traversing deserts, plains covered with soda, with no deeper hollow than a prairie dog hole tenanted by owls. . . ."

Perhaps in those lines he had seen the most of man's journey through the centuries. At all events he had coined two incomparable phrases, the "mindprint" which marked man's strange passage through the millennia and which differentiated him completely from the bones of all those creatures that lay strewn in the basement rocks of the planet, and that magnificent expression "another civilization," coined to apply to nature. That "civilization" contained for Thoreau the mysterious hieroglyphs left by a deer mouse, or the preternatural winter concealment of a moth's cocoon in which leaves were made to cooperate. He saw in the dancing of a fox on snow-whipped Walden ice "the fluctuations of some mind."

Thoreau had extended his thought-prints to something beyond what we of this age would call the natural. He would read them into nature itself, see, in other words, some kind of trail through that prairie for outlaws that had always intimidated him. On mountain tops, he had realized a star's substance, sensed a nature "not bound to be kind to man." Nevertheless he confided firmly to his diary, "the earth which I have *seen* cannot bury me." He searches desperately, all senses alert, for a way to read these greater hieroglyphs in which the tiny interpretable minds of our forerunners are embedded. We, with a sharper knowledge of human limitations and a devotion to the empirical fact, may deny to ourselves the reality of this other civilization within whose laws and probabilities we exist. Thoreau reposed faith in the consistency of nature's habits, but only up to a point, for he was a student of change.

As Alfred North Whitehead was to remark long afterward, "We are in the world and the world is in us"—a phrase that all artists should contemplate. Something, some law of a greater civilization, sustains nature from moment to moment within and above the void of non-being. "I hold," maintains the process philosopher, "that these unities of existence, these occasions of experience are the really real things which in their collective unity compose the evolving universe." In spite of today's emphasis upon the erratic nature of the submicroscopic particle there is, warns Whitehead the mathematician, "no valid inference from mere possibility to matter of fact; or, in other words, from mere mathematics to concrete nature. . . . Apart from metaphysical presupposition there can be no civilization." I doubt if Whitehead had ever perused Thoreau's journals, yet both return to the word "civilization," that strange on-going otherness of interlinked connections that makes up the nature that we know, just as human society and its artistic productions represent it in miniature, even to its eternal novelty.

Now Thoreau was a stay-at-home who traveled much in his mind, both in travel literature and beside Walden Pond. I, by circumstance, directly after delivering a lecture at Concord and gazing in my turn at Walden, was forced immediately to turn and fly west to the badlands and dinosaur-haunted gulches of Montana, some of its natives wild, half-civilized, still, in the way that Thoreau had viewed one of his Indian guides in Maine: "He shall spend a sunny day, and in this century be my contemporary. Why read history, then, if the ages and the generations are now? He lives three thousand years deep into time, an age not yet described by poets." As I followed our mixed-breed Cheyenne, as ambivalent toward us as the savage blood in his veins demanded, it came to me, as it must have come to many others, that seeing is not the same thing as understanding.

One man sees with indifference a leaf fall; another with the vision of Thoreau invokes the whole of that nostalgic world which we call autumn. One man sees a red fox running through a shaft of sunlight and lifts a rifle; another lays a restraining hand upon his companion's arm and says, "Please. There goes the last wild gaiety in the world. Let it live, let it run." This is the role of the alchemist, the true, if sometimes inarticulate artist. He transmutes the cricket's song in an autumn night to an aching void in the heart; snowflakes become the flying years. And when, as archaeologist, he lifts from the encrusting earth those forgotten objects Thoreau called "fossil thoughts," he is giving depth and tragedy and catharsis to the one great drama that concerns us most, the supreme mystery, man. Only man is capable of comprehending all he was and all that he has failed to be.

On those sun-beaten uplands over which we wandered, every chip of quartzite, every patinized flint, gleamed in our eyes as large as the monuments of other lands. Our vision in that thin air was incredibly enhanced and prolonged. Thoreau had conceived of nature as a single reflecting eye, the Walden eye of which he strove to be a solitary part, to apprehend with all his being. It was chance that had brought me in the span of a day to the dinosaur beds of Montana. Thoreau would have liked that. He had always regarded such places as endowed with the vapors of Nox, places where rules were annulled. He had called arrowheads mindprints. What then would he have termed a tooth of *Tyrannosaurus rex* held in my palm? The sign of another civilization, another order of mind? Or that tiny Cretaceous mammal which was a step on the way to ourselves? Surely it represented mind in embryo, our mind, but not of our devising. What would he have called it—that miracle of a bygone moment, the annulment of what had been, to be replaced by an eye, the artist's eye, that nature had never heretofore produced among her creatures? Would these have answered for him on this giant upland, itself sleeping like some tired dinosaur with outspread claws? Would he have simply called it "nature," as we sometimes do, scarcely knowing how to interpret the looming inchoate power out of which we have been born? Or would he have labeled nature itself a mindprint beyond our power to read or to interpret?

A man might sketch Triceratops, but the alphabet from which it was assembled had long since disappeared. As for man, how had his own alphabet been constructed? The nature in which he momentarily resided was a journal in which the script was always changing, like the dancing footprints of the fox on icy Walden Pond. Here, exposed about me, was the great journal Thoreau had striven to read, the business, in the end, that had taken him beyond Walden. He would have been too wise, too close to earth, too intimidated, to have called such a journal human. It was palpably inscribed from a star's substance. Tiny and brief in that journal were the hieroglyphs of man. Like Thoreau, we had come to the world's end, but not to the end of nature, not to the end of time. All that could be read was that we had a past; that was something no other life on the planet had learned. There was, we had also ascertained, a future.

In the meantime, Thoreau would have protested, there is the eye, the sun and the eye. "Nothing must be postponed; find eternity in each moment." But how few of us are endowed to sustain Thoreau's almost diabolical vision. Here and here alone the true alchemist of Jung's thought must come to exist in each of us. It is ours to transmute, not iron, not copper, not gold, but our tracks through nature, see them finally attended by self-knowledge, by the vision of the universal eye, that faculty possessed by the alchemist at Walden Pond.

"Miasma and infection come from within," he once wrote. It was as if he sought the cleanliness of flint patinized by the sun of ages, the artifact, the mindprint from which the mind itself had departed. It is something that perhaps only a few artists like Piranesi have understood amidst cromlechs, shards, and broken cities. It is man's final act as an alchemist to find the philosopher's stone in a desert-varnished flint and to watch himself, his mind, his species, evaporate into the air and sun that once had nourished the dinosaurs. Man alone knows the way he came; man alone is the alchemical animal who can vaporize himself in an utter cleansing, either by the powers of art alone, or, more terribly, by that dread device which began its active life at Los Alamos more than thirty years ago.

On a great hill in Montana on the day I had flown from Walden, I picked up a quartz knife that had the look of ten thousand years about it. It was as clean as the sun and I knew suddenly what Thoreau had been thinking about his arrowheads, his mindprints. They were free at last. They had aged out of human history, out of corruption. They were joined to that other civilization, evidence of some power that ran all through nature. They were a sign now beyond man, like all those other traceries of the frost that Thoreau had studied so avidly for evidence of some greater intelligence.

For just a moment I was back at Walden with a mind beyond infection by man, the mind of an alchemist who knew instinctively how laws might be annulled and great civilizations rise evanescent as toadstools on an autumn night. I too had taken on a desert varnish. I might have been a man but, if so, a man from whom centuries had been flayed away. I was being transmuted, worn down. There was flint by my hand that had not moved for millennia. It had ceased to radiate a message and whatever message I, as man, had carried there from Walden was also forgotten.

I lay among logs of petrified wood and found myself already

stiffening. Nature was bound somewhere; the great mind was readying some new experiment but not, perhaps, for man. I sighed a little with the cleanliness of that release. I slept deep under the great sky. I slept sound. For a moment as I drowsed I thought of the little stone marked "Henry" in the Concord cemetery. He would have known, I thought—the great alchemist had always known—and then I slept. It was Henry who had once written "the best philosophy is all untrue," untrue, that is, for man. Across an untamed prairie one's footprints must always be altering, that was the condition of the world, the only one that mattered, the only one for art.

## III

But why, some midnight questioner persisted in my brain, why had he left that sunny doorway of his hut in Walden for unknown mysterious business? Had he not written as though he had settled down forever? Why had Channing chronicled Thoreau's grievous disappointments? What had he been seeking and how had it affected him? If Walden was the opening chapter of a life, might not there still be a lurking message, a termination, a final chapter beyond his recorded death?

It was evident that he had seen the whole of American culture as copper-tinted by its antecedents, its people shadowy and gigantic as figures looming indistinctly in some Indian-summer haze. He had written of an old tree near Concord penetrated by a flying arrow with the shaft still attached. Some of the driving force of that flint projectile still persisted in his mind. Perhaps indeed those points that had once sung their message through every glade of the eastern woodland had spoken louder than the telegraph harp to which his ears had been attuned at Walden. Protest as he would, cultivate sauntering as he would, abhor as he would the rootless travelers whose works he read by lamplight, he was himself the eternal traveler. On the mountains of New Hampshire he had found "small and almost uninhabited ponds, apparently without fish, sources of rivers, still and cold, strange as condensed clouds." He had wandered without realizing it back into the time of the first continental ice recession.

"It is not worth the while to go around the world to count the cats in Zanzibar," he once castigated some luckless explorer, but why then this peering into lifeless tarns or engrossing himself with the meteoritic detritus of the Appalachians? Did he secretly wish to come to a place of no more life, where a man might stiffen into immobility as I had found myself freezing into the agate limbs of petrified trees in Montana? A divided man, one might say with surety. The bold man of abrasive village argument, the defender of John Brown, the advocate of civil disobedience, the spokesman who supplied many of the phrases which youthful revolutionaries hurled at their elders in the sixties of this century, felt the world too large for him.

As a college graduate he wept at the thought of leaving Concord. Emerson's well-meant efforts to launch him into the intellectual life of New York had failed completely. He admitted that he would gladly fall "into some crevice along with leaves and acorns." To Emerson's dismay he captained huckleberry parties among children and was content to be a rural surveyor, wandering over the farms and woodlots he could not own, save for his all-embracing eye. "There is no more fatal blunderer," he protested, "than he who consumes the greater part of life getting a living." He had emphasized that contemplative view at Walden, lived it, in fact, to the point where the world came finally to accept him as a kind of rural Robinson Crusoe who, as the cities grew, it might prove wise to emulate.

"I sat in my sunny doorway," he ruminated, "from sunrise till noon, rapt in a revery, amidst the pines and hickories and sumachs, in undisturbed solitude and stillness, while the birds sang around or flitted noiseless through the house, until by the sun falling in at my west window, or the noise of some traveller's wagon on the distant highway, I was reminded of the lapse of time. I grew in those seasons like corn in the night."

This passage would seem to stand for the serene and timeless life of an Oriental sage, a well-adjusted man, as the psychiatrists of our day would have it. Nevertheless this benign façade is deceptive.

There is no doubt that Thoreau honestly meant what he said at the time he said it, but the man was storm-driven. He would not be content with the first chapter of his life; he would, like a true artist, dredge up dreams even from the bottom of a pond.

In the year 1837 Thoreau confided abruptly to his journal: "Truth strikes us from behind, and in the dark." Thoreau's life was to be comparatively short and ill-starred. Our final question must, therefore, revolve, not about wanderings in autumn fields, not the drowsing in pleasant doorways where time stood still forever, but rather upon the leap of that lost arrow left quivering in an ancient oak. It was, in symbol, the hurtling purposeful arrow of a seemingly aimless life. It has been overlooked by Thoreau's biographers, largely because they have been men of the study or men of the forest. They have not been men of the seashore, or men gifted with the artist's eye. They have not trudged the naturalist's long miles through sea sand, where the war between two elements leaves even the smallest object magnified, as the bleached bone or broken utensil can be similarly magnified only on the dead lake beaches of the west.

Thoreau had been drawn to Cape Cod in 1849, a visit he had twice repeated. It was not the tourist resort it is today. It was still the country of men on impoverished farms, who went to sea or combed the beaches like wreckers seeking cargo. On those beaches, commented Thoreau, in a posthumous work which he was never destined to see in print, "a house was rarely visible . . . and the solitude was that of the ocean and the desert combined." The ceaseless roar of the surf, the strands of devil's-apron, the sun jellies, the stories of the drowned cast on the winter coast awoke in Thoreau what must have been memories of Emerson's shipwrecked friend Margaret Fuller. Here, recorded the chronicler, was a wilder, less human nature. Objects on the beach, he noted, were always more grotesque and dilated than upon approach they proved to be. A cast-up pair of gloves suggested the reality of hands.

Thoreau's account in *Cape Cod* of the Charity House to which his wanderings led him takes on a special meaning. I think it embodies something of a final answer to Channing's question about Thoreau's disappointment in his fellow men. Published two years after his death, it contains his formulation of the end of his business, or perhaps I should say of his quest. Hidden in what has been dismissed as a mere book of travel is an episode as potentially fabulous as Melville's great white whale.

First, however, I must tell the story of another coast because it will serve to illuminate Thoreau's final perception. A man, a shore dweller on Long Island Sound, told me of his discovery in a winter dawn. All night there had been a heavy surf and freezing wind. When he came to stroll along his beach at morning he had immediately seen a lifeboat cast upon the shingle and a still, black figure with the eastern sun behind it on the horizon. Gripped by a premonition he ran forward. The seaman in oilskins was alone and stiffly upright. A compass was clutched in his numb fingers. The man was sheeted in ice. Ice over his beard, his clothing, his hands, ice over his fixed, open eyes. Had he made the shore alive but too frozen to move? No one would ever know, just as no one would ever know his name or the sinking vessel from which he came. With desperate courage he had steered a true course through a wild night of breakers only to freeze within sight of help.

In those fishing days on Cape Cod, Thoreau came to know many such stories—vessels without weather warnings smashed in the winter seas, while a pittance of soaked men, perhaps, gained the shore. The sea, the intolerable sea, tumbled with total indifference the bodies of the dead or the living who were tossed up through the grinding surf of winter. These were common events in the days of sail.

The people who gained a scant living along that coast entertained, early in the nineteenth century, the thought that a few well-stocked sheds, or "Charity Houses," might enable lost seamen who made the shore to warm and feed themselves among the dunes till rescued. The idea was to provide straw and matches and provender, supervised and checked at intervals by some responsible person. Impressed at first by this signal beneficence of landsmen, Thoreau noted the instructions set down for the benefit of mariners. Finally, he approached one such Charity House. It appeared, he commented, "but a stage to the grave." The chimney had fallen. As he and his companion wished to gain an idea of a "humane house," they put their eyes, by turns, to a knothole in the door. "We had,"

Thoreau comments ironically, "some practice at looking inward—the pupil becomes enlarged. Nature is never so dark that a patient eye may not prevail over it."

So there, at last, he saw the end of his journey, of the business begun at Walden. He was peering into the Charity House of man, upon a Cape Cod beach. For frozen, shipwrecked mariners he saw a fireplace with no matches, no provisions, no straw upon the floor. "We looked," he said, "into the bowels of mercy, and for bread we found a stone." Shivering like castaways, "we looked through the knothole into that night without a star, until we concluded it was not a *humane* house at all." The arrow Thoreau had followed away from Walden had pierced as deep as Captain Ahab's lance. No wonder the demoniacal foxes leaping at Thoreau's window had urged him to begone. He had always looked for a crevice into the future. He had peered inward instead. It was ourselves who were rudimental men.

Recently I had a letter from one of my students who is working in the Arctic and who has a cat acquired somewhere in his travels. The cat, he explained to me, hunts in the barrens behind the Eskimo village. Occasionally it proudly brings in a lemming or a bird to his hut. The Eskimo were curious about the unfamiliar creature.

"Why does he do that?" my friend was asked.

"Because he is a good cat," my student explained. "He shares his game."

"So, so." The old men nodded wisely. "It is true for the man and for the beast—the good man and the good beast. They share, yes indeed. They share the game."

I think my young quick-witted friend had momentarily opened the eye of winter. Before laying aside his letter, I thought of the eye of Walden as I had seen it under the summer sun. It was the sharing that had impressed the people of the ice and it was a great sharing of things seen that Thoreau had attempted at his pond. A hundred years after his death people were still trying to understand what he was about. They were still trying to get both eyes open. They were still trying to understand that the town surveyor had brought something to share with his fellows, something that, if they partook of it, might transpose them to another world.

# WALDEN: THOREAU'S UNFINISHED BUSINESS

I had thought, staring across an angular gravestone at Concord and again as I held my wind-varnished flint in Montana, that "sharing" could be the word. It was appropriate, even though Thoreau in a final bitterness had felt sharing to be as impoverished as the Charity House for sailors—a knothole glimpse into the human condition. How then should the artist see? By an eye applied to a knothole? By a magnification of sand-filled gloves washed up on a beach? Could this be the solitary business that led Thoreau on his deathbed to mutter, whether in irony or confusion, "one world at a time"?

This is the terror of our age. How should we see? In what world are we? For we have fallen out of nature and see sometimes more and sometimes less. We see the past, the looming future, and then, so fearfully is the eye confused, that it stares inverted into a Charity House that appears to reflect a less than human heart. Is this Thoreau's final surrealist vision, his glance through the knothole into the "humane house"? It would appear at least to be a glimpse from one of those two great alternating eyes at Walden Pond from which in the end he had fled—the blind eye of winter and that innocent blue pupil beside which he had once drowsed when time seemed endless. Both are equally real, as the great poets and prophets have always known, but it was Thoreau's tragic destiny to see with eyes strained beyond endurance man subsiding into two wrinkled gloves grasping at the edge of infinity. It is his final contribution to literature, the final hidden conclusion of an unwritten life whose first chapter Morris had rightly diagnosed as Walden.

There is an old Biblical saying that our days are prolonged and every vision fails us. This I would dispute. The vision of the great artist does not fail. It sharpens and refines with age until everything extraneous is pared away. "Simplify," Thoreau had advocated. Two gloves, devoid of flesh, clutching the stones of the ebbing tide become, transmuted, the most dreadful object in the world.

"There has been nothing but the sun and eye from the beginning," Thoreau had written when his only business was looking and he grew, as he expressed it, "like corn in the night." The sun and the eye are the two aspects of nature which are irremediably linked. But the eye of man constitutes an awesome crystal whose diffractions are far greater than those of any Newtonian prism.

We see, as artists, as scientists, each in his own way, through the inexorable lens we cannot alter. In a nature which Thoreau recognized as unfixed and lawless anything might happen. The artist's endeavor is to make it happen—the unlawful, the oncoming world, whether endurable or mad, but shaped, shaped always by the harsh angles of truth, the truth as glimpsed through the terrible crystal of genius. This is the one sure rule of that other civilization which we have come to know is greater than our own. Thoreau called it, from the first, "unfinished business," when he turned and walked away from his hut at Walden Pond.

# The Lethal
# Factor

The Great Olduvai Gorge in East Africa has been appropriately called the Grand Canyon of human evolution. Here a million, perhaps two million, years of human history are recorded in the shape of successive skulls and deposits of stone tools. The elusive story of the long road man has traveled is glimpsed momentarily in eroded strata and faded bone. Olduvai is now famous all over the world. Only to those who have the habit of searching beyond the obvious, however, may it have occurred that this precipitous rift through time parallels and emphasizes a similar rift in ourselves—a rift that lies like a defacing crack across our minds and consequently many of our institutions. From its depths we can hear the rumble of the torrent from which we have ascended and sense the disastrous ease with which both individual men and civilizations can topple backward and be lost.

Brooding upon the mysteries of time and change, a great and thoughtful scholar, Alfred North Whitehead, many years ago recorded his thoughts in a cryptic yet profound observation. He said, in brief, "We are . . . of infinite importance, because as we perish we are immortal." Whitehead was not speaking in ordinary theological terms. He was not concerned in this passage with the survival of the human personality after death—at least as a religious conception. He was, instead, struggling with that difficult idea which he describes as the "prehension of the past," the fact that the world we know, even as it perishes, remains an elusive, unfixed element in the oncoming future.

The organic world, as well as that superorganic state which exists in the realm of thought, is, in truth, prehensile in a way that the inorganic world is not. The individual animal or plant in the course of its development moves always in relation to an unseen future toward which its forces are directed: the egg is broken and a snake writhes away into the grass; the acorn seedling, through many seasons, contorts itself slowly into a gnarled, gigantic oak. Similarly, life moves against the future in another, an evolutionary, sense. The creature existing now—this serpent, this bird, this man—has only to leave progeny in order to stretch out a gray, invisible hand into the evolutionary future, into the nonexistent.

With time, the bony fin is transformed into a paw, a round, insectivore eye into the near-sighted gaze of a scholar. Moreover, all along this curious animal extension into time, parts of ourselves are flaking off, breaking away into unexpected and unforeseen adventures. One insectivore fragment has taken to the air and become a vampire bat, while another fragment draws pictures in a cave and creates a new prehensile realm where the shadowy fingers of lost ideas reach forward into time to affect our world view and, with it, our future destinies and happiness.

Thus, since the dawn of life on the planet, the past has been figuratively fingering the present. There is in reality no clearly separable past and future either in the case of nerve and bone or within the less tangible but equally real world of history. Even the extinct dead have plucked the great web of life in such a manner that the future still vibrates to their presence. The mammalian world was for a long time constricted and impoverished by the dominance of the now vanished reptiles. Similarly, who knows today what beautiful creature remains potential only because of man's continued existence, or what renewed manifestations of creative energy his presence inhibits or has indeed destroyed forever.

As the history of the past unrolls itself before the eyes of both paleontologists and archaeologists, however, it becomes evident, so far as the biological realm is concerned, that by far the greater proportion of once-living branches on the tree of life are dead, and to this the archaeologist and historian must add dead stone, dead letters, dead ideas, and dead civilizations. As one gropes amid all this attic dust it becomes ever more apparent that some lethal factor, some arsenical poison, seems to lurk behind the pleasant show of the natural order or even the most enticing cultural edifices that man has been able to erect.

In the organic world of evolution three facts, so far as we can perceive, today seem to determine the death of species: the irreversibility of the organic process in time; high specialization which, in the end, limits new adaptive possibilities; the sudden emergence of spectacular enemies or other environmental circumstances which overwhelm or ambush a living form so suddenly that the slow adjustive process of natural selection cannot be made to function. This third principle, one could say, is the factor which, given the other two limitations upon all forms of life, will result in extinction. As a drastic example one could point to the destruction of many of the larger creatures as man has abruptly extended his sway over both hemispheres and into many different environmental zones.

The past century has seen such great accessions of knowledge in relation to these natural events, as well as a growing consciousness of man's exposure to similar dangers, that there is an increasing tendency to speculate upon our own possibilities for survival. The great life web which man has increasingly plucked with an abruptness unusual in nature shows signs of "violence in the return," to use a phrase of Francis Bacon's. The juvenile optimism about progress which characterized our first scientific years was beginning early in this century to be replaced by doubts which the widely circulated *Decline of the West* by Oswald Spengler documents only too well. As the poet J. C. Squire says, we can turn

> the great wheel backward until Troy unburn,
> . . . and seven Troys below
> Rise out of death and dwindle . . .

We can go down through the layers of dead cities until the gold becomes stone, until the jewels become shells, until the palace is a hovel, until the hovel becomes a heap of gnawed bones.

Are the comparisons valid? The historians differ. Is there hope? A babble of conflicting voices confuses us. Are we safe? On this point I am sure that every person of cultivation and intelligence would answer with a resounding "No!" Spengler— not the optimist—was right in prophesying that this century would be one marked by the rise of dictators, great wars, and augmented racial troubles. Whether he was also right in foreseeing this century as the onsetting winter of Western civilization is a more difficult problem.

Faustian, space-loving man still hurls his missiles skyward. His tentacular space probes seem destined to palpate the farthest rim of the solar system. Yet honesty forces us to confess that this effort is primarily the product of conflict, that millions are now employed in the institutions erected to serve that conflict, that government and taxes are increasingly geared to it, that in another generation, if not now, it will have become traditional. Men who have spent their lives in the service of these institutions will be reluctant to dissolve them. A vested interest will exist on both sides of the iron curtain. The growing involution of this aspect of Western culture may well come to resemble the ingrowth and fantasies of that ritualized belief in *mana* which characterized late Polynesian society.

It is upon this anthropological note that I should like to examine the nature of the human species—the creature who at first glance appears to have escaped from the specialized cul-de-sac which has left his late-existing primate relative, the gorilla, peering sullenly from the little patch of sheltered bush that yet remains to him. I have said that some lethal factor seems to linger in man's endeavors. It is for this reason that I venture these words from a discipline which has long concerned itself with the origins, the illusions, the symbols, and the folly as well as the grandeur of civilizations whose records are lost and whose temples are fallen. Yet the way is not easy. As Herman Melville has written in one great perceptive passage:

> By vast pains we mine into the pyramid; by
> horrible gropings we come to the central room;
> with joy we espy the sarcophagus; but we lift
> the lid—and no body is there!—appallingly
> vacant, as vast, is the soul of man!

I have spent a sizable number of my adult years among the crude stones of man's Ice Age adventurings. The hard, clean flint in the mountain spring defines and immortalizes the race that preceded us better than our own erratic fabrications distinguish our time. There is as yet no sharp edge to our image. Will it be, in the end, the twisted gantrys on the rocket bases, or telephone wires winding voiceless through the high Sierras, or the glass from space-searching observatories pounded into moonstones in the surf on a sinking coast?

What makes the symbol, finally, for another age as the pyramids for theirs—writing for five thousand years man's hope against the sky? Before we pass, it is well to think of what our final image as a race may be—the image that will give us a kind of earthly immortality or represent, perhaps, our final collective visage in eternity. But it is to the seeds of death within us that we must address ourselves before we dare ask this other final question of what may stand for us when all else is fallen and gone down. We shall not begin with Western society, we shall begin with man. We shall open that symbolic sepulcher of which Melville speaks. We shall grope in the roiling, tumultuous darkness for that unplumbed vacancy which Melville termed so ironically the soul of man.

Since the days of Lyell and Hutton, who perceived, beneath the romantic geological catastrophism of their age, that the prosaic and unnoticed works of wind and sun and water were the real shapers of the planet, science has been adverse to the recognition of discontinuity in natural events. (It should be said in justice to Sir Charles Lyell, however, that in combating the paroxysmal theories which preoccupied his contemporaries he maintained, nevertheless, that "minor convulsions and changes are . . . a *vera causa,* a force and mode of operation which we know to be true.") Nevertheless the rise of modern physics, with its emphasis on quantum theory in the realm of particles, and even certain aspects of Mendelian genetics serve to remind us that there are still abroad in nature hidden powers which, on occasion, manifest themselves in an unpredictable fashion. On a more dramatic scale no one to date has been quite able to account satisfactorily for that series of rhythmic and overwhelming catastrophes which we call the Ice Age. It is true that we no longer cloak such mysteries in an aura of supernaturalism, but they continue to remind us, nevertheless, of the latent forces still lurking within nature.

Another of these episodes is reflected in the origins of the human mind. It represents, in a sense, a quantum step: the emergence of genuine novelty. It does so because the brain brought into being what would have been, up until the time of its appearance, an inconceivable event—the world of culture. The *mundus alter*—this other intangible, faery world of dreams, fantasies, invention—has been flowing through the heads of men since the first ape-man succeeded in cutting out a portion of his environment and delineating it in a transmissible word. With that word a world arose which will die only when the last man utters the last meaningful sound.

It is a world that lurks, real enough, behind the foreheads of men; it has transformed their natural environment. It has produced history, the unique act out of the natural world about us. "The foxes have their holes," the words are recorded of the apostle Matthew, "the wild birds have their nests, but the Son of Man has no where to lay his head." Two thousand years ago in the Judean desert men recognized that the instinctive world of the animals had been lost to man. Henceforward he would pass across the landscape as a wanderer who, in a sense, was outside of nature. His shadow would grow large in the night beside the glare of his red furnaces. Fickle, erratic, dangerous, he would wrest from stone and deep-veined metal powers hitherto denied to living things. His restless mind would try all paths, all horrors, all betrayals. In the strange individual talents nourished in his metropolises, great music would lift him momentarily into some pure domain of peace. Art would ennoble him; temptation and terror pluck his sleeve. He would believe all things and believe nothing. He would kill for shadowy ideas more ferociously than other creatures kill for food, then, in a generation or less, forget what bloody dream had so oppressed him.

Man stands, in other words, between the two most disparate kingdoms upon earth: the flesh and the spirit. He is lost between an instinctive mental domain he has largely abandoned and a realm of thought through which still drift ghostly shadows of his primordial past. Like all else that lingers along the borders of one world while gazing into another, he is imperfectly adapted. It is not only the sea lion from the deep waters that inches itself painfully up the shore into the unfamiliar sunlight. So does man in the deep interior of his mind occasionally clamber far up into sunlit meadows where his world is changed and where, in the case of some few, for such is the way of evolution, there is no return to lower earth. It has taken us far longer to discover the scars of evolution in our brains than to interpret the vestigial organs tucked into odd crannies of our bodies or the wounds and aches that reveal to us that we have not always walked upon two feet.

Alfred Russel Wallace perceived in 1864 that in man the rise of the most remarkable specialization in the organic world—the human brain—had to a considerable degree outmoded the evolution of specialized organs. The creature who could clothe himself in fur or take it off at will, who could, by extension of himself into machines, fly, swim, or roll at incredible speeds, had simultaneously mastered all of earth's environments with the same physical body. Paradoxically, this profound biological specialization appeared to have produced an organ devoted to the sole purpose of escaping specialization. No longer could man be trapped in a single skin, a single climate, a single continent, or even a single culture. He had become ubiquitous. The wind wafted his little craft to the ends of the earth, seeds changed their substance under his hands, the plague hesitated and drew back before his cities. Even his body appeared destined to remain relatively stable since he had become the supremely generalized animal whose only mutability lay in his intelligence as expressed upon his instruments and weapons.

A creature who sets out upon a new road in the wilderness, however, is apt to encounter unexpected dangers, particularly if he ventures into that invisible and mysterious environmental zone, that "other world" which has been conjured up by the sheer power of thought. Man, when he moved from the animal threshold into dawning intellectual consciousness, no longer could depend upon the instinctive promptings that carry a bird upon the wing.

Although it is difficult to penetrate into that half-world of the past, it is evident that order, simple order, must have rapidly become a necessity for survival in human groups across whose members the inchoate thoughts and impulses of the freed mind must have run as alarming vagaries. Man must, in fact, have walked the knife edge of extinction for untold years. As he defined his world he also fell victim to the shadows that lay behind it. He did not accept it, like the animal, as a thing given. He bowed to stone and heard sprites in running water. The entire universe was talking about him and his destiny. He knew the powers and heard the voices. He formulated their wishes for himself. He shaped out of his own drives and timidities the rules and regulations which reintroduced into his world a kind of facsimile of his lost instinctive animal order and simplicity.

By means of custom, strengthened by supernatural enforcement, the violent and impulsive were forced into conformity. There was a way—the way of the tribe. The individual conformed or perished. There was only one way, and one people, the tribe. That there were many tribes and many ways into the future no one knew, and at first in the wide emptiness of the world it scarcely mattered. It was enough that there was some kind of way or path. Even the Neanderthals had known this and had provided meat and tools that the dead might need upon their journey.

If we pause and contemplate this dim and unhistorical age for a moment it is, as I have intimated, with the thought that it reveals a rift or schism in man's endeavors that runs through his life in many aspects and throughout his history. The great historians have spoken of universal history as, in the words of Lord Acton, "an illumination of the soul." They have ventured to foresee the eventual reunion of man and the meeting of many little histories, ultimately, in the great history of man's final unification. It may be so. Yet whether we peer backward into the cloudy mirror of the past or look around us at the moment, it appears that behind every unifying effort in the life of man there is an opposite tendency to disruption, as if the force symbolized in the story of the Tower of Babel had been felt by man since the beginning. Eternally he builds, and across the smooth façade of his institutional structures there runs this ancient crack, this primordial flaw out of old time. We of this age have not escaped it.

Scarcely had man begun dimly and uncertainly to shape his new-found world of culture than it split into many facets. Its "universal" laws were unfortunately less than those of the nature out of which he had emerged. The customs were, in reality, confined to this island, that hill fort, or the little tribe by the river bank. The people's conception of themselves was similarly circumscribed. *They* were the people. Those who made strange sounds in a different tongue or believed in other gods were queer and, at best, tolerated for trading purposes if they did not encroach upon tribal territory.

In some parts of the world this remote life, untouched by self-questioning of any sort, this ancient way of small magical dealings with animals and wood spirits and man, has persisted into modern times. It is a comparatively harmless but ensorcelled world in which man's innate capacities are shut up in a very tiny ring and held latent through the long passage of millennia. There are times when one wonders whether it is only a very rare accident that releases man from the ancient, hypnotic sleep into which he so promptly settled after triumphing in his first human endeavor—that of organizing a way of life, controlling the seasons, and, in general, setting up his own microscopic order in the vast shadow of the natural world. It is worth a passing thought upon primitive capacities that perhaps no existing society has built so much upon so little.

Nevertheless the rift persisted and ran on. The great neolithic empires arose and extended across the old tribal boundaries. The little peoples were becoming the great people. The individual inventor and artist, released from the restrictions of a low-energy society, enriched the whole culture. The arts of government increased. As wealth arose, however, so war, in a modern sense, also arose. Conquest empires, neolithic and classic, largely erased the old tribalism, but a long train of miseries followed in their wake. Slavery, merciless exploitation such as our paleolithic ancestors never imagined in their wildest dreams, disrupted the society and in the end destroyed both the individual and the state.

There began to show across the face of these new empires not alone the symptoms of a bottomless greed but what, in the light of times to come, was more alarming: the very evident fact that, as human rule passed from the village to the empire, the number of men who could successfully wield power for long-term social purposes grew less. Moreover, the long chain of bureaucracy from the ruler to the ruled made for greater inefficiency and graft. Man was beginning to be afflicted with bigness in his affairs, and with bigness there often emerges a dogmatic rigidity. The system, if bad, may defy individual strength to change it and simply run its inefficient way until it collapses. It is here that what we may call involution in the human drama becomes most apparent.

There tend to arise in human civilization institutions which monopolize, in one direction or another, the wealth and attention of the society, frequently to its eventual detriment and increasing rigidity. These are, in a sense, cultural overgrowths, excessively ornate societal excrescences as exaggerated as some of the armor plate that adorned the gigantic bodies of the last dinosaurs. Such complications may be as relatively harmless as a hyperdeveloped caste system in which no social fluidity exists, or as dangerous as military institutions that employ increasingly a disproportionate amount of the capital and attention of the state and its citizens.

In one of those profound morality plays which C. S. Lewis is capable of tossing off lightly in the guise of science fiction, one of his characters remarks that in the modern era the good appears to be getting better and the evil more terrifying. It is as though two antipathetic elements in the universe were slowly widening the gap between them. Man, in some manner, stands at the heart of this growing rift. Perhaps he contains it within himself. Perhaps he feels the crack slowly widening in his mind and his institutions. He sees the finest intellects, which in the previous century concerned themselves with electric light and telephonic communication, devote themselves as wholeheartedly to missiles and supersonic bombers. He finds that the civilization which once assumed that only barbarians would think of attacking helpless civilian populations from the air has, by degrees, come to accept the inevitability of such barbarism.

Hope, if it is expressed by the potential candidates for mass extermination in this age of advanced destruction, is expressed, not in terms of living, but in those of survival, such hope being largely premised on confidence in one's own specialists to provide a nuclear blanket capable of exceeding that of the enemy. All else gives way before the technician and the computer specialist running his estimates as to how many million deaths it takes, and in how many minutes, before the surviving fragment of a nation—if any—sues for peace. Nor, in the scores of books analyzing these facts, is it easy to find a word spared to indicate concern for the falling sparrow, the ruined forest, the contaminated spring—all, in short, that still spells to man a life in nature.

One of these technicians wrote in another connection involving the mere use of insecticides, which I here shorten and paraphrase: "Balance of nature? An outmoded biological concept. There is no room for sentiment in modern science. We shall learn to get along without birds if necessary. After all, the dinosaurs disappeared. Man merely makes the process go faster. Everything changes with time." And so it does. But let us be as realistic as the gentleman would wish. It may be we who go. I am just primitive enough to hope that somehow, somewhere, a cardinal may still be whistling on a green bush when the last man goes blind before his man-made sun. If it should turn out that we have mishandled our own lives as several civilizations before us have done, it seems a pity that we should involve the violet and the tree frog in our departure.

To perpetrate this final act of malice seems somehow disproportionate, beyond endurance. It is like tampering with the secret purposes of the universe itself and involving not only man but life in the final holocaust—an act of petulant, deliberate blasphemy.

It is for this reason that Lewis's remark about the widening gap between good and evil takes on such horrifying significance in our time. The evil man may do has this added significance about it: it is not merely the evil of one tribe seeking to exterminate another. It is, instead, the thought-out willingness to make the air unbreathable to neighboring innocent nations and to poison, in one's death throes, the very springs of life itself. No greater hypertrophy of the institution of war has ever been observed in the West. To make the situation more ironic, the sole desire of every fifth-rate nascent nationalism is to emulate Russia and America, to rattle rockets, and, if these are too expensive, then at least to possess planes and a parade of tanks. For the first time in history a divisive nationalism, spread like a contagion from the West, has increased in virulence and blown around the world.

A multitude of states are now swept along in a passionate hunger for arms as the only important symbol of prestige. Yearly their number increases. For the first time in human history the involutional disease of a single civilization, that of the West, shows signs of becoming the disease of all contemporary societies. Such, it would appear, is one of the less beneficial aspects of the communications network that we have flung around the world. The universal understanding which has been the ultimate goal sought by the communications people, that shining Telstar through which we were to promote the transmission of wisdom, bids fair, instead, to promote unsatisfied hunger and the enthusiastic reception of irrationalities that embed themselves all too readily in the minds of the illiterate.

Man may have ceased to teeter uncertainly upon his hind legs; his strange physical history may be almost over. But within his mind he is still hedged about by the shadows of his own fear and uncertainty; he still lingers at the borders of his dark and tree-filled world. He fears the sunlight, he fears truth, he fears himself. In the words of Thomas Beddoes, who looked long into that world of shadows:

> Nature's polluted.
> There's man in every secret corner of her
> Doing damned wicked deeds. Thou art, old world,
> A hoary, atheistic, murdering star.

This is the dark murmur that rises from the abyss beneath us and that draws us with uncanny fascination.

If I were to attempt to spell out in a sentence the single lethal factor at the root of declining or lost civilizations up to the present, I would be forced to say adaptability. I would have to remark, paradoxically, that the magnificent specialization of gray matter which has opened to us all the climates of the earth, which has given us music, surrounded us with luxury, entranced us with great poetry, has this one flaw: it is too adaptable. In breaking free from instinct and venturing naked into a universe which demands constant trial and experiment, a world whose possibilities were unexplored and are unlimited, man's hunger for experience became unlimited also. He has the capacity to veer with every wind or, stubbornly, to insert himself into some fantastically elaborated and irrational social institution only to perish with it.

It may well be that some will not call this last piece of behavior adaptation. Yet it is to be noted that only extreme, if unwise, adaptability would have allowed man to contrive and inhabit such strange structures. When men in the mass have once attached themselves to a cultural excrescence that grows until it threatens the life of the society, it is almost impossible to modify their behavior without violence. Yet along with this, as I have remarked, fervid waves of religious or military enthusiasm may sweep through a society and then vanish with scarcely a trace.

It would take volumes to chronicle the many facets of this problem. It is almost as though man had at heart no image, but only images, that his soul was truly as vacant and vast as Melville intimated in the passage I quoted earlier. Man is mercurial and shifting. He can look down briefly into the abyss and say, smiling, "We are beasts from the dark wood. We will never be anything else. We are not to be trusted. Never on this earth. We have come from down there." This view is popular in our time. We speak of the fossil ape encrusted in our hearts. This is one image of many that man entertains of himself. Another was left by a man who died 2000 years ago.

I have mentioned before the collective symbol that a civilization sometimes leaves to posterity and the difficulty one has with our own because of the rapidity with which our technology has altered and the restless flickering of our movement from one domain of life to another. A few months ago I read casually in my evening newspaper that our galaxy is dying. That great wheel of fire of which our planetary system is an infinitesimal part was, so the report ran, proceeding to its end. The detailed evidence was impressive. Probably, though I have not attempted to verify the figures, the spiral arm on which we drift is so vast that it has not made one full circle of the wheel since the first man-ape picked up and used a stone.

I saw no use in whispering behind my hand at the club, next morning, "They say the galaxy is dying." I knew well enough that man, being more perishable than stars, would be gone billions of years before the edge of the Milky Way grew dark. It was not that aspect of the human episode which moved me. Instead it was the sudden realization of what man could do on so gigantic a scale even if, as yet, his personal fate eluded him. Out there millions of light-years away from earth, man's hands were already fumbling in the coal-scuttle darkness of a future universe. The astronomer was fore-shortening time—just as on a shorter scale eclipses can be foretold, or an apparently empty point in space can be shown as destined to receive an invisibly moving body. So man, the short-lived midge, is reaching into and observing events he will never witness in the flesh. In a psychological second, on this elusive point we call the present, we can watch the galaxy drift into darkness.

The materiality of the universe, Alfred North Whitehead some-where remarks, is measured "in proportion to the restriction of memory and anticipation." With consciousness, memory, extended through the written word and the contributions of science, pene-trates further and further into both aspects of time's unknown do-main—that is, the past and the future. Although individual men do not live longer, we might say that the reach of mind in the universe and its potential control of the natural order is enormously mag-nified.

Material substance no longer dominates the spiritual life. There is not space here to explore all aspects of this fascinating subject, or the paradoxes with which our burgeoning technology have presented us. This strange capacity of the mind upon which we exercise so little thought, however, means that man both remains within the histori-cal order, and, at the same time, passes beyond it.

We are present in history, we may see history as meaningless or purposeful, but as the heightened consciousness of time invades our thinking, our ability to free our intellects from a narrow and self-centered immediacy should be intensified. It is this toward which Whitehead was directing his thought: that all responsible decisions are acts of compassion and disinterest; they exist within time and history but they are also outside of it, unique and individual and, because individual, spiritually free. In the words of Erich Frank,

"History and the world do not change, but man's attitude to the world changes."

I wonder if we understand this point, for it is the crux of this essay, and though I have mentioned modern thinkers, it leads straight back to the New Testament. A number of years ago in a troubled period of my life I chanced to take a cab from an airport outside a large eastern city. My route passed through the back streets of a run-down area of dilapidated buildings. I remember passing a pathetic little cemetery whose smudged crosses, dating from another era, were now being encroached upon and overshadowed by the huge gray tanks of an oil refinery. The shadow of giant machines now fell daily across the hill of the dead. It was almost a visible struggle of the symbols to which I have earlier referred—the cross that marks two thousand years of Western culture, shrinking, yet still holding its little acre in the midst of hulking beams and shadows where now no sunlight ever fell.

I felt an unreasoned distaste as we jounced deeper into these narrow alleyways, or roared beneath giant bridges toward a distant throughway. Finally, as we cut hastily through a slightly more open section, I caught a glimpse of a neighborhood church—a church of evident poverty, of a sect unknown, and destined surely to vanish from that unsavory spot. It was an anachronism as doomed as the cemetery. We passed, and a moment later, as though the sign had been hanging all that time in the cab before me, instead of standing neatly in the yard outside the church, my conscious mind unwillingly registered the words:

> Christ died to save mankind.
> Is it nothing to you, all ye that pass by?

I looked at that invisible hanging sign with surprise, if not annoyance. By some I have been castigated because I am an evolutionist. In one church which I had attended as the guest of a member I had been made the covert object of a sermon in which I had recognizably played the role of a sinning scientist. I cannot deny that the role may have fitted me, but I could not feel that the hospitality, under the circumstances, was Christian. I had seen fanatical sectarian signs of ignorant and contentious sects painted on rocks all over America, particularly in desert places. I had gazed unmoved on them all.

But here on a plain white board that would not remove itself from my eyes, an unknown man in the shadow of one of the ugliest neighborhoods in America had in some manner lifted that falling symbol from the shadow of the refinery tanks and thrust it relentlessly before my eyes. There was no evading it. "Is it nothing to you?" I was being asked—I who passed by, who had indeed already passed and would again ignore much more sophisticated approaches to religion.

But the symbol, one symbol of many in the wilderness of modern America, still exerted its power over me; a dozen lines of thinking, past and present, drew in upon me. Nothing eventful happened in the outside world. Whatever took place happened within myself. The cab sped on down the throughway.

But before my mind's eye, like an ineradicable mote, persisted the vision of that lost receding figure on the dreadful hill of Calvary who whispered with his last breath, "It is finished." It was not for himself he cried—it was for man against eternity, for us of every human generation who perform against the future the acts which justify creation or annul it. This is the power in the mind of man, a mindprint, if you will, an insubstantial symbol which holds like a strained cable the present from falling into the black abyss of nothingness. This is why, if we possess great fortitude, each one of us can say against the future he has not seen, "It is finished."

At that moment we will have passed beyond the reach of time into a still and hidden place where it was said, "He who loses his life will find it." And in that place we will have found an ancient and an undistorted way.

# The Illusion of
# the Two Cultures

Not long ago an English scientist, Sir Eric Ashby, remarked that "to train young people in the dialectic between orthodoxy and dissent is the unique contribution which universities make to society." I am sure that Sir Eric meant by this remark that nowhere but in universities are the young given the opportunity to absorb past tradition and at the same time to experience the impact of new ideas—in the sense of a constant dialogue between past and present—lived in every hour of the student's existence. This dialogue, ideally, should lead to a great winnowing and sifting of experience and to a heightened consciousness of self which, in turn, should lead on to greater sensitivity and perception on the part of the individual.

Our lives are the creation of memory and the accompanying power to extend ourselves outward into ideas and relive them. The finest intellect is that which employs an invisible web of gossamer running into the past as well as across the minds of living men and which constantly responds to the vibrations transmitted through these tenuous lines of sympathy. It would be contrary to fact, however, to assume that our universities always perform this unique function of which Sir Eric speaks, with either grace or perfection; in fact our investment in man, it has been justly remarked, is deteriorating even as the financial investment in science grows.

More than thirty years ago, George Santayana had already sensed this trend. He commented, in a now-forgotten essay, that one of the strangest consequences of modern science was that as the visible

267

wealth of nature was more and more transferred and abstracted, the mind seemed to lose courage and to become ashamed of its own fertility. "The hard-pressed natural man will not indulge his imagination," continued Santayana, "unless it poses for truth; and being half-aware of this imposition, he is more troubled at the thought of being deceived than at the fact of being mechanized or being bored; and he would wish to escape imagination altogether."

"Man would wish to escape imagination altogether." I repeat that last phrase, for it defines a peculiar aberration of the human mind found on both sides of that bipolar division between the humanities and the sciences, which C. P. Snow has popularized under the title of *The Two Cultures*. The idea is not solely a product of this age. It was already emerging with the science of the seventeenth century; one finds it in Bacon. One finds the fear of it faintly foreshadowed in Thoreau. Thomas Huxley lent it weight when he referred contemptuously to the "caterwauling of poets."

Ironically, professional scientists berated the early evolutionists such as Lamarck and Chambers for overindulgence in the imagination. Almost eighty years ago John Burroughs observed that some of the animus once directed by science toward dogmatic theology seemed in his day increasingly to be vented upon the literary naturalist. In the early 1900s a quarrel over "nature faking" raised a confused din in America and aroused W. H. Hudson to some dry and pungent comment upon the failure to distinguish the purposes of science from those of literature. I know of at least one scholar who, venturing to develop some personal ideas in an essay for the layman, was characterized by a reviewer in a leading professional journal as a worthless writer, although, as it chanced, the work under discussion had received several awards in literature, one of them international in scope. More recently, some scholars not indifferent to humanistic values have exhorted poets to leave their personal songs in order to portray the beauty and symmetry of molecular structures.

Now some very fine verse has been written on scientific subjects, but, I fear, very little under the dictate of scientists as such. Rather there is evident here precisely that restriction of imagination against which Santayana inveighed; namely, an attempt to constrain literature itself to the delineation of objective or empiric truth, and to dismiss the whole domain of value, which after all constitutes the very nature of man, as without significance and beneath contempt.

Unconsciously, the human realm is denied in favor of the world of pure technics. Man, the tool user, grows convinced that he is himself only useful as a tool, that fertility except in the use of the scientific imagination is wasteful and without purpose, even, in some indefinable way, sinful. I was reading J. R. R. Tolkien's great symbolic trilogy, *The Fellowship of the Ring,* a few months ago, when a young scientist of my acquaintance paused and looked over my shoulder. After a little casual interchange the man departed leaving an accusing remark hovering in the air between us. "I wouldn't waste my time with a man who writes fairy stories." He might as well have added, "or with a man who reads them."

As I went back to my book I wondered vaguely in what leafless landscape one grew up without Hans Christian Andersen, or Dunsany, or even Jules Verne. There lingered about the young man's words a puritanism which seemed the more remarkable because, as nearly as I could discover, it was unmotivated by any sectarian religiosity unless a total dedication to science brings to some minds a similar authoritarian desire to shackle the human imagination. After all, it is this impossible, fertile world of our imagination which gave birth to liberty in the midst of oppression, and which persists in seeking until what is sought is seen. Against such invisible and fearful powers, there can be found in all ages and in all institutions —even the institutions of professional learning—the humorless man with the sneer, or if the sneer does not suffice, then the torch, for the bright unperishing letters of the human dream.

One can contrast this recalcitrant attitude with an 1890 reminiscence from that great Egyptologist Sir Flinders Petrie, which steals over into the realm of pure literature. It was written, in unconscious symbolism, from a tomb:

"I here live, and do not scramble to fit myself to the requirements of others. In a narrow tomb, with the figure of Néfermaat standing on each side of me—as he has stood through all that we know as human history—I have just room for my bed, and a row of good reading in which I can take pleasure after dinner. Behind me is that

Great Peace, the Desert. It is an entity—a power—just as much as the sea is. No wonder men fled to it from the turmoil of the ancient world."

It may now reasonably be asked why one who has similarly, if less dramatically, spent his life among the stones and broken shards of the remote past should be writing here about matters involving literature and science. While I was considering this with humility and trepidation, my eye fell upon a stone in my office. I am sure that professional journalists must recall times when an approaching deadline has keyed all their senses and led them to glance wildly around in the hope that something might leap out at them from the most prosaic surroundings. At all events my eyes fell upon this stone.

Now the stone antedated anything that the historians would call art; it had been shaped many hundreds of thousands of years ago by men whose faces would frighten us if they sat among us today. Out of old habit, since I like the feel of worked flint, I picked it up and hefted it as I groped for words over this difficult matter of the growing rift between science and art. Certainly the stone was of no help to me; it was a utilitarian thing which had cracked marrow bones, if not heads, in the remote dim morning of the human species. It was nothing if not practical. It was, in fact, an extremely early example of the empirical tradition which has led on to modern science.

The mind which had shaped this artifact knew its precise purpose. It had found out by experimental observation that the stone was tougher, sharper, more enduring than the hand which wielded it. The creature's mind had solved the question of the best form of the implement and how it could be manipulated most effectively. In its day and time this hand ax was as grand an intellectual achievement as a rocket.

As a scientist my admiration went out to that unidentified workman. How he must have labored to understand the forces involved in the fracturing of flint, and all that involved practical survival in his world. My uncalloused twentieth-century hand caressed the yellow stone lovingly. It was then that I made a remarkable discovery.

In the mind of this gross-featured early exponent of the practical approach to nature—the technician, the no-nonsense practitioner of survival—two forces had met and merged. There had not been room in his short and desperate life for the delicate and supercilious separation of the arts from the sciences. There did not exist then the refined distinctions set up between the scholarly percipience of reality and what has sometimes been called the vaporings of the artistic imagination.

As I clasped and unclasped the stone, running my fingers down its edges, I began to perceive the ghostly emanations from a long-vanished mind, the kind of mind which, once having shaped an object of any sort, leaves an individual trace behind it which speaks to others across the barriers of time and language. It was not the practical experimental aspect of this mind that startled me, but rather that the fellow had wasted time.

In an incalculably brutish and dangerous world he had both shaped an instrument of practical application and then, with a virtuoso's elegance, proceeded to embellish his product. He had not been content to produce a plain, utilitarian implement. In some wistful, inarticulate way, in the grip of the dim aesthetic feelings which are one of the marks of man—or perhaps I should say, some men—this archaic creature had lingered over his handiwork.

One could still feel him crouching among the stones on a long-vanished river bar, turning the thing over in his hands, feeling its polished surface, striking, here and there, just one more blow that no longer had usefulness as its criterion. He had, like myself, enjoyed the texture of the stone. With skills lost to me, he had gone on flaking the implement with an eye to beauty until it had become a kind of rough jewel, equivalent in its day to the carved and gold-inlaid pommel of the iron dagger placed in Tutankhamen's tomb.

All the later history of man contains these impractical exertions expended upon a great diversity of objects, and, with literacy, breaking even into printed dreams. Today's secular disruption between the creative aspect of art and that of science is a barbarism that would have brought lifted eyebrows in a Cro-Magnon cave. It is a product of high technical specialization, the deliberate blunting of wonder, and the equally deliberate suppression of a phase of our humanity in the name of an authoritarian institution, science, which has taken on, in our time, curious puritanical overtones. Many scientists seem unaware of the historical reasons for this development or the fact that the creative aspect of art is not so remote from that of science as may seem, at first glance, to be the case.

I am not so foolish as to categorize individual scholars or scientists. I am, however, about to remark on the nature of science as an institution. Like all such structures it is apt to reveal certain behavioral rigidities and conformities which increase with age. It is no longer the domain of the amateur, though some of its greatest discoverers could be so defined. It is now a professional body, and with professionalism there tends to emerge a greater emphasis upon a coherent system of regulations. The deviant is more sharply treated, and the young tend to imitate their successful elders. In short, an "Establishment"—a trade union—has appeared.

Similar tendencies can be observed among those of the humanities concerned with the professional analysis and interpretation of the works of the creative artist. Here too, a similar rigidity and exclusiveness make their appearance. It is not that in the case of both the sciences and the humanities standards are out of place. What I am briefly cautioning against is that too frequently they afford an excuse for stifling original thought or constricting much latent creativity within traditional molds.

Such molds are always useful to the mediocre conformist who instinctively castigates and rejects what he cannot imitate. Tradition, the continuity of learning, are, it is true, enormously important to the learned disciplines. What we must realize as scientists is that the particular institution we inhabit has its own irrational accretions and authoritarian dogmas which can be as unpleasant as some of those encountered in sectarian circles—particularly so since they are frequently unconsciously held and surrounded by an impenetrable wall of self-righteousness brought about because science is regarded as totally empiric and open-minded by tradition.

This type of professionalism, as I shall label it in order to distinguish it from what is best in both the sciences and humanities, is characterized by two assumptions: that the accretions of fact are cumulative and lead to progress, whereas the insights of art are, at best, singular, and lead nowhere, or, when introduced into the realm of science, produce obscurity and confusion. The convenient label "mystic" is, in our day, readily applied to men who pause for simple wonder, or who encounter along the borders of the known that "awful power" which Wordsworth characterized as the human imagination. It can, he says, rise suddenly from the mind's abyss and enwrap the solitary traveler like a mist.

We do not like mists in this era, and the word imagination is less and less used. We like, instead, a clear road, and we abhor solitary traveling. Indeed one of our great scientific historians remarked not long ago that the literary naturalist was obsolescent if not completely outmoded. I suppose he meant that with our penetration into the biophysical realm, life, like matter, would become increasingly represented by abstract symbols. To many it must appear that the more we can dissect life into its elements, the closer we are getting to its ultimate resolution. While I have some reservations on this score, they are not important. Rather, I should like to look at the symbols which in the one case denote science and in the other constitute those vaporings and cloud wraiths that are the abomination, so it is said, of the true scientist but are the delight of the poet and literary artist.

Creation in science demands a high level of imaginative insight and intuitive perception. I believe no one would deny this, even though it exists in varying degrees, just as it does, similarly, among writers, musicians, or artists. The scientist's achievement, however, is quantitatively transmissible. From a single point his discovery is verifiable by other men who may then, on the basis of corresponding data, accept the innovation and elaborate upon it in the cumulative fashion which is one of the great triumphs of science.

Artistic creation, on the other hand, is unique. It cannot be twice discovered, as, say, natural selection was discovered. It may be imitated stylistically, in a genre, a school, but, save for a few items of technique, it is not cumulative. A successful work of art may set up reverberations and is, in this, just as transmissible as science, but there is a qualitative character about it. Each reverberation in another mind is unique. As the French novelist François Mauriac has remarked, each great novel is a separate and distinct world operating under its own laws with a flora and fauna totally its own. There is communication, or the work is a failure, but the communication releases our own visions, touches some highly personal chord in our own experience.

The symbols used by the great artist are a key releasing our humanity from the solitary tower of the self. "Man," says Lewis Mumford, "is first and foremost the self-fabricating animal." I shall merely add that the artist plays an enormous role in this act of self-creation. It is he who touches the hidden strings of pity, who searches our hearts, who makes us sensitive to beauty, who asks questions about fate and destiny. Such questions, though they lurk always around the corners of the external universe which is the peculiar province of science, the rigors of the scientific method do not enable us to pursue directly.

And yet I wonder.

It is surely possible to observe that it is the successful analogy or symbol which frequently allows the scientist to leap from a generalization in one field of thought to a triumphant achievement in another. For example, Progressionism in a spiritual sense later became the model contributing to the discovery of organic evolution. Such analogies genuinely resemble the figures and enchantments of great literature, whose meanings similarly can never be totally grasped because of their endless power to ramify in the individual mind.

John Donne gave powerful expression to a feeling applicable as much to science as to literature when he said devoutly of certain Biblical passages: "The literall sense is always to be preserved; but the literall sense is not alwayes to be discerned; for the literall sense is not alwayes that which the very letter and grammar of the place presents." A figurative sense, he argues cogently, can sometimes be the most "literall intention of the Holy Ghost."

It is here that the scientist and artist sometimes meet in uneasy opposition, or at least along lines of tension. The scientist's attitude is sometimes, I suspect, that embodied in Samuel Johnson's remark that, wherever there is mystery, roguery is not far off.

Yet surely it was not roguery when Sir Charles Lyell glimpsed in a few fossil prints of raindrops the persistence of the world's natural forces through the incredible, mysterious aeons of geologic time. The fossils were a symbol of a vast hitherto unglimpsed order. They are, in Donne's sense, both literal and symbolic. As fossils they merely denote evidence of rain in a past era. Figuratively they are more. To the perceptive intelligence they afford the hint of lengthened natural order, just as the eyes of ancient trilobites tell us similarly of the unchanging laws of light. Equally, the educated mind may discern in a scratched pebble the retreating shadow of vast ages of ice and gloom. In Donne's archaic phraseology these objects would bespeak the principal intention of the Divine Being—that is, of order beyond our power to grasp.

Such images drawn from the world of science are every bit as powerful as great literary symbolism and equally demanding upon the individual imagination of the scientist who would fully grasp the extension of meaning which is involved. It is, in fact, one and the same creative act in both domains.

Indeed evolution itself has become such a figurative symbol, as has also the hypothesis of the expanding universe. The laboratory worker may think of these concepts in a totally empirical fashion as subject to proof or disproof by the experimental method. Like Freud's doctrine of the subconscious, however, such ideas frequently escape from the professional scientist into the public domain. There they may undergo further individual transformation and embellishment. Whether the scholar approves or not, such hypotheses are now as free to evolve in the mind of the individual as are the creations of art. All the resulting enrichment and confusion will bear about it something suggestive of the world of artistic endeavor.

As figurative insights into the nature of things, such embracing conceptions may become grotesquely distorted or glow with added philosophical wisdom. As in the case of the trilobite eye or the fossil raindrop, there lurks behind the visible evidence vast shadows no longer quite of that world which we term natural. Like the words in Donne's Bible, enormous implications have transcended the literal expression of the thought. Reality itself has been superseded by a greater reality. As Donne himself asserted, "The substance of the truth is in the great images which lie behind."

It is because these two types of creation—the artistic and the scientific—have sprung from the same being and have their points of contact even in division that I have the temerity to assert that,

275

in a sense, the "two cultures" are an illusion, that they are a product of unreasoning fear, professionalism, and misunderstanding. Because of the emphasis upon science in our society, much has been said about the necessity of educating the layman and even the professional student of the humanities upon the ways and the achievements of science. I admit that a barrier exists, but I am also concerned to express the view that there persists in the domain of science itself an occasional marked intolerance of those of its own membership who venture to pursue the way of letters. As I have remarked, this intolerance can the more successfully clothe itself in seeming objectivity because of the supposed open nature of the scientific society. It is not remarkable that this trait is sometimes more manifest in the younger and less secure disciplines.

There was a time, not too many centuries ago, when to be active in scientific investigation was to invite suspicion. Thus it may be that there now lingers among us, even in the triumph of the experimental method, a kind of vague fear of that other artistic world of deep emotion, of strange symbols, lest it seize upon us or distort the hard-won objectivity of our thinking—lest it corrupt, in other words, that crystalline and icy objectivity which, in our scientific guise, we erect as a model of conduct. This model, incidentally, if pursued to its absurd conclusion, would lead to a world in which the computer would determine all aspects of our existence; one in which the bomb would be as welcome as the discoveries of the physician.

Happily, the very great in science, or even those unique scientist-artists such as Leonardo, who foreran the emergence of science as an institution, have been singularly free from this folly. Darwin decried it even as he recognized that he had paid a certain price in concentrated specialization for his achievement. Einstein, it is well known, retained a simple sense of wonder; Newton felt like a child playing with pretty shells on a beach. All show a deep humility and an emotional hunger which is the prerogative of the artist. It is with the lesser men, with the institutionalization of method, with the appearance of dogma and mapped-out territories, that an unpleasant suggestion of fenced preserves begins to dominate the university atmosphere.

As a scientist, I can say that I have observed it in my own and others' specialties. I have had occasion, also, to observe its effects in the humanities. It is not science *per se;* it is, instead, in both regions of thought, the narrow professionalism which is also plainly evident in the trade union. There can be small men in science just as there are small men in government or business. In fact it is one of the disadvantages of big science, just as it is of big government, that the availability of huge sums attracts a swarm of elbowing and contentious men to whom great dreams are less than protected hunting preserves.

The sociology of science deserves at least equal consideration with the biographies of the great scientists, for powerful and changing forces are at work upon science, the institution, as contrasted with science as a dream and an ideal of the individual. Like other aspects of society, it is a construct of men and is subject, like other social structures, to human pressures and inescapable distortions.

Let me give an illustration. Even in learned journals, clashes occasionally occur between those who would regard biology as a separate and distinct domain of inquiry and the reductionists who, by contrast, perceive in the living organism only a vaster and more random chemistry. Understandably, the concern of the reductionists is with the immediate. Thomas Hobbes was expressing a similar point of view when he castigated poets as "working on mean minds with words and distinctions that of themselves signifie nothing, but betray (by their obscurity) that there walketh . . . another kingdome, as it were a kingdome of fayries in the dark." I myself have been similarly criticized for speaking of a nature "beyond the nature that we know."

Yet consider for a moment this dark, impossible realm of "fayrie." Man is not totally compounded of the nature we profess to understand. He contains, instead, a lurking unknown future, just as the man-apes of the Pliocene contained in embryo the future that surrounds us now. The world of human culture itself was an unpredictable fairy world until, in some pre-ice-age meadow, the first meaningful sounds in all the world broke through the jungle babble of the past, the nature, until that moment, "known."

It is fascinating to observe that, in the very dawn of science, Francis Bacon, the spokesman for the empirical approach to nature, shared with Shakespeare, the poet, a recognition of the creativeness which adds to nature, and which emerges from nature as "an art which nature makes." Neither the great scholar nor the great poet had renounced this "kingdome of fayries." Both had realized what Henri Bergson was later to express so effectively, that life inserts a vast "indetermination into matter." It is, in a sense, an intrusion from a realm which can never be completely subject to prophetic analysis by science. The novelties of evolution emerge; they cannot be predicted. They haunt, until their arrival, a world of unimaginable possibilities behind the living screen of events, as these last exist to the observer confined to a single point on the time scale.

Oddly enough, much of the confusion that surrounded my phrase, "a nature beyond the nature that we know," resolves itself into pure semantics. I might have pointed out what must be obvious even to the most dedicated scientific mind—that the nature which we know has been many times reinterpreted in human thinking, and that the hard, substantial matter of the nineteenth century has already vanished into a dark, bodiless void, a web of "events" in space-time. This is a realm, I venture to assert, as weird as any we have tried, in the past, to exorcise by the brave use of seeming solid words. Yet some minds exhibit an almost instinctive hostility toward the mere attempt to wonder or to ask what lies below that microcosmic world out of which emerge the particles which compose our bodies and which now take on this wraithlike quality.

Is there something here we fear to face, except when clothed in safely sterilized professional speech? Have we grown reluctant in this age of power to admit mystery and beauty into our thoughts, or to learn where power ceases? I referred earlier to one of our own forebears on a gravel bar, thumbing a pebble. If, after the ages of building and destroying, if after the measuring of light-years and the powers probed at the atom's heart, if after the last iron is rust-eaten and the last glass lies shattered in the streets, a man, some savage, some remnant of what once we were, pauses on his way to the tribal drinking place and feels rising from within his soul the inexplicable mist of terror and beauty that is evoked from old ruins—even the ruins of the greatest city in the world—then, I say, all will still be well with man.

# THE ILLUSION OF THE TWO CULTURES

And if that savage can pluck a stone from the gravel because it shone like crystal when the water rushed over it, and hold it against the sunset, he will be as we were in the beginning, whole—as we were when we were children, before we began to split the knowledge from the dream. All talk of the two cultures is an illusion; it is the pebble which tells man's story. Upon it is written man's two faces, the artistic and the practical. They are expressed upon one stone over which a hand once closed, no less firm because the mind behind it was submerged in light and shadow and deep wonder.

Today we hold a stone, the heavy stone of power. We must perceive beyond it, however, by the aid of the artistic imagination, those humane insights and understandings which alone can lighten our burden and enable us to shape ourselves, rather than the stone, into the forms which great art has anticipated.

# How Natural Is "Natural"?

In the more obscure scientific circles which I frequent there is a legend circulating about a late distinguished scientist who, in his declining years, persisted in wearing enormous padded boots much too large for him. He had developed, it seems, what to his fellows was a wholly irrational fear of falling through the interstices of that largely empty molecular space which common men in their folly speak of as the world. A stroll across his living-room floor had become, for him, something as dizzily horrendous as the activities of a window washer on the Empire State Building. Indeed, with equal reason he could have passed a ghostly hand through his own ribs.

The quivering network of his nerves, the awe-inspiring movement of his thought, had become a vague cloud of electrons interspersed with the light-year distances that obtain between us and the farther galaxies. This was the natural world which he had helped to create, and in which, at last, he had found himself a lonely and imprisoned occupant. All around him the ignorant rushed on their way over the illusion of substantial floors, leaping, though they did not see it, from particle to particle, over a bottomless abyss. There was even a question as to the reality of the particles which bore them up. It did not, however, keep insubstantial newspapers from being sold, or insubstantial love from being made.

Not long ago I became aware of another world perhaps equally natural and real, which man is beginning to forget. My thinking began in New England under a boat dock. The lake I speak of has been pre-empted and civilized by man. All day long in the vacation season high-speed motorboats, driven with the reckless abandon common to the young Apollos of our society, speed back and forth, carrying loads of equally attractive girls. The shores echo to the roar of powerful motors and the delighted screams of young Americans with uncounted horsepower surging under their hands. In truth, as I sat there under the boat dock, I had some desire to swim or to canoe in the older ways of the great forest which once lay about this region. Either notion would have been folly. I would have been gaily chopped to ribbons by teen-age youngsters whose eyes were always immutably fixed on the far horizons of space or upon the dials which indicated the speed of their passing. There was another world, I was to discover, along the lake shallows and under the boat dock, where the motors could not come.

As I sat there one sunny morning when the water was peculiarly translucent, I saw a dark shadow moving swiftly over the bottom. It was the first sign of life I had seen in this lake, whose shores seemed to yield little but washed-in beer cans. By and by the gliding shadow ceased to scurry from stone to stone over the bottom. Unexpectedly, it headed almost directly for me. A furry nose with gray whiskers broke the surface. Below the whiskers green water foliage trailed out in an inverted V as long as his body. A muskrat still lived in the lake. He was bringing in his breakfast.

I sat very still in the strips of sunlight under the pier. To my surprise the muskrat came almost to my feet with his little breakfast of greens. He was young, and it rapidly became obvious to me that he was laboring under an illusion of his own, and that he thought animals and men were still living in the Garden of Eden. He gave me a friendly glance from time to time as he nibbled his greens. Once, even, he went out into the lake again and returned to my feet with more greens. He had not, it seemed, heard very much about men. I shuddered. Only the evening before I had heard a man describe with triumphant enthusiasm how he had killed a rat in the garden because the creature had dared to nibble his petunias. He had even showed me the murder weapon, a sharp-edged brick.

On this pleasant shore a war existed and would go on until nothing remained but man. Yet this creature with the gray, appealing face wanted very little: a strip of shore to coast up and down, sunlight and moonlight, some weeds from the deep water. He was an edge-of-the-world dweller, caught between a vanishing forest and a deep lake pre-empted by unpredictable machines full of chopping blades. He eyed me near-sightedly, a green leaf poised in his mouth. Plainly he had come with some poorly instructed memory about the lion and the lamb.

"You had better run away now," I said softly, making no movement in the shafts of light. "You are in the wrong universe and must not make this mistake again. I am really a very terrible and cunning beast. I can throw stones." With this I dropped a little pebble at his feet.

He looked at me half blindly, with eyes much better adjusted to the wavering shadows of his lake bottom than to sight in the open air. He made almost as if to take the pebble up into his forepaws. Then a thought seemed to cross his mind—a thought perhaps tele-pathically received, as Freud once hinted, in the dark world below and before man, a whisper of ancient disaster heard in the depths of a burrow. Perhaps after all this was not Eden. His nose twitched carefully; he edged toward the water.

As he vanished in an oncoming wave, there went with him a natural world, distinct from the world of girls and motorboats, distinct from the world of the professor holding to reality by some great snowshoe effort in his study. My muskrat's shoreline universe was edged with the dark wall of hills on one side and the waspish drone of motors farther out, but it was a world of sunlight he had taken down into the water weeds. It hovered there, waiting for my disappearance. I walked away, obscurely pleased that darkness had not gained on life by any act of mine. In so many worlds, I thought, how natural is "natural"—and is there anything we can call a natural world at all?

## II

Nature, contended John Donne in the seventeenth century, is the common law by which God governs us. Donne was already aware of

the new science and impressed by glimpses of those vast abstractions
which man was beginning to build across the gulfs of his ignorance.
Donne makes, however, a reservation which rings strangely in the
modern ear. If nature is the common law, he said, then Miracle is
God's Prerogative.

By the nineteenth century, this spider web of common law had
been flung across the deeps of space and time. "In astronomy,"
meditated Emerson, "vast distance, but we never go into a foreign
system. In geology, vast duration, but we are never strangers. Our
metaphysic should be able to follow the flying force through all its
transformations."

Now admittedly there is a way in which all these worlds are real
and sufficiently natural. We can say, if we like, that the muskrat's
world is naïve and limited, a fraction, a bare fraction, of the world
of life: a view from a little pile of wet stones on a nameless shore.
The view of the motor speedsters in essence is similar and no less
naïve. All would give way to the priority of that desperate professor,
striving like a tired swimmer to hold himself aloft against the soft
and fluid nothingness beneath his feet. In terms of the modern
temper, the physicist has penetrated the deepest into life. He has
come to that place of whirling sparks which are themselves phan-
toms. He is close upon the void where science ends and the manifes-
tation of God's Prerogative begins. "He can be no creature," argued
Donne, "who is present at the first creation."

Yet there is a way in which the intelligence of man in this era of
science and the machine can be viewed as having taken the wrong
turning. There is a dislocation of our vision which is, perhaps, the
product of the kind of creatures we are, or at least conceive ourselves
to be. Man, as a two-handed manipulator of the world about him,
has projected himself outward upon his surroundings in a way impos-
sible to other creatures. He has done this since the first half-human
man-ape hefted a stone in his hand. He has always sought mastery
over the materials of his environment, and in our day he has pierced
so deeply through the screen of appearances that the age-old distinc-
tions between matter and energy have been dimmed to the point of
disappearance. The creations of his clever intellect ride in the skies
and the sea's depths; he has hurled a great fragment of metal at the

283

moon, which he once feared. He holds the heat of suns within his hands and threatens with it both the lives and the happiness of his unborn descendants.

Man, in the words of one astute biologist, is "caught in a physiological trap and faced with the problem of escaping from his own ingenuity." Pascal, with intuitive sensitivity, saw this at the very dawn of the modern era in science. "There is nothing which we cannot make natural," he wrote, and then, prophetically, comes the full weight of his judgment upon man: "there is nothing natural which we do not destroy." *Homo faber*, the toolmaker, is not enough. There must be another road and another kind of man lurking in the mind of this odd creature, but whether the attraction of that path is as strong as the age-old primate addiction to taking things apart remains to be seen.

We who are engaged in the life of thought are likely to assume that the key to an understanding of the world is knowledge, both of the past and of the future—that if we had that knowledge we would also have wisdom. It is not my intention here to decry learning, but only to say that we must come to understand that learning is endless and that nowhere does it lead us behind the existent world. It may reduce the prejudices of ignorance, set our bones, build our cities. In itself it will never make us ethical men. Yet because ours, we conceive, is an age of progress, and because we know more about time and history than any men before us, we fallaciously equate ethical advance with scientific progress in a point-to-point relationship. Thus as society improves physically, we assume the improvement of the individual and are all the more horrified at those mass movements of terror which have so typified the first half of the twentieth century.

On the morning of which I want to speak, I was surfeited with the smell of mortality and tired of the years I had spent in archaeological dustbins. I rode out of a camp and across a mountain. I would never have believed, before it happened, that one could ride into the past on horseback. It is true I rode with a purpose, but that purpose was to settle an argument within myself.

It was time, I thought, to face up to what was in my mind—to the dust and the broken teeth and the spilled chemicals of life seeping away into the sand. It was time I admitted that life was of the earth, earthy, and could be turned into a piece of wretched tar. It was time I consented to the proposition that man had as little to do with his fate as a seed blown against a grating. It was time I looked upon the world without spectacles and saw love and pride and beauty dissolve into effervescing juices. I could be an empiricist with the best of them. I would be deceived by no more music. I had entered a black cloud of merciless thought, but the horse, as it chanced, worked his own way over that mountain.

I could hear the sudden ring of his hooves as we came cautiously treading over a tilted table of granite, past the winds that blow on the high places of the world. There were stones there so polished that they shone from the long ages that the storms had rushed across them. We crossed the divide then, picking our way in places scoured by ancient ice action, through boulder fields where nothing moved, and yet where one could feel time like an enemy hidden behind each stone.

If there was life on those heights, it was the thin life of mountain spiders who caught nothing in their webs, or of small gray birds that slipped soundlessly among the stones. The wind in the pass caught me head on and blew whatever thoughts I had into a raveling stream behind me, until they were all gone and there was only myself and the horse, moving in an eternal dangerous present, free of the encumbrances of the past.

We crossed a wind that smelled of ice from still higher snowfields, we cantered with a breeze that came from somewhere among cedars, we passed a gust like Hell's breath that had risen straight up from the desert floor. They were winds and they did not stay with us. Presently we descended out of their domain, and it was curious to see, as we dropped farther through gloomy woods and canyons, how the cleansed and scoured mind I had brought over the mountain began, like the water in those rumbling gorges, to talk in a variety of voices, to debate, to argue, to push at stones or curve subtly around obstacles. Sometimes I wonder whether we are only endlessly repeating in our heads an argument that is going on in the world's foundations among crashing stones and recalcitrant roots.

"Fall, fall, fall," cried the roaring water and the grinding pebbles in the torrent. "Let go, come with us, come home to the place without light." But the roots clung and climbed and the trees pushed up, impeding the water, and forests filled even the wind with their sighing and grasped after the sun. It is so in the mind. One can hear the rattle of falling stones in the night, and the thoughts like trees holding their place. Sometimes one can shut the noise away by turning over on the other ear, sometimes the sounds are as dreadful as a storm in the mountains, and one lies awake, holding, like the roots that wait for daylight. It was after such a night that I came over the mountain, but it was the descent on the other side that suddenly struck me as a journey into the aeons of the past.

I came down across stones dotted with pink and gray lichens— a barren land dreaming life's last dreams in the thin air of a cold and future world.

I passed a meadow and a meadow mouse in a little shower of petals struck from mountain flowers. I dismissed it—it was almost my own time—a pleasant golden hour in the age of mammals, lost before the human coming. I rode heavily toward an old age far backward in the reptilian dark.

I was below timber line and sinking deeper and deeper into the pine woods, whose fallen needles lay thick and springy over the ungrassed slopes. The brown needles and the fallen cones, the stiff, endless green forests, were a mark that placed me in the Age of Dinosaurs. I moved in silence now, waiting a sign. I saw it finally, a green lizard on a stone. We were far back, far back. He bobbed his head uncertainly at me, and I reined in with the nostalgic intent, for a moment, to call him father, but I saw soon enough that I was a ghost who troubled him and that he would wish me, though he had not the voice to speak, to ride on. A man who comes down the road of time should not expect to converse—even with his own kin. I made a brief, uncertain sign of recognition, to which he did not respond, and passed by. Things grew more lonely. I was coming out upon the barren ridges of an old sea beach that rose along the desert floor. Life was small and grubby now. The hot, warning scarlet of peculiar desert ants occasionally flashed among the stones. I had lost all trace of myself and thought regretfully of the lizard who might have directed me.

A turned-up stone yielded only a scorpion who curled his tail in a kind of evil malice. I surveyed him reproachfully. He was old enough to know the secret of my origin, but once more an ancient, bitter animus drawn from that poisoned soil possessed him and he raised his tail. I turned away. An enormous emptiness by degrees possessed me. I was back almost, in a different way, to the thin air over the mountain, to the end of all things in the cold starlight of space.

I passed some indefinable bones and shells in the salt-crusted wall of a dry arroyo. As I reined up, only sand dunes rose like waves before me and if life was there it was no longer visible. It was like coming down to the end—to the place of fires where we began. I turned about then and let my gaze go up, tier after tier, height after height, from crawling desert bush to towering pine on the great slopes far above me.

In the same way animal life had gone up that road from these dry, envenomed things to the deer nuzzling a fawn in the meadows far above. I had come down the whole way into a place where one could lift sand and ask in a hollow, dust-shrouded whisper, "Life, what is it? Why am I here? Why am I here?"

And my mind went up that figurative ladder of the ages, bone by bone, skull by skull, seeking an answer. There was none, except that in all that downrush of wild energy that I had passed in the canyons there was this other strange organized stream that marched upward, gaining a foothold here, tossing there a pine cone a little farther upward into a crevice in the rock.

And again one asked, not of the past this time, but of the future, there where the winds howled through open space and the last lichens clung to the naked rock, "Why did we live?" There was no answer I could hear. The living river flowed out of nowhere into nothing. No one knew its source or its departing. It was an apparition. If one did not see it there was no way to prove that it was real.

No way, that is, except within the mind itself. And the mind, in some strange manner so involved with time, moving against the cutting edge of it like the wind I had faced on the mountain, has yet its own small skull-borne image of eternity. It is not alone that I can reach out and receive within my head a handsbreadth replica of the far fields of the universe. It is not because I can touch a trilobite and know the fall of light in ages before my birth. Rather, it lies in the fact that the human mind can transcend time, even though trapped, to all appearances, within that medium. As from some remote place, I see myself as child and young man, watch with a certain dispassionate objectivity the violence and tears of a remote youth who was once I, shaping his character, for good or ill, toward the creature he is today. Shrinking, I see him teeter at the edge of abysses he never saw. With pain I acknowledge acts undone that might have saved and led him into some serene and noble pathway. I move about him like a ghost, that vanished youth. I exhort, I plead. He does not hear me. Indeed, he too is already a ghost. He has become me. I am what I am. Yet the point is, we are not wholly given over to time—if we were, such acts, such leaps through that gray medium, would be impossible. Perhaps God himself may rove in similar pain up the dark roads of his universe. Only how would it be, I wonder, to contain at once both the beginning and the end, and to hear, in helplessness perhaps, the fall of worlds in the night?

This is what the mind of man is just beginning to achieve—a little microcosm, a replica of whatever it is that, from some unimaginable "outside," contains the universe and all the fractured bits of seeing which the world's creatures see. It is not necessary to ride over a mountain range to experience historical infinity. It can descend upon one in the lecture room.

I find it is really in daylight that the sensation I am about to describe is apt to come most clearly upon me, and for some reason I associate it extensively with crowds. It is not, you understand, an hallucination. It is a reality. It is, I can only say with difficulty, a chink torn in a dimension life was never intended to look through. It connotes a sense beyond the eye, though the twenty years' impressions are visual. Man, it is said, is a time-binding animal, but he was never intended for this. Here is the way it comes.

I mount the lecturer's rostrum to address a class. Like any work-worn professor fond of his subject, I fumble among my skulls and papers, shuffle to the blackboard and back again, begin the patient translation of three billion years of time into chalk scrawls and uncertain words ventured timidly to a sea of young, impatient faces. Time does not frighten them, I think enviously. They have, most of them, never lain awake and grasped the sides of a cot, staring upward into the dark while the slow clock strokes begin.

"Doctor." A voice diverts me. I stare out nearsightedly over the class. A hand from the back row gesticulates. "Doctor, do you believe there is a direction to evolution? Do you believe, Doctor . . . Doctor, do you believe? . . ." Instead of the words, I hear a faint piping, and see an eager scholar's face squeezed and dissolving on the body of a chest-thumping ape. "Doctor, is there a direction?"

I see it then—the trunk that stretches monstrously behind him. It winds out of the door, down dark and obscure corridors to the cellar, and vanishes into the floor. It writhes, it crawls, it barks and snuffles and roars, and the odor of the swamp exhales from it. That pale young scholar's face is the last bloom on a curious animal extrusion through time. And who among us, under the cold persuasion of the archaeological eye, can perceive which of his many shapes is real, or if, perhaps, the entire shape in time is not a greater and more curious animal than its single appearance?

I too am aware of the trunk that stretches loathsomely back of me along the floor. I too am a many-visaged thing that has climbed upward out of the dark of endless leaf falls, and has slunk, furred, through the glitter of blue glacial nights. I, the professor, trembling absurdly on the platform with my book and spectacles, am the single philosophical animal. I am the unfolding worm, and mud fish, the weird tree of Igdrasil shaping itself endlessly out of darkness toward the light.

I have said this is not an illusion. It is when one sees in this manner, or a sense of strangeness halts one on a busy street to verify the appearance of one's fellows, that one knows a terrible new sense has opened a faint crack into the Absolute. It is in this way alone that one comes to grips with a great mystery, that life and time bear some curious relationship to each other that is not shared by inanimate things.

It is in the brain that this world opens. To our descendants it may become a commonplace, but me, and others like me, it has made a castaway. I have no refuge in time, as others do who troop homeward at nightfall. As a result, I am one of those who linger furtively over coffee in the kitchen at bedtime or haunt the all-night restaurants. Nevertheless, I shall say without regret: there are hazards in all professions.

## III

It may seem at this point that I have gone considerably round about in my examination of the natural world. I have done so in the attempt to indicate that the spider web of law which has been flung, as Emerson indicated, across the deeps of time and space and between each member of the living world has brought us some quite remarkable, but at the same time disquieting, knowledge. In rapid summary, man has passed from a natural world of appearances invisibly controlled by the caprice of spirits to an astronomical universe visualized by Newton, through the law of gravitation, as operating with the regularity of a clock.

Newton, who remained devout, assumed that God, at the time of the creation of the solar system, had set everything to operating in its proper orbit. He recognized, however, certain irregularities of planetary movement which, in time, would lead to a disruption of his perfect astronomical machine. It was here, as a seventeenth-century scholar, that he felt no objection to the notion that God interfered at periodic intervals to correct the deviations of the machine.

A century later Laplace had succeeded in dispensing with this last vestige of divine intervention. Hutton had similarly dealt with supernaturalism in earth-building, and Darwin, in the nineteenth century, had gone far toward producing a similar mechanistic explanation of life. The machine that began in the heavens had finally been installed in the human heart and brain. "We can make everything natural," Pascal had truly said, and surely the more naïve forms of worship of the unseen are vanishing.

Yet strangely, with the discovery of evolutionary, as opposed to purely durational, time, there emerges into this safe-and-sane mechanical universe something quite unanticipated by the eighteenth-century rationalists—a kind of emergent, if not miraculous, novelty.

I know that the word "miraculous" is regarded dubiously in scientific circles because of past quarrels with theologians. The word has been defined, however, as an event transcending the known laws of nature. Since, as we have seen, the laws of nature have a way of being altered from one generation of scientists to the next, a little taste for the miraculous in this broad sense will do us no harm. We forget that nature itself is one vast miracle transcending the reality of night and nothingness. We forget that each one of us in his personal life repeats that miracle.

Whatever may be the power behind those dancing motes to which the physicist has penetrated, it makes the light of the musk-rat's world as it makes the world of the great poet. It makes, in fact, all of the innumerable and private worlds which exist in the heads of men. There is a sense in which we can say that the planet, with its strange freight of life, is always just passing from the unnatural to the natural, from that Unseen which man has always reverenced to the small reality of the day. If all life were to be swept from the world, leaving only its chemical constituents, no visitor from another star would be able to establish the reality of such a phantom. The dust would lie without visible protest, as it does now in the moon's airless craters, or in the road before our door.

Yet this is the same dust which, dead, quiescent, and unmoving, when taken up in the process known as life, hears music and responds to it, weeps bitterly over time and loss, or is oppressed by the looming future that is, on any materialist terms, the veriest shadow of nothing. How natural was man, we may ask, until he came? What forces dictated that a walking ape should watch the red shift of light beyond the island universes or listen by carefully devised antennae to the pulse of unseen stars? Who, whimsically, conceived that the plot of the world should begin in a mud puddle and end—where, and with whom? Men argue learnedly over whether life is chemical chance or antichance, but they seem to forget that the life *in* chemicals may be the greatest chance of all, the most mysterious and unexplainable property in matter.

"The special value of science," a perceptive philosopher once wrote, "lies not in what it makes of the world, but in what it makes of the knower." Some years ago, while camping in a vast eroded area in the West, I came upon one of those unlikely sights which illuminate such truths.

I suppose that nothing living had moved among those great stones for centuries. They lay toppled against each other like fallen dolmens. The huge stones were beasts, I used to think, of a kind that man ordinarily lived too fast to understand. They seemed inanimate because the tempo of the life in them was slow. They lived ages in one place and moved only when man was not looking. Sometimes at night I would hear a low rumble as one drew itself into a new position and subsided again. Sometimes I found their tracks ground deeply into the hillsides.

It was with considerable surprise that while traversing this barren valley I came, one afternoon, upon what I can only describe as a very remarkable sight. Some distance away, so far that for a little space I could make nothing of the spectacle, my eyes were attracted by a dun-colored object about the size of a football, which periodically bounded up from the desert floor. Wonderingly, I drew closer and observed that something ropelike which glittered in the sun appeared to be dangling from the ball-shaped object. Whatever the object was, it appeared to be bouncing faster and more desperately as I approached. My surroundings were such that this hysterical dance of what at first glance appeared to be a common stone was quite unnerving, as though suddenly all the natural objects in the valley were about to break into a jig. Going closer, I penetrated the mystery.

The sun was sparkling on the scales of a huge blacksnake which was partially looped about the body of a hen pheasant. Desperately the bird tried to rise, and just as desperately the big snake coiled and clung, though each time the bird, falling several feet, was pounding the snake's body in the gravel. I gazed at the scene in astonishment. Here in this silent waste, like an emanation from nowhere, two bitter and desperate vapors, two little whirlwinds of contending energy, were beating each other to death because their plans—something, I suspected, about whether a clutch of eggs was to turn into a thing with wings or scales—this problem, I say, of the onrushing nonexistent future, had catapulted serpent against bird.

The bird was too big for the snake to have had it in mind as prey. Most probably, he had been intent on stealing the pheasant's eggs and had been set upon and pecked. Somehow in the ensuing scuffle he had flung a loop over the bird's back and partially blocked her wings. She could not take off, and the snake would not let go. The snake was taking a heavy battering among the stones, but the high-speed metabolism and tremendous flight exertion of the mother bird were rapidly exhausting her. I stood a moment and saw the blood-shot glaze deepen in her eyes. I suppose I could have waited there to see what would happen when she could not fly; I suppose it might have been worth scientifically recording. But I could not stand that ceaseless, bloody pounding in the gravel. I thought of the eggs somewhere about, and whether they were to elongate and writhe into an armor of scales or eventually to go whistling into the wind with their wild mother.

So I, the mammal, in my way supple, and less bound by instinct, arbitrated the matter. I unwound the serpent from the bird and let him hiss and wrap his battered coils around my arm. The bird, her wings flung out, rocked on her legs and gasped repeatedly. I moved away in order not to drive her farther from her nest. Thus the serpent and I, two terrible and feared beings, passed quickly out of view.

Over the next ridge, where he could do no more damage, I let the snake, whose anger had subsided, slowly uncoil and slither from my arm. He flowed away into a little patch of bunch grass—aloof, forgetting, unaware of the journey he had made upon my wrist, which throbbed from his expert constriction. The bird had con-tended for birds against the oncoming future; the serpent writhing into the bunch grass had contended just as desperately for serpents. And I, the apparition in that valley—for what had I contended?— I who contained the serpent and the bird and who read the past long written in their bodies.

Slowly, as I sauntered dwarfed among overhanging pinnacles, as the great slabs which were the visible remnants of past ages laid their enormous shadows rhythmically as life and death across my face, the answer came to me. Man could contain more than himself. Among these many appearances that flew, or swam in the waters, or wavered momentarily into being, man alone possessed that unique ability.

The Renaissance thinkers were right when they said that man, the Microcosm, contains the Macrocosm. I had touched the lives of creatures other than myself and had seen their shapes waver and blow like smoke through the corridors of time. I had watched, with sudden concentrated attention, myself, this brain, unrolling from the seed like a genie from a bottle, and casting my eyes forward, I had seen it vanish again into the formless alchemies of the earth.

For what then had I contended, weighing the serpent with the bird in that wild valley? I had struggled, I am now convinced, for a greater, more comprehensive version of myself.

## IV

I am a man who has spent a great deal of his life on his knees, though not in prayer. I do not say this last pridefully, but with the feeling that the posture, if not the thought behind it, may have had some final salutary effect. I am a naturalist and a fossil hunter, and I have crawled most of the way through life. I have crawled downward into holes without a bottom, and upward, wedged into crevices where the wind and the birds scream at you until the sound of a falling pebble is enough to make the sick heart lurch. In man, I know now, there is no such thing as wisdom. I have learned this with my face against the ground. It is a very difficult thing for a man to grasp today, because of his power; yet in his brain there is really only a sort of universal marsh, spotted at intervals by quaking green islands representing the elusive stability of modern science—islands frequently gone as soon as glimpsed.

It is our custom to deny this; we are men of precision, measurement and logic; we abhor the unexplainable and reject it. This, too, is a green island. We wish our lives to be one continuous growth in knowledge; indeed, we expect them to be. Yet well over a hundred years ago Kierkegaard observed that maturity consists in the discovery that "there comes a critical moment where everything is reversed, after which the point becomes to understand more and more that there is something which cannot be understood."

When I separated the serpent from the bird and released them in that wild upland, it was not for knowledge; not for anything I had learned in science. Instead, I contained, to put it simply, the serpent and the bird. I would always contain them. I was no longer one of the contending vapors; I had embraced them in my own substance and, in some insubstantial way, reconciled them, as I had sought reconciliation with the muskrat on the shore. I had transcended feather and scale and gone beyond them into another sphere of reality. I was trying to give birth to a different self whose only expression lies again in the deeply religious words of Pascal, "You would not seek me had you not found me."

I had not known what I sought, but I was aware at last that something had found me. I no longer believed that nature was either natural or unnatural, only that nature now appears natural to man. But the nature that appears natural to man is another version of the muskrat's world under the boat dock, or the elusive sparks over which the physicist made his trembling passage. They were appearances, specialized insights, but unreal because in the constantly onrushing future they were swept away.

What had become of the natural world of that gorilla-headed little ape from which we sprang—that dim African corner with its chewed fish bones and giant Ice Age pigs? It was gone more utterly than my muskrat's tiny domain, yet it had given birth to an unimaginable thing—ourselves—something overreaching the observable laws of that far epoch. Man since the beginning seems to be awaiting an event the nature of which he does not know. "With reference to the near past," Thoreau once shrewdly commented, "we all occupy the region of common sense, but in the prospect of the future we are, by instinct, transcendentalists." This is the way of the man who makes nature "natural." He stands at the point where the miraculous comes into being, and after the event he calls it "natural." The imagination of man, in its highest manifestations, stands close to the doorway of the infinite, to the world beyond the nature that we know. Perhaps, after all, in this respect man constitutes the exertion of that act which Donne three centuries ago called God's Prerogative.

Man's quest for certainty is, in the last analysis, a quest for meaning. But the meaning lies buried within himself rather than in the void he has vainly searched for portents since antiquity. Perhaps the first act in its unfolding was taken by a raw beast with a fearsome head who dreamed some difficult and unimaginable thing denied his fellows. Perhaps the flashes of beauty and insight which trouble us so deeply are no less prophetic of what the race might achieve. All that prevents us is doubt—the power to make everything natural without the accompanying gift to see, beyond the natural, to that inexpressible realm in which the words "natural" and "supernatural" cease to have meaning.

Man, at last, is face to face with himself in natural guise. "What we make natural, we destroy," said Pascal. He knew, with superlative insight, man's complete necessity to transcend the worldly image that this word connotes. It is not the outward powers of man the toolmaker that threaten us. It is a growing danger which has already afflicted vast areas of the world—the danger that we have created an unbearable last idol for our worship. That idol, that uncreate and ruined visage which confronts us daily, is no less than man made natural. Beyond this replica of ourselves, this countenance already grown so distantly inhuman that it terrifies us, still beckons the lonely figure of man's dreams. It is a nature, not of this age, but of the becoming—the light once glimpsed by a creature just over the threshold from a beast, a despairing cry from the dark shadow of a cross on Golgotha long ago.

Man is not totally compounded of the nature we profess to understand. Man is always partly of the future, and the future he possesses a power to shape. "Natural" is a magician's word—and like all such entities, it should be used sparingly lest there arise from it, as now, some unglimpsed, unintended world, some monstrous caricature called into being by the indiscreet articulation of worn syllables. Perhaps, if we are wise, we will prefer to stand like those forgotten humble creatures who poured little gifts of flints into a grave. Perhaps there may come to us then, in some such moment, a ghostly sense that an invisible doorway has been opened—a doorway which, widening out, will take man beyond the nature that he knows.

# The Inner Galaxy

There is strong archaeological evidence to show that with the birth of human consciousness there was born, like a twin, the impulse to transcend it.

—Alan McGlashan

## I

Many years ago, I, with another youth of my own age whom I had persuaded to make the journey with me, walked throughout the day up a great mountain. There was a famous astronomical observatory upon the mountain. On certain nights, according to the guidebooks, the lay public might come to the observatory and look upon some remote planetary object. They could also hear a lecture.

The youth and I, who had much eager interest but no money, were unable to join one of the numerous tours organized from the tourist hotels in the valley. Instead, we had trudged for many hours in order to arrive before the crowds of visitors might frustrate our hopes for a glimpse of those far worlds about which we had read so avidly.

This was long ago, and we were naïve young men. We thought that, though we were poor, we would be welcome upon the mountain because of our desire to learn. There were reputed to dwell in the observatory men of wisdom who we hoped would receive us kindly since we, too, wished to gaze upon the wonders of outer space. We were, indeed, very unskilled in the ways of the adult world. As it turned out, we were never permitted to see the men of wisdom, or to gaze through the magic glass into outer space. I rather suspect that the eminent astronomers had not taken youths like us into their calculations. There was, it seemed, a relationship we had never suspected between the hotels in the valley and the men who inhabited the observatory upon the mountain.

Although by laborious effort we had succeeded in arriving before the busloads of tourists from the hotels, we were thrust forth and told to take our chances after the tourists had been accommodated. As busload after busload of people roared up before the observatory, we saw that this was an indirect dismissal. It would be dawn before our turn came, if, indeed, they chose to accept us at all.

The guard eyed us and our clothes with sullen distaste. Though it was freezing cold upon the mountain, it was plain we were not welcome in the inn that catered to the tourists. Reluctantly, with a few coins from our little store of change we purchased a bit of chocolate. We looked at each other. Wearily and without a word, we turned and began our long descent through the dark. It would take many hours; nor were we sustained by having seen the shining planet upon which our hopes were fixed.

This was my first experience of the commercial side of outer space, and though I now serve upon a committee that encourages the young in a direction once denied me, I feel that this youthful experience contributed to a certain growing introspection and curiosity about the relationship of science to the world about it.

Something was seriously wrong upon that mountain and among the wise men who flourished there. Knowledge, I had learned in the bleak wind by the shut door, was not free, and many to whom that observatory was only a passing curiosity had easier access to it than we who had climbed painfully for many hours. My memory is from the far days of the 1920s, and I realize that we now beckon enticingly to the youth interested in space where before we ignored him. I still have an uncomfortable feeling, however, that it is the circumstances, and not the actors, which have changed. I remain oppressed by the thought that the venture into space is meaningless unless it coincides with a certain interior expansion, an ever-growing universe within, to correspond with the far flight of the galaxies our telescopes follow from without.

Upon that desolate peak my mind had turned finally inward. It is from that domain, that inner sky, that I choose to speak—a world of dreams, of light and darkness that we will never escape, even on the far edge of Arcturus. The inward skies of man will accompany him across any void upon which he ventures and will be with him to the end of time. There is just one way in which that inward world differs from outer space. It can be more volatile and mobile, more terrible and impoverished, yet withal more ennobling in its self-consciousness, than the universe that gave it birth. To the educators of this revolutionary generation, the transformations we may induce in that inner sky loom in at least equal importance with the work of those whose goals are set beyond the orbit of the moon.

No one needs to be told that different and private worlds exist in the heads of men. But in a day when some men are listening by radio telescope to the rustling of events at the ends of the universe, the universe of others consists of hopeless poverty amidst the filthy garbage of a city lot. A taxi man I know thinks that the stars are just "up there" and as soon as our vehicles are perfected we can all take off like crowds of summer tourists to Cape Cod. This man expects, and I fear has been encouraged to expect, that such flights will solve the population problem. Again, while I was sitting one night with a poet friend watching a great opera performed in a tent under arc lights, the poet took my arm and pointed silently. Far up, blundering out of the night, a huge Cecropia moth swept past from light to light over the posturings of the actors.

"He doesn't know," my friend whispered excitedly. "He's passing through an alien universe brightly lit but invisible to him. He's in another play; he doesn't see us. He doesn't know. Maybe it's happening right now to us. Where are we? Whose is the *real* play?"

Between the universe of the moth and the poet, I sat confounded. My mind went back to the heads of alabaster that the kings of the old Egyptian empire sought to endow with eternal life, replacing thus against accident their own frail and perishable brains for the passage through eternity. The pharaohs, like the moth among the arc lights, had been entranced by the flaming journey of the sun. Some had even constructed, hopefully, their own solar boats. Perhaps, I thought, those boats symbolized the frail vessel of which Plato was later to speak—that vessel on which to risk the voyage of life, or, rather, eternity, which was inevitably man's compulsive interest. As for me, I had come to seek wisdom no longer upon the improvised rafts of proud philosophies. I had seen the moth burn in its passage through the light. I had seen all the vessels fail but one —that word which Plato sought, and which none could long identify or hold.

There *was* a real play, but it was a play in which man was destined always to be a searcher, and it would be his true nature he would seek. The fragile vessel was himself, and not among the stars upon the mountain. Was not that what Plotinus had implied? Then if a man were to write further, I considered, he would write of that— of the last things.

## II

Several years ago, a man in a small California town suffered an odd accident. The accident itself was commonplace. But the psychological episode accompanying it seems so strange that I recount it here. I had been long engaged upon a book I was eager to finish. As I walked, abstracted and alone, toward my office one late afternoon, I caught the toe of my shoe in an ill-placed drain. Some trick of mechanics brought me down over the curb with extraordinary violence. A tremendous crack echoed in my ears. When I next opened my eyes I was lying face down on the sidewalk. My nose was smashed over on one side. Blood from a gash on my forehead was cascading over my face.

Reluctantly I explored further, running my tongue cautiously about my mouth and over my teeth. Under my face a steady rivulet of blood was enlarging to a bright red pool on the sidewalk. It was then, as I peered nearsightedly at my ebbing substance there in the brilliant sunshine, that a surprising thing happened. Confusedly, painfully, indifferent to running feet and the anxious cries of witnesses about me, I lifted a wet hand out of this welter and murmured in compassionate concern, "Oh, don't go. I'm sorry, I've done for you."

The words were not addressed to the crowd gathering about me. They were inside and spoken to no one but a part of myself. I was quite sane, only it was an oddly detached sanity, for I was addressing blood cells, phagocytes, platelets, all the crawling, living, indepen-

dent wonders that had been part of me and now, through my folly
and lack of care, were dying like beached fish on the hot pavement.
A great wave of passionate contrition, even of adoration, swept
through my mind, a sensation of love on a cosmic scale, for mark
that this experience was, in its way, as vast a catastrophe as would
be that of a galaxy consciously suffering through the loss of its solar
systems.

I was made up of millions of these tiny creatures, their toil, their
sacrifices, as they hurried to seal and repair the rent fabric of this
vast being whom they had unknowingly, but in love, compounded.
And I, for the first time in my mortal existence, did not see these
creatures as odd objects under the microscope. Instead, an echo of
the force that moved them came up from the deep well of my being
and flooded through the shaken circuits of my brain. I was their
galaxy, their creation. For the first time, I loved them consciously,
even as I was plucked up and away by willing hands. It seemed to
me then, and does now in retrospect, that I had caused to the
universe I inhabited as many deaths as the explosion of a supernova
in the cosmos.

Weeks later, recovering, I paid a visit to the place of the accident.
A faint discoloration still marked the sidewalk. I hovered over the
spot, obscurely troubled. They were gone, utterly destroyed—those
tiny beings—but the entity of which they had made a portion still
persisted. I shook my head, conscious of the brooding mystery that
the poet Dante impelled into his great line: "the love that moves the
sun and other stars."

The phrase does not come handily to our lips today. For a century
we have chosen to talk continuously about the struggle for existence,
about man the brawling half-ape and bestial fighter. We have ex-
plored with wavering candles the dark cellars of our subconscious
and been appalled by the faces we have encountered there. It will
do no harm, therefore, if we choose to examine the history of that
great impulse—love, compassion, call it what one will—which, how-
ever discounted in our time, moved the dying Christ on Golgotha
with a power that has reached across two thousand weary years.

"The conviction of wisdom," wrote Montaigne in the sixteenth
century, "is the plague of man." Century after century, humanity

studies itself in the mirror of fashion, and ever the mirror gives back distortions, which for the moment impose themselves upon man's real image. In one period we believe ourselves governed by immutable laws; in the next, by chance. In one period angels hover over our birth; in the following time we are planetary waifs, the product of a meaningless and ever-altering chemistry. We exchange halos in one era for fangs in another. Our religious and philosophical conceptions change so rapidly that the theological and moral exhortations of one decade become the wastepaper of the next epoch. The ideas for which millions yielded up their lives produce only bored yawns in a later generation.

"We are, I know not how," Montaigne continued, "double in ourselves, so that what we believe we disbelieve, and cannot rid ourselves of what we condemn."

This complex, many-faceted, self-conscious creature now examines himself in the mirror held up to him by the modern students of prehistory. Increasingly he asks of the bony fragments recovered from pre-ice-age strata, not whether they are related to himself, but what manner of creature they proclaim us to be. Of the answer that may come up from underground we are all too evidently afraid. There are even those who have dared prematurely to announce the verdict. "Look," they say, "at the dark instincts that drive you. Look deep into your bloody, fossil, encrusted hearts. Then you will know man. You will know him from the caves to the Berlin wall. Thus he is and thus he will remain. It is written in his bones."

Yet the moment the words are said and documented, either the data are seized upon to give ourselves a fearsome picture to delight and excuse the black side of our natures or, strangely, even beautifully, the picture begins to waver and to change. St. Francis of the birds broods by the waters; Gilbert White of Selborne putters harmlessly with the old pet tortoise in his garden. Ishi, the primitive gentle philosopher, steps real as life from the Sierra forest—the idyllic man denounced as an invention of Rousseau's, yet the product of a world more primitive than black Africa today.

"Double in ourselves" we are, said Montaigne. Now with that doubleness in mind let us look once more into the fossil past, full into the hollow sockets of the half-men from whom we sprang. Their bones are known; their remains have been turning up for over a century in almost every area of the Old World land mass. They have been found in the caves and gravels of Ice Age Europe, in the cemented breccias of deposits near Peking, in Asian coastal isles like Java, shaken at intervals by turbulent volcanoes. They have been found, as well, in the high uplands of eastern Africa and in the grottoes of the Holy Land.

Nevertheless, the faces of our ancestors remain forever unknown to us even as they stare from the illustrations of the poorest and most obscure textbook. The color of their skins is lost, the texture of their hair unknown, the expression of their once living features is as masked as those of the anonymous cadaver that represents collective humanity in the pages of medical textbooks. It is the same gray anonymity in which man's formidable enemy, the saber-toothed tiger, is lost, or even the dinosaur.

In the case of man, the representations are particularly ungratifying. Man is a creature volatile of expression, and across his features in a day may flow happiness and remorse, rage and charity. Individually, as on a modern street, one should be able to sight the sly, the brutal, and the benignant. If, in the world of fossils, however, we seek the soul of man himself, we are forced to draw it from the empty sockets of skulls or the representations of artists quick to project their own conceptions of the past upon the indifferent dead.

It is man's folly, as it is perhaps a sign of his spiritual aspirations, that he is forever scrutinizing and redefining himself. A mole, so far as we can determine, is content with its dim world below the grass roots, a snow leopard with being what he is—a drifting ghost in a blizzard. Man, by contrast, is marked by a restless inner eye, which in periods of social violence such as characterize our age, grows clouded with anxiety. There are times when our bodies seem to waver from within and bulge lumpishly with the shape of contending forces.

There is danger as well as wisdom, however, in such self-scrutiny. Man, unlike the lower creatures locked safely within their particular endowed natures, possesses freedom. He can define and redefine his own humanity, his own conception of himself. In so doing, he may give wings to the spirit or reshape himself into something more genuinely bestial than any beast of prey obeying its own nature. In this ability to take on the shape of his own dreams, man extends beyond visible nature into another and stranger realm. It is part of each person's individual evolutionary status that he possesses this power in unequal degrees.

Few of us can be saints; few of us are total monsters. To the degree that we let others project upon us erroneous or unbalanced conceptions of our natures, we may unconsciously reshape our own image to less pleasing forms. It is one thing to be "realistic," as many are fond of saying, about human nature. It is another thing entirely to let that consideration set limits to our spiritual aspirations or to precipitate us into cynicism and despair. We are protean in many things, and stand between extremes. There is still great room for the observation of John Donne, however, that "no man doth refine and exalt Nature to the heighth it would beare."

As one surveys the artistic conceptions of the past, whether sculptured or drawn, one frequently encounters an adenoidal, open-mouthed brute with a club representing Neanderthal man. Then, by contrast, we encounter a neatly groomed model of Peking man, looking as clear-eyed and intelligent as a broker on his way to the Stock Exchange. Something is obviously wrong here. The well-groomed Peking specimen belongs on the same anatomical level as Pithecanthropus, sometimes represented in older illustrations as possessing snarling fangs. The fangs are a figment of the artist's imagination. They have been stolen from our living relative, the gorilla. The mispictured adenoidal moron with the club is known to have buried his dead with offerings and to have cared for the injured and maimed among his kind.

Men are subjects of society. It is true that they carry bits and pieces of their past about with them, but they also covertly examine in the social mirror of their minds the way they look. Thus there is a quality of illusion about all of us. Emerson knew this well when he asked, in one of his more profound moments, "Why do men feel that the natural history of man has never been written, but he is always leaving behind what you have said of him, and it becomes old and books of metaphysics worthless?"

This comment of Emerson's is perhaps one of the most difficult pieces of wisdom that man has to learn. We are inclined to visualize our psychological make-up as fixed—as something bestowed upon the first man. In pre-evolutionary times, the human mind, with its reason, its conscience, its free will, was regarded as divinely and immediately created in the human organism just as it stands today.

With the rise of Darwinian evolution in the mid-nineteenth century, the concept of the stably endowed species correctly gave way to the notion of man and other animal forms as transient, imperfect, forever moving from one set of conditions to another. "Cosmic nature," wrote Thomas Huxley, Darwin's colleague and defender, "is no school of virtue. . . . For his successful progress as far as the savage state, man has been largely indebted to those qualities which he shares with the ape and the tiger."

No intelligent person today, surveying the low skull vault and heavy brow ridges of fossil man, can deny that man has changed through the aeons of prehistory, however difficult may seem the road he has traveled. Natural selection has undoubtedly played a leading role in that process. Here we must proceed with care, if we are not to fall into fallacious reasoning. Otherwise we will emerge from our survey of the past with another set of stereotypes as to the nature of man, which may well prove to be just as rigid and dogmatic as those developed in pre-evolutionary thought—stereotypes that have been thrust forward even today as evidence of man's bestial nature.

Man's altruistic and innately cooperative character has brought him along the road to civilization far more than the qualities of the ape and tiger of Huxley's analysis. These are bad metaphors at best. The ape is a largely inoffensive social animal, the tiger a solitary carnivorous hunter. To lump them in a comparison with man is spectacular but confusing. As for the fearful war of nature painted by the early evolutionists and symbolized by the tiger, we know today that even the great carnivores exist, normally, in balance with their prey. When satiated and not involved in the hunt, they may stroll scarcely noticed among the herd creatures they stalk.

Some members of the Darwinian circle could only conceive of man achieving his high intellect through the heavy selection of incessant war. Today we know that early man was small and scant in numbers and that most of his efforts must have been given over to food-getting rather than conflict. This is not to minimize his destructive qualities, but his long-drawn-out, helpless childhood, during which his growing brain matured, could only have flourished in the safety of a stable family organization—groups marked by altruistic and long-continued care of the young.

The nineteenth-century evolutionists, and many philosophers still today, are obsessed by struggle. They try to define natural selection in one sense only—something that Darwin himself avoided. They ignore all man's finer qualities—generosity, self-sacrifice, universe-searching wisdom—in the attempt to enclose him in the small capsule that contained the brain of proto-man. Such writers often fail to explore man's growing sense of beauty, the language that has opened and defined his world, the little gifts he came to lay beside his dead.

None of these acts could have been prophesied before man came. They reveal something other than what the pure materialist would be able to draw out of the dark concourse of matter before the genuine emergence of these novel human phenomena into time. There is no definition or description of man possible by reducing him to ape or tree shrew. Once, it is true, the shrew contained him, but he is gone. He has broken from the opened seed pod of the prehominid brain, a thistledown now drifting toward the empty spaces of the universe. He is full of the lights and visions—yes, and the fearful darknesses—of the next age of man.

The world we now know is open-ended, unpredictable. Man has partially domesticated himself; in this lies the story of his strange nature, of that love which transcends the small Darwinian matters of tribal cooperation and safety. For man, be it noted, can love the music of Ariel's isle, or, in his heart, that ideal city of the Greeks which is not and yet is forever.

The law of selection that acts upon living creatures in the wild is frequently repressive. A coat color a little off tone and visible, a variation in instinct, may make for death. The powerful creative surge from the under-darkness of nature is held in check, awaiting, perhaps, a season that never comes; the white stag is struck down by the hunter. It is this unending struggle that those who would picture man from the beginning as a monster of terror would delineate—the man with the stone striking down in barbaric rage, not only his game, but his brother and his son.

Natural selection is real but at the same time it is a shifting chimera, less a "law" than making its own law from age to age. Let us see, before we approach what I shall call domesticated man, what mutual aid can mean in the life of a European sea bird, the common tern. This bird lacks the careful concealing coloration of some of nature's species. It is variable in matters of egg form and nest shape. Capricious deviation in all these features prevails among the terns. The conformist pressures of natural selection have here given way to the creative forces of random mutation. The potential hidden in nature has flowered into a greater variety of behavior. Thus what we call natural selection, "the war of nature," can either enclose living creatures in specialized prisons or, on occasion, open amazing doorways into unsuspected worlds. Even such a lowly relative of man as the existing lemur Propithecus, which lives in groups, may exhibit marked individual variation, because these animals recognize and behave differently toward one another. Conformity has here given way to selective pressure for at least limited physical diversity and corresponding individuality of behavior.

Though the case of man is complicated, it seems evident that just such a remarkable doorway opened when man, as a social animal, fell under selective forces that no longer severely channeled the nature of his mind or the minds of his aberrant offspring. Through language, this creature could communicate his dreams around the cave fires. Inevitably, a great wealth of intellectual diversity, and consequent selective mating, based upon mutual attraction, would emerge from the dark storehouse of nature. The cruel and the gentle would sit at the same fireside, dreaming already in the Stone Age the different dreams they dream today.

The visionary was already awaiting the eternal city; the gifted musician sat hearing in his brain sounds that did not yet exist. All waited upon and yet possessed, in some dim way, the future in their heads. Abysmal darkness and great light lay invisibly about their camps. The phantom cities of the far future awaited latent talents for which, in that unspecialized time, there was no name.

Above all, some of them, a mere handful in any generation perhaps, loved—they loved the animals about them, the song of the wind, the soft voices of women. On the flat surfaces of cave walls the three dimensions of the outside world took animal shape and form. Here—not with the ax, not with the bow—man fumbled at the door of his true kingdom. Here, hidden in times of trouble behind silent brows, against the man with the flint, waited St. Francis of the birds—the lovers, the men who are still forced to walk warily among their kind.

## III

I am middle-aged now, and like the Egyptian heads of buried stone, or like the gentle ones who came before me, I am resigned to wait out man's lingering barbarity. I have walked much to the sea, not knowing what I seek. The west headland I visit is always boiling, even on calm days. Spume leaps up from the sea caverns of buried reefs and the blue and purple of the turbulent waters are roiled and twisted with clashing and opposed currents. I go there frequently and sit for hours on an old whiskey crate half-buried in the sand.

Staring into those uncertain and treacherous waters with their unexpected and lifting apparitions is like looking into the future. You can see its forces constantly gathering, expending themselves, streaming away and streaming back, contorting or violently lifting into huge and grotesque shapes. The meaning escapes one, but day after day the harpy gulls scream and mew over it and the crabs scuttle like spiders along its edge, waving threatening pincers.

But I wander.

On one occasion, there was just this broken crate in the sand, myself, and the sea—and then this other. I only became aware of him after several days had passed. I first encountered him when I had ventured at low tide up to the verge of the reef beyond which burst that leaping, spouting thunder, which, in my isolated wanderings, I had come to conceive of as containing the future. As I reached the flat, slippery stones over which passed a constant surf, I saw a gray wing tilt upward and move a few feet farther on. It was a big gray-backed gull, who slid quietly down again amidst the encrusted sea growth. He moved just enough, out of old and wise judgment, to keep me at arm's length, no more. He was no longer with his kind, hovering and mewing over the outer rock masses of a dubious future. He had a space of his own on the last edge of the present. He fed there upon such things as the sea brought. He was old and he rested, if one could be said to rest amidst such waters.

I disturbed him once by coming closer, whereupon he rose and tilted slightly in the blast from over the reef. If I did not move, neither did he. Since I am not one to go rushing over dangerous crevices, we achieved, after some days, a dignified relationship. We were both gray, and disinclined toward a future that had come to have little meaning to either of us. We stood or sat a little apart and ignored each other, being, after all, creatures diverse.

Every morning when I came he was there. He was growing thinner, but he still rose at my coming and hovered low upon his great seagoing wings. Then I would seek my box and he would swoop back to the little space that contained his last of life. I came to look for this bird as though we shared some sane, enormously simple secret amidst a little shingle of hard stones and broken beach.

After several days he was gone. A sector of my own life had been sheared away with his going. I shied a stone uncertainly toward the still-spouting future. Nothing came of it; no hand reached out, no shape emerged. The only rational shape had been that aged gull, too wise to venture more than a tilting wing's length upward in such air. Finally, the extremest edge of his space had hesitantly touched mine. Neither of us had much farther to go, and the harsh simplicity of it was somehow appropriate and gratifying. A little salt-washed rock had contained us both.

Here, I thought, is where I shall abide my ending, in the mind at least. Here where the sea grinds coral and bone alike to pebbles, and the crabs come in the night for the recent dead. Here where everything is transmuted and transmutes, but all is living or about to live.

It was here that I came to know the final phase of love in the mind of man—the phase beyond the evolutionists' meager concentration upon survival. Here I no longer cared about survival—I merely loved. And the love was meaningless, as the harsh Victorian Darwinists would have understood it or even, equally, those harsh modern materialists of whom Lord Dunsany once said: "It is very seldom that the same man knows much of science, and about the things that were known before ever science came."

I felt, sitting in that desolate spot upon my whiskey crate, a love without issue, tenuous, almost disembodied. It was a love for an old gull, for wild dogs playing in the surf, for a hermit crab in an abandoned shell.

It was a love that had been growing through the unthinking demands of childhood, through the pains and rapture of adult desire. Now it was breaking free, at last, of my worn body, still containing but passing beyond those other loves. Now, at last, it was truly "the bright stranger, the foreign self," of which Emerson had once written.

Through shattered and receding skulls, growing ever smaller behind us in the crannies of a broken earth, a stranger had crept and made his way. But precisely how he came, and what might be his destiny, except that it is not wholly of our time or this our star, we do not know.

Perhaps it is always the destined role of the compassionate to be strangers among men. To fail and pass, to fail and come again. For the seed of man is thistledown, and a puff of breath may govern it, or a word from a poet torment it into greatness. There are few among us who can notice the passage of a moth's wing across an opera tent at midnight and ask ourselves, "Whose is the real play?"

I had turned to the young man who spoke those words as to one whose eye reached farther than the giant lens upon the mountain in my youth. Before us had seemed to stretch the infinite pathways of space down which, like the questing moth, it was henceforth man's doom to wander. But the void had become to me equally an interior void—the void of our own minds—a sea as infinite as the one before which I had been meditating.

Amidst the fall of waters on that desolate shore I watched briefly an exquisitely shaped jellyfish pumping its little umbrella sturdily along only to subside with the next wave on the strand. "Love makyth the lover and the living matters not," an old phrase came hesitantly to my lips. We would win, I thought steadily, if not in human guise then in another, for love was something that life in its infinite prodigality could afford. It was the failures who had always won, but by the time they won they had come to be called successes. This is the final paradox, which men call evolution.

# HONORS AND AWARDS

## AWARDS

Athenaeum Of Philadelphia Literary Award, Literary Award Committee, Athenaeum of Philadelphia, for *Darwin's Century*, 1959
Science Award, Phi Beta Kappa, for *Darwin's Century*, 1959
Page One Award, Newspaper Guild of Philadelphia, for literary work, 1960
Burroughs Medal, the John Burroughs Memorial Association, Inc., American Museum of Natural History, for *The Firmament of Time*, 1961
Le Comte du Nouy Award, American Foundation, for *The Firmament of Time*, 1961
Award in literature at the Philadelphia Arts Festival, 1962
Citation for outstanding accomplishment as a teacher and scholar, Department of Public Instruction, Commonwealth of Pennsylvania, 1962
Philadelphia Art Alliance Award for distinguished achievement in literature, 1967
Athenaeum of Philadelphia Literary Award, for *The Night Country*, 1973
Distinguished Nebraskan Award, Nebraska Society of Washington, D.C., 1974
Bradford Washburn Award, Boston Museum of Science, for outstanding contribution toward public understanding of science, 1976
Christopher Award, The Christophers, for *All the Strange Hours*, 1976

Joseph Wood Krutch Medal, Humane Society of the United States, for significant contribution towards the improvement of life and environment, 1976

National Award of Distinction, Graduate School of Education Alumni Association, University of Pennsylvania, 1976

## HONORARY DEGREES

| | | |
|---|---|---|
| Western Reserve University | 1959 | L.H.D. |
| Franklin & Marshall College | 1960 | Sc.D. |
| New York University | 1960 | L.H.D. |
| University of Nebraska | 1960 | Litt.D. |
| Alfred University | 1963 | LL.D. |
| Washington College | 1963 | L.H.D. |
| Brown University | 1964 | Litt.D. |
| Pace College | 1964 | L.H.D. |
| Hahnemann Medical College | 1965 | Sc.D. |
| Northern Michigan University | 1966 | L.H.D. |
| Kalamazoo College | 1967 | L.H.D. |
| University of British Columbia | 1967 | Sc.D. |
| University of Chattanooga | 1968 | Litt.D. |
| University of Puget Sound | 1968 | Sc.D. |
| Southern Methodist University | 1969 | Sc.D. |
| Hope College | 1970 | L.H.D. |
| St. Lawrence College | 1970 | Sc.D. |
| University of Bridgeport | 1970 | LL.D. |
| Ursinus College | 1971 | Litt.D. |
| Clarkson College of Technology | 1972 | Sc.D. |
| Hamilton College | 1972 | Sc.D. |
| LaSalle College | 1972 | Sc.D. |
| Lewis & Clark College | 1972 | L.H.D. |
| Monmouth College | 1972 | Litt.D. |
| St. Joseph's College | 1972 | Sc.D. |
| Butler University | 1973 | L.H.D. |
| Dickinson College | 1973 | LL.D. |
| Medical College of Pennsylvania | 1973 | L.H.D. |
| Middlebury College | 1973 | Doctor of Civil Law |

| | | |
|---|---|---|
| Kenyon College | 1974 | L.H.D. |
| Lehigh University | 1974 | Sc.D. |
| Southampton College of Long | | |
| Island University | 1974 | Sc.D. |
| Regis College | 1975 | F.A.D. |
| Trinity College | 1975 | L.H.D. |
| Muhlenberg College | 1976 | Litt.D. |
| University of Wisconsin, Green | | |
| Bay | 1976 | (special citation) |

## SOCIETIES

### Fellow

American Academy of Arts and Sciences
American Anthropological Association (Vice President, 1948)
American Association for the Advancement of Science (Vice President and chairman, history of science section, 1969)
World Academy of Arts and Sciences

### Member

American Association of Physical Anthropologists
American Institute of Human Paleontology (President 1949–1952)
American Philosophical Society
National Institute of Arts and Letters
National Research Council
Philadelphia Anthropological Society (Vice President 1947, President 1948)
Sigma Upsilon
Sigma Xi (President, University of Pennsylvania chapter, 1975–1976)
Society for American Archaeology
Wistar Society

### Honorary Member

Phi Beta Kappa

# Acknowledgments

# ACKNOWLEDGMENTS

"The Fire Apes," copyright © 1949 by Harper's Magazine. All rights reserved.

"Easter: The Isle of Faces," copyright © 1962 by Loren Eiseley, originally appeared in *Holiday*.

"The Winter of Man," © 1972 by The New York Times Company. Reprinted by permission.

"Thoreau's Vision of the Natural World," afterword by Loren Eiseley for *The Illustrated World of Thoreau*, edited by Howard Chapnick, copyright © 1974 by Howard Chapnick. Used by permission of Grosset & Dunlap, Inc.

"Man: The Lethal Factor," copyright © 1963 by *American Scientist*. Reprinted by permission.

The poems, copyright © 1930, 1935, 1936, 1939, 1941, 1942, 1943, 1964 by Loren Eiseley, first appeared in the following publications: *American Mercury:* "Leaving September." *American Poetry Journal:*"Nocturne in Silver." *Ladies' Home Journal:* "Let the Red Fox Run." *New York Herald Tribune:* "Dusk Interval." *Poetry:* "The Spider" and "Tasting the Mountain Spring." *Prairie Schooner:* "Winter Sign," "October Has the Heart," and "The Fishers." *Voices:* "Things Will Go."

# ABOUT THE AUTHOR

LOREN EISELEY was born on September 2, 1907, the son of a prairie artist and a sometime itinerant actor, both descendants of pioneers. In spite of poverty and hardship, he early gained from his mother a feeling for natural beauty, and from his father an appreciation of poetry. After a boyhood among the sunflower forests of eastern Nebraska and the high plains farther west, he spent the depression years doing odd jobs, riding the rails, sporadically attending college, until he found a vocation in science. His career culminated as Benjamin Franklin Professor of Anthropology and the History of Science at the University of Pennsylvania, where he also served a term as Provost and was Curator of Early Man at the University Museum.

Eiseley is widely known as a naturalist, a humanist, and a poet. In addition to his own books, his work has appeared in numerous anthologies of English prose, as well as in scientific journals. For many years he lectured frequently at leading universities throughout the United States.

| DATE | | | |
|------|------|------|------|
|      |      |      |      |
|      |      |      |      |
|      |      |      |      |
|      |      |      |      |
|      |      |      |      |
|      |      |      |      |
|      |      |      |      |
|      |      |      |      |
|      |      |      |      |
|      |      |      |      |
|      |      |      |      |
|      |      |      |      |